Fathers' Rights

Fathers' Rights

Hard-hitting & Fair Advice

for Every Father

Involved in a Custody Dispute

JEFFERY M. LEVING

with

KENNETH A. DACHMAN, Ph.D.

Basic Books

A Member of the Perseus Books Group

Grateful acknowledgment is made for the use of excerpts from essays by David Blasco, Michael Korts, David Riley, C. W. Smith, and Kip Eastman from *The Fathers' Book: Shared Experiences,* Carol Kort and Ronnie Friedland, eds. (Boston: G. K. Hall, 1986).

Published by Basic Books,
A Member of the Perseus Books Group

Designed by Elliott Beard

Library of Congress Cataloging-in-Publication Data

Leving, Jeffrey.
    Fathers' rights : hard-hitting & fair advice for every father involved in a custody dispute / Jeffrey Leving with Kenneth A. Dachman. — 1st ed.
        p. cm.
    Includes index.
    ISBN 0–465–02443–2 (cloth)
    ISBN 0–465–023622 (paper)

    1. Custody of children—United States—Popular works. 2. Divorced fathers—Legal status, laws, etc.—United States—Popular works.
    I. Dachman, Ken. II. Title.
    KF547.Z9L48   1997
    346.7301'7—dc20
    [347.30617]   96-43232

10 9 8 7 6 5 4
RRD 02 01 00 99

Dedication

For my daughter, "Sheeba," the reason I look forward to each new day. And in loving memory of my father, Al. I wish we could have had more time.

J. L.

For Gina, Jillian, and David, who bring me boundless joy. And for Leonard Dachman. He dragged himself to work every morning and sang me to sleep most every night. What a fine example you are, Dad.

K. D.

Contents

1
A Father's Rights, a Child's Needs 1

2
Inexcusable Bias, Unacceptable Consequences 24

3
Basic Training 52

4
An Honorable Peace 79

5
Going to War 116

6
The Aftermath   167

7
Paternity Issues   193

8
Recommendations for Reform   203

Acknowledgments

I couldn't do what I do without the finest team of pro-father trial lawyers ever assembled under one roof: William G. Dowling, James M. Hagler, Matthew C. Arnoux, Christopher L. Ingrim, Michael W. Ochoa, Michael S. Schiffman, Caryn Kenik, Fred McDonald, and Richard Doerr. Thank you all.

J. L.

My sincerest gratitude to our fine literary agent, James Levine, for his insightful comments and passionate contribution to this truly collaborative effort. And special thanks to John Whalen, a gifted man and unwitting mentor.

K. D.

Introduction

During fifteen years as a domestic relations attorney committed to the assertion and protection of fathers' rights, I've traveled all over the United States in service to a cause I fervently believe to be essential to the preservation of the American family.

The thousands of disenfranchised dads I've met—and society's indifference to their plight—created and sustained the inspiration for this book. My need to share what I've learned can be traced back to hundreds of encounters very similar to a modest gathering that occurred on Father's Day, 1993. . . .

Outside, the suburban park was filled with families playing in the summer sunshine. Dads and moms and kids were flying kites, slinging Frisbees, scaling jungle gyms, roller-blading, skipping rope, biking, triking, tossing baseballs back and forth.

In a poorly lit, badly ventilated classroom in the basement of the park's community center, a quiet Father's Day gathering was under way. A dozen completely average men sipped vending-machine coffee and shared sad, soul-wrenching tales of loss, loneliness, anger, and pain.

The men were divorced dads. All had been forced to the periphery of their children's lives, excluded from parental decisions, and stripped of the respect and moral authority inherent in a normal father-child relationship.

Most of these fathers could not even see their children regularly. "I called my ex-wife Thursday to see what time I could pick my daughter up for the weekend," said Ben. "She laughed and hung up."

Robert nodded knowingly. "My wife took my kids to Florida in April," he said. "I'm not even sure where they are."

"I know where my son is," said Tom. "He lives with his mother not more than five minutes from my house. I haven't had any time with him in almost a year. I took him to a ball game just after he turned seven. We had a great time. A couple of days later, my ex convinced a judge that the kid didn't want to see me anymore. My lawyer and I have been to court I don't know how many times trying to get a judge to let me see my son or at least talk to him. We keep getting turned down." Tom's voice cracked. "She's teaching the kid to hate me," he said. "And I don't even know why."

"My wife surprised me," said Chuck. "We had serious problems with each other, but I thought we were pretty decent parents. We worked different shifts, so each of us spent about the same amount of time with the kids. When we got divorced, I guess I just assumed not much would change. I thought I'd still be with them a lot. I found an apartment near the house, so I'd be nearby if they needed me, and so it'd be easy for them to come over. For a while things were fine. But then my ex found out I was dating someone. All of a sudden seeing the kids became real complicated. They were always sick, or out with friends, or their mother had other plans. What it's coming down to is I see them when she feels like letting me see them."

"Sounds like the same situation I'm in," said Steve. "When you do finally get them, it's awkward, really uncomfortable. It's like you're some relative from out of town instead of their father. You feel like you have to entertain them every second, and buy 'em everything they see. You wait and wait to be with them, and when you do, you spend all your time at the movies, or the arcade, or the mall."

"My kids live with their mother six hundred miles from here. Airline fare wars let me see them a couple of days every six weeks or so," said Brad. "It's not nearly enough. I don't even know what their rooms are like. I don't know anything about their school, or their teachers. I've never met their friends; I have no idea how they spend their time. I call them every few days, but they're little kids, they can't tell me all the things I want to know. I can't put my mind at ease. I constantly worry about them getting into accidents, getting sick. I can't even help them with the little things, like a broken bike, or homework. I miss them badly, I feel like they're growing up without me."

One by one, the men in the basement offered their experiences with the divorce process and the family court system.

Finally, the discussion turned to practical matters. "What can we do to stay in our kids' lives?" someone asked.

The pages that follow are filled with equitable, effective, and realistic answers to that vital question. You'll find no deceitful guerrilla tactics, and no antiwoman ravings. You will find the information and guidance you need to preserve your relationship with your children and to ease the trauma that divorce inevitably inflicts upon them.

Psychologists tell us that except for the death of someone we love, no other life experience is more stressful than divorce. A divorce decree documents the official termination of a life in which both spouses have shared countless hopes, dreams, and expectations. A mutual history ends; an investment of years of energy and commitment returns nothing. The impact of divorce is staggering, affecting not only the divorcing couple but their families, their friends, and most of all, their children.

Divorce litigation is an attempt to impose order and structure to resolve intensely intimate, incredibly complex human conflicts. In the best possible world, couples would never part. In the next best possible world, our family courts would assist estranged couples in dissolving their unions fairly, quickly, and cleanly.

Sadly, that ideal is rarely approached. Men and women already suffering severe emotional trauma and obviously in dire need of help and support turn to the courts and find themselves entangled in a system that brings them exactly the opposite of what they require. Too often, a dangerous free-fall ensues, as, at every step in the divorce process, the legal system deepens marital wounds, serving up revenge and recrimination much more often than it dispenses compassion and justice.

Our legal system is geared toward winning and losing—not necessarily the fair resolution of an estranged couple's mutual problems. Litigation relies heavily on classic adversarial proceedings, in which each lawyer is *obligated* to try to win. The traditional quest for victory, coupled with the highly charged atmosphere surrounding many divorces, often incites domestic relations attorneys to extreme levels of advocacy and breeds a win-at-all-costs attitude that encourages distortion, trickery, slander, and harassment. Family court judges generally aren't problem solvers, either; too often they behave more like claims processors. The courts determine which side has the best presentation, the most ducks in the correct rows. In many jurisdictions, custody decisions have become a matter of routine; rarely are a case's underlying issues satisfactorily addressed.

Believe me when I tell you that, as a father, you do not want to become involved in prolonged adversarial divorce litigation. Your life, your standard of living, and, most important, your relationship with your children will almost surely be damaged. Divorce litigation, with its search-and-destroy mentality, its frequent deployment of children as weapons, and its glaring ineffectiveness in preserving any semblance of family structure, is consuming many more men, women, and children than it helps.

Few relationships disintegrate instantaneously. The end is usually the result of a long history of wrongs, disappointments, and unfulfilled expectations; a decline in sharing, caring, and concern. Years together have left each spouse with a complex, highly personal agenda—an array of grievances each feels must be redressed before life can go on. Divorcing couples who expect the courts to settle these disputes are not going to like what they find as they struggle through the litigation process.

Fathers, especially, will encounter almost unbearable frustration, but adversarial divorce doesn't treat anyone gently. Both parents can expect extreme emotional stress and severe financial strain. The children, often after witnessing a demeaning, destructive battle in which Mom and Dad (each supported by a band of "experts") claw and maul one another, are required to "choose" one parent and banish the other. Children forced into this traumatic and unnatural situation are subject to what some psychologists would classify as legalized abuse.

Fortunately, with careful planning, a degree of flexibility, and a measure of self-control, you may not have to subject yourself or your children to the torments and torture of adversarial divorce litigation.

This book will provide you with several better ways to legally dissolve your marriage. Each of the approaches I'll present is more respectful, more honorable, more humane, and less traumatic than litigation. Perhaps most important, each is much more likely to get you what you and your children need to fashion a new life.

When you've evaluated all your options, I'm confident you'll agree that litigation—the most extreme way to end a marriage—should be your last recourse, not your first.

Acting in your children's behalf, I'll present convincing evidence that a "shared-parenting" agreement is often the only truly equitable solution to a custody dispute, and undeniably the best available antidote for emotional and developmental difficulties experienced by children of divorce. Decades of research and the experience of thousands of estranged couples will demonstrate the communication, cooperation, and creativity necessary to establish and maintain a parental partnership that will survive long after the end of an unsatisfactory marriage.

Of course, having been a frontline participant in family law for well over a decade, I know that dissolution of some relationships can be accomplished only in court. Should you find yourself involved in a custody battle, this book will offer information that I know will prove invaluable in protecting you and your children. If you must fight for your kids, I'll show you how to fight to win. While family law is an arena where negotiation is almost always preferable to warfare, both approaches require the same degree of preparation and an identical level of motivation.

Let us proceed, then, determining what must be done, planning how we'll do it, and always keeping in mind an extremely useful guiding principle concisely expressed in the old adage . . .

Hope for the best; plan for the worst.

—*J. L.*

1
A Father's Rights, a Child's Needs

The sacred rights of mankind are not to be rummaged for among old parchments or musty records. They are written, as with a sunbeam in the whole volume of nature, by the hand of the divinity himself; and can never be erased by mortal power.

Alexander Hamilton said that in 1775.

Two hundred and twenty years later, a divorced father's final few words to a family court judge distilled Hamilton's sentiment to its visceral essence.

"A man has the right to be his children's father," the man asserted. His simple, heartfelt statement clearly defines the acknowledgment, validation, deference, and protection that divorced fathers (and all fathers) feel they have a right to demand from our legal system. And the body of family law does indeed attempt to affirm the inviolate nature of the father-child relationship—primarily, and most relevantly, in statutes addressing issues of custody, support, access, alienation, and authority.

Our judicial establishment's efforts to understand and formalize the complex and primal bond between parents and children would, I suspect, disappoint and perhaps alarm Alexander Hamilton. The faded parchments and musty records he deplored have evolved into massive libraries of rules, orders, procedures, and formulas. In the ornery, litigious United States of the present, a father seeking enforcement of the natural rights Hamilton viewed as sacred will find knowledge more useful than moral force.

The following review provides a basic introduction to family law, an essential guide to the statutes most likely to assist, or hinder, your efforts to remain a father to your children as your legal relationship with their mother is dissolved. If a fight is necessary, these statutes are your only weapons.

It's important to keep in mind that the legal safeguards and remedies provided to fathers by our domestic relations laws are also available to mothers. (In fact, as we'll demonstrate in chapter 3, mothers are far more likely to benefit from the judiciary's protective arsenal than are fathers.) It's also essential to remember that this review shows the law at its best, as it should be, as the Constitution promises it will be—free of the antifather contempt and bias that infects so many family courts.

Custody

Under the law, custody has two distinct components. *Legal custody* gives a parent the legal authority to make decisions about a child's upbringing. *Physical custody* is the right of a parent to maintain physical control of a child. The children of a divorced couple live with the parent who is awarded physical custody. An award of *sole custody* grants control of a child's life to one parent. That parent's home becomes the child's legal residence, and the child becomes that parent's legal responsibility. *Divided custody* is an arrangement allowing children to live with each parent for part of the year. The parent with whom the children are residing at any given time has legal custody. *Split custody* is an allocation of parental rights in which each parent is granted sole custody of some of the couple's children. *Joint custody* theoretically grants both parents equal legal rights and responsibilities. A variety of residential options are possible under joint custody, including *bird's nest custody*—an arrangement allowing the children to remain in the family home while the parents take turns moving in and out.

Until about twenty-five years ago, custody of a divorcing couple's children was, by statute, presumptively awarded to the children's mother. The "tender years doctrine," a tenet of family law for more than 100 years, required that young children (of tender years) be kept with their mothers after divorce. The basis for this mandate was the widely held belief that women were more "naturally suited" to parenthood than men. It was not until the early 1970s that a political commitment to racial and gender equality forced repeal of the tender years doctrine (unfortunately, the overt gender bias inherent in the concept has survived). New custody laws enacted across the United States declared that "the best interests of the children" must be the primary consideration in custody decisions.

"The best interests of the children" is a highly subjective standard touching all aspects of a divorcing couple's relationship with each other and with their children. Typically, family law requires the court to consider "all relevant factors" when attempting to fashion a custody arrangement that truly accommodates a child's best interests. Most family court judges rely on some combination of the following criteria:

The Parents' Wishes. A court will almost always approve custody provisions that the divorcing couple have designed themselves. Parental agreements do not, however, deprive a family court of its power to act in the best interests of the child. Occasionally, courts use this power to alter or overrule a divorcing couple's custody arrangements. Not surprisingly, a judge is unlikely to award custody to a parent who is not prepared for custodial responsibilities or whose stated desire for custody seems to be based on financial gain or personal satisfaction rather than a child's interests.

The Child's Preference. A child's wishes are given more or less weight, depending on the child's age, education, and demonstrated maturity. In some states, a child's custodial preference cannot be considered unless the child is at least twelve years old. In a few states, a child's preference *must* be honored if the child is fourteen or older.

Siblings. While courts overwhelmingly prefer to keep siblings together, circumstances frequently arise that warrant split-custody decisions. Siblings who constantly fight are often separated at the request of their parents. To honor children's wishes, a father is sometimes awarded custody of an older son while his daughter continues to live with her mother.

Environmental Stability. A child's comfort in and satisfaction with home life, school, friends, and daily activities are significant considerations for most family court judges. Divorce itself is a traumatic disruption to children's lives; courts are reluctant to approve custody requests that are likely to result in additional anxiety and destabilization. A child's "established living pattern" in a familiar home, school, community, and religious institution should be altered only if there is a compelling need to do so.

Violence or the Threat of Violence. No family court should knowingly allow a child to be exposed to domestic violence or the threat of violence. It doesn't matter whether the violence, or the threat, is directed against the child or against someone else. A potential for violence based on past conduct is usually considered a valid indicator of future danger.

Mental and Physical Health. If a child suffers from a mental or physical disability, the court must decide which parent can best meet the child's special needs. The physical and mental health of the divorcing parents also comes under close scrutiny. Mental illnesses or physical impediments severe enough to endanger a child or debilitating enough to deprive a child of a parent's care and companionship will almost always hamper a parent's chances for custody in the eyes of the court. Evidence of rehabilitation can mitigate these concerns.

Lifestyle. A family court evaluates a wide range of factors in its attempt to determine the effects (both positive and negative) that parents' lifestyles are likely to have on the well-being of children. Courts do not generally look kindly on parents who engage in criminal activity, substance abuse, sexual misconduct, promiscuity, or homosexuality. Cohabitation is viewed harshly by some courts, barely noticed by others. The time that each parent's lifestyle leaves available for child-rearing activities is also closely examined. A parent willing to revamp a daily work schedule to devote more time to child care has a clear advantage over a parent whose days and nights are consumed by the demands of a career. Because medical science has recently made clear the dangers of secondary smoke, a nonsmoking parent is often preferable to a smoker.

Everything Else. The majority of family court judges will consider any and all information presented to them in their attempts to determine what is—and what is not—in the best interests of a divorcing couple's children. Best-interest factors cited by one court or another in recent years include:

The age and sex of the child.

Emotional ties between parent and child.

The ability of a parent to provide vocational guidance.

School quality.

The willingness of a parent to promote communication and contact between the child and the other parent.

Availability of medical care.

The cultural background of the children and the parents.

Residential circumstances (cleanliness, living space, safety of the neighborhood, and the like).

Race (in cases involving interracial marriages).

Interference with a child's relationship with the other parent.

The effectiveness and appropriateness of parental discipline.

Wealth.

A child's integration into a "new" family (a stepmother and her children or a stepfather and his children).

To the surprise of many divorcing couples, religion generally plays an insignificant role in custody decisions—primarily because the First Amendment of the Constitution prohibits family courts from considering religion or religious beliefs unless physical, emotional, or mental harm to a child caused by religious practices is alleged. On the other hand, a court will generally not interfere with a divorcing couple's agreement specifying how religious training will be provided.

Joint Custody

Within the past decade, legal and social service experts have united to convince several states to assert, through legislation, that the best interests of a divorcing couple's children are more adequately and more humanely served when both parents are involved in their children's lives. This can be accomplished through joint custody. Typically, this precept is expressed in language similar to the following excerpt from the Illinois Marriage and Dissolution of Marriage Act:

The court shall presume that the maximum involvement and co-operation of both parents regarding the physical, mental, moral and emotional well-being of their child is in the best interests of the child.

The lieutenant governor of Illinois, Robert Kustra, who was a state senator when he sponsored the Illinois Joint Custody Act (legislation I coauthored) in 1986, said he did so because "evidence warranted a joint custody law to ensure that both parents participated in the upbringing of their children." In testimony before a legislative committee considering divorce reform, New York State Supreme Court judge Richard Lattner called joint custody "an appealing concept" that allowed the courts to "escape an agonizing decision and avoid even the appearance of sexual discrimination." Joint custody's most significant feature, Lattner testified, was that it "allowed both parents an equal voice in child rearing decisions."

Joint custody may be joint legal custody (parents share all major decision-making powers), joint physical custody (children spend significant time living with each parent), or a combination of both. Divorced couples who share physical custody of their children almost always share legal custody too. Joint legal custody, on the other hand, frequently occurs without an agreement to share physical custody.

In some jurisdictions, joint custody can be vetoed by one of the parents; in others it may be imposed despite the objections of even both parents. In several states, a joint custody order may not be awarded if evidence demonstrates that the divorcing parents are unable to cooperate with each other. As an Illinois court recently noted, "Joint custody is dependent upon the following: the best interests of the child; agreement of the parents and their mutual ability to cooperate; geographic distance between the parents; and the relationships previously established between the child and the parents. Since joint custody requires extensive contact and intensive communication, it cannot work between belligerent parents."

Most joint custody statutes emphasize that joint custody does not necessarily mean equal parenting time. Typically, a joint parenting agreement (see pp.109–115.) must meet several specific standards. The pact (or order) must clearly indicate how each parent will contribute to a child's care and how major decisions affecting the child's life will be made. The joint parenting agreement must also include a clause spelling out how disputes will be resolved (usually through mediation) and that there be periodic reviews of the agreement.

Access

When a parent is awarded sole or primary physical custody of children in a divorce action, family law provisions should attempt to protect the other parent's access to the children by granting (and enforcing) "visitation" rights. Most noncustodial parents, family therapists, and social scientists detest calling the time that parents and children spend together "visitation." Nevertheless, that's what the law calls it. A family court judge can deny a noncustodial parent's visitation rights _only_ when the court has strong evidence that visitation would be dangerous or detrimental to the child.

Family courts generally have avoided establishing specific standards that, if met, would constitute adequate visitation—and, thus, adequate parental access. How often and how long a noncustodial parent can visit children is typically determined on a case-by-case basis. Usually, the court orders visitation at "reasonable times and places" and asks the parents to work out the details. This open-ended instruction is intended to allow parents a degree of flexibility in meshing now separate household schedules. If a divorcing couple is unable to agree on a visitation schedule, the court can order a fixed schedule.

Interference with visitation can be (but is not often) regarded as contempt of court. Sanctions imposed to punish violation of a family court's visitation orders can include fines, forfeiture of child support, and sometimes incarceration. (In a well-publicized example of the sanction process, I read that Cyndi Garvey, ex-wife of former baseball star Steve Garvey, spent several nights in jail after being convicted of interference with her former husband's visitation rights.)

In cases in which a noncustodial parent has a well-documented history of violent, abusive, or otherwise destructive behavior (especially if that behavior has been directed toward children), the court is empowered to require that visitation take place only under supervision. When a court orders supervision, an adult third party (other than the parent) must be present at all times during the visit. The supervising adult may be a friend or relative or child-care professional chosen by the parents (and approved by the court), or someone appointed directly by the court. Occasionally, supervised visits are ordered to protect a noncustodial parent from false accusations of child abuse or other unacceptable conduct.

In situations where the impending geographic relocation of one parent seriously interferes with the other parent's access to a child, the parent whose access rights are in jeopardy may ask the court for modification of custody or visitation orders. When a move of substantial distance is involved, the court may switch custody from one parent to the other or alter visitation schedules to allow the child to live with one parent during the school year and the other parent during summers. Another commonly used remedy is a court order requiring the relocating parent to pay all expenses associated with the noncustodial parent's visits.

Unlawful interference with a parent's right of access to a child occurs when one parent wrongfully deprives the other of court-ordered custody or visitation privileges. In most states, denying parental access by concealing the child or taking the child out of state is a felony—a form of kidnapping.

The Parental Kidnapping Prevention Act, a federal statute in force since 1980, addresses the prosecution and punishment of parents guilty of kidnapping their own children. This law also requires all states to recognize and enforce the custody and visitation decisions of courts in other states rather than making new, possibly contradictory rulings on custody or visitation. Locator services operated by many states and the federal government assist parents in finding children who may have been kidnapped by the other parent.

The International Child Abduction Remedies Act enabled the United States to join twenty-nine other countries in an agreement to provide for the prompt return of children wrongfully removed or illegally detained within the borders of the participating nations. The pact ensures that custody and access laws of each member nation are respected and enforced in all jurisdictions throughout the alliance. Common rules and procedures are used to settle custody and access disputes that cross international borders.

Within the United States—until recently—a parent who disagreed with family court decisions governing access to a child could move to another state in search of a more favorable judicial climate. Since the enactment of the Uniform Child Custody Jurisdiction Act it's unlikely that such a change of scenery will be effective. The UCCJA, now in force in all fifty states and the District of Columbia, requires judges to acknowledge and honor valid decrees and orders issued by courts in other states. Conflicting decisions and the subsequent shuttling of children back and forth between states has largely been eliminated.

Protection

A parent has the right (and the duty) to protect his child, and the child's future, from harm. A parent involved in a divorce action must use the family court system to assert this right (and fulfill this obligation). A divorced or divorcing parent who becomes aware of dangerous behavior or damaging influences that threaten his children's physical safety or emotional well-being can ask the court to protect the children by removing them from the source of the immediate or potential danger. A court-ordered award of sole custody or the severe restriction of visitation rights are the standard methods for ensuring children's safety. These actions may be taken if the court is shown clear and convincing evidence that children are seriously endangered by a parent's lifestyle, a parent's behavior, or the environment in which a parent forces the children to live.

Documented cases of child abuse—in any form—meet the court system's serious endangerment standard. Physical, emotional, or sexual mistreatment of a child is child abuse.

Physical abuse is any action that inflicts grave physical damage, even if the injury is temporary. Corporal punishment that causes bruising, bleeding, or burning is physical abuse. So is the denial of food, water, shelter, or medical treatment. While the difference between acceptable physical discipline and physical abuse has never been defined in law, most courts (and most parents) know when the boundary between the two has been crossed.

Emotional abuse includes derogatory language and parental conduct calculated to destroy or seriously undermine a child's dignity and self-esteem. Constantly berating a child, humiliating a child in the presence of family, friends, or teachers, or isolating the child from the outside world for extended periods of time are examples of emotional abuse. Relentless insults or mockery are other forms of this destructive behavior.

The legal definition of sexual abuse encompasses virtually all actions involving a child intended to lead to the sexual gratification of either the child or a participating adult. While the most common forms of sexual abuse are outright sexual acts (fondling, intercourse, oral copulation), this category of child abuse may also include placing the child in sexually compromising positions, using the child to produce pornography, requiring the child to wear seductive clothing, and indulging in forms of physical discipline more commonly associated with adult sexuality than parental behavior. Whether the child consents to sexual activity or is forced to participate is irrelevant in determining if sexual mistreatment has occurred.

Neglect may also constitute serious endangerment. Courts have revoked the custodial rights of parents who have left young children alone for hours or days; parents whose primary meal-planning function has been leaving paint chips within easy reach; parents who failed to treat, or even notice, the serious physical or mental illnesses of children; and parents who were unable or unwilling to provide a clean, warm room for their children to sleep in.

Elements of a custodial parent's lifestyle may be judged dangerous, or potentially dangerous, to a child, even if the child is not directly involved in that lifestyle. A lifestyle that brings potentially harmful relationships into a child's life, for example, can be considered to be dangerous enough to warrant removal of the child. A recent family court case provides a vivid example. . . .

Sam and Vera

Sam filed for divorce when he learned that his wife, Vera, was involved in an ongoing homosexual relationship with a young woman named Joni. Sam moved from the marital residence, and a family court granted Vera temporary custody of the couple's three-year-old daughter, Tracy. Sam was awarded visitation rights. He petitioned the court for permanent custody of Tracy, and while the divorce process moved slowly toward its conclusion, Sam saw his daughter as often as he could, frequently taking her to her paternal grandparents' farm, where father and child would plant flowers and vegetables or go rock hunting.

When Sam was accused of having violated the court's temporary custody order by removing Tracy from Vera's care for six weeks, he was cited for contempt of court. He reluctantly returned Tracy to her mother, who retained custody for about a year as litigation wore on. During that period, Sam's visits with Tracy included several verbal confrontations with Vera and her lesbian partner, Joni. They called him "worthless." Sam referred to them in equally unflattering terms. Sam wasn't proud of himself for resorting to such juvenile behavior, but the pain of watching his family crumble (and being helpless to stop it) made it difficult for him to keep his composure.

When Sam and Vera's custody hearing finally got under way, some disturbing facts came to the court's attention. Testimony revealed that Vera had met Joni sixteen months prior to Sam's termination of the marriage. Vera was a nurse at a chemical dependency rehabilitation center at the time, and Joni was one of her patients. Just before entering the rehab facility, Joni had attempted suicide—after six years of abusing alcohol, marijuana, cocaine, quaaludes, amphetamines, and tranquilizers. Joni had been sexually abused as a child and had become pregnant at age twelve.

Joni told the court that she was recovering from her chemical dependencies and that she believed her relationship with Vera was healthy and permanent. Joni also testified that she felt she had the ability and authority to discipline and correct Vera's daughter, Tracy. Joni admitted that she had written Vera an alarming letter in which she expressed her concerns: "[T]oo many of today's victims are tomorrow's abusers"; "[B]lood comes up a lot in my mind when I look at my life"; [I had a dream] "about people being shot and that suddenly [I] was standing over them with a gun in my hand." And Joni had a dream where she killed Tracy.

Sam's expert witness, a pediatric psychologist, testified that Joni's past and ongoing instability imposed a real threat to Tracy's well-being. The psychologist was particularly concerned about Joni's age (eighteen at the time of the hearing), her history of child abuse (the expert agreed with Joni's observation that abuse victims frequently became abusers), and the relatively short time Joni had been free of chemical dependencies. Vera's expert, a psychiatrist specializing in marital and sexual dysfunction, testified that Tracy had "prospered" under Vera's care and that Vera's lifestyle choices did not harm her daughter in any way.

The court awarded custody of Tracy to Sam, based on several findings:

> Vera's open and continuing cohabitation with a lesbian lover indicated to the court that Vera was unlikely to keep her lifestyle choice from infringing on her relationship with Tracy.

> Vera's choice of Joni as a partner posed an unacceptable risk to Tracy because of Joni's serious emotional problems, her history of drug abuse, and her past and present instability.

> Tracy, it appeared to the court, was not Vera's highest priority.

Sam, the child's father, was better able, on the whole, to provide for Tracy's physical, mental, and emotional needs.

Vera appealed the custody award, claiming that her choice of lifestyle should not have been a factor in determining the best interests of her child. The appeal enabled the state's supreme court to uphold, and clarify, the decision. "The mother exhibited gross character defects . . . [when, using her position as a nurse, she] actively recruited [Joni] who was a minor [at the time], to engage in an illicit and criminal sexual relationship," the appeals court ruled. Vera's conduct, the court said, demonstrated "a propensity to feed her sexual appetite without regard to morals, ethics or law." The court found that Vera had "abused her position [as a nurse] to take advantage of an underage drug addict" and that her behavior was "not only reprehensible, but criminal."

The court rejected Vera's contention that her relationship with Joni should not have been considered in resolving a custody dispute, noting that a family court judge is instructed by statute to evaluate "all relevant factors" in awarding custody rights. Among factors the law deems relevant, the appeals court pointed out, is the "interrelationship of the child with any person who may affect the child's best interest." Joni certainly fit that description, the court said. "[Joni] is an 18-year-old teenager who, at the time of the hearing, was still undergoing counseling for sexual abuse and for recent drug abuse. [Joni] admitted writing a letter to [Vera] . . . where she dreamed about killing [the child in question]. . . . Her past and present emotional problems pose a risk to [the child] and provide a high degree of instability in the household."

The potential harm a child faces in living with an alcoholic, a drug addict, a child abuser, or a criminal are obvious. On the other hand, the lifestyle of a custodial parent who lives with a lover or occasionally drinks or uses marijuana is rarely sufficient cause to withdraw custody (except in extremely conservative jurisdictions). A parent's discreet, stable relationship with another adult is not, in itself, usually considered harmful to children, nor is the infrequent indulgence in recreational chemicals not approved by some segments of society.

A Better Life

A good parent is much more than a security guard. Parental rights and responsibilities extend far beyond a commitment to protect children from harm. If a noncustodial parent believes that court-ordered custody provisions subject a child to unnecessary trauma or that custody arrangements impede the treatment of correctable educational or developmental difficulties, the parent generally has the right to request a custody change under the "best interests" standard.

The numerous cases in which family courts have ordered custody modifications in effect to provide children with opportunities for better, more normal lives include the following examples.

Billy, the ten-year-old son of a Kansas couple who divorced when Billy was eight, lived with his mother. Soon after his parents' divorce, Billy encountered troubles at school and in his neighborhood. His grades plummeted (from a B average to barely above a D); he started fistfights or shoving matches at least once a week; and he was caught shoplifting candy bars and magazines.

Billy's mother, busy with a full-time job and membership in two church groups, could not find the time to supervise Billy's homework. She disliked confrontation of any kind, which may have been why her infrequent attempts to discipline Billy were ineffective and why she never asked her ex-spouse to help.

Billy's father was unaware of his son's problems until a parent-teacher conference brought them to his attention. Realizing that he might be able to provide the attention, discipline, and assistance that Billy seemed to be missing, the father volunteered to assume custody. He promised to rearrange his work schedule to be available for Billy each day after school. He would see that Billy completed his homework assignments, help with the boy's studies, and, should the need arise, administer appropriate discipline.

Billy's mother refused to agree to the revised custody arrangement, so Billy's father brought the matter to the family court that had issued the original custody decree. The court examined the circumstances and correctly awarded Billy's father temporary custody. When Billy's performance at school (and his general behavior) improved, that custody order became permanent. While Billy's mother was a capable, loving parent, the court ruled, living with his father afforded Billy the structure and attention the child needed at that point in his life. In short, Billy's best interests were recognized and served.

A thousand miles east, and a year later, Len and Rita were divorced. Rita was awarded custody of the couple's six-year-old daughter.

When Rita moved five times in fourteen months, Len asked the court for a custody transfer, contending that Rita's frequent change of residence deprived his daughter of the stability a child needs to develop happily and normally. Rita argued that the child was accustomed to moving and that it was beneficial for her daughter to experience a variety of people and places while growing up.

The court decided that the establishment of roots in a secure, stable setting would improve the quality of the child's life. "A familiar, comfortable home environment, with the opportunity to adjust to school, and to make friends, is crucial to a child's well being," the court ruled in the order that gave Len custody of his daughter.

Interference and Alienation

A clearly stated (though infrequently enforced) aim of family law is the protection of the special reciprocal relationship between parent and child. All parents, including divorced parents, should have the right to their children's love, honor, and respect. Regardless of how custody and visitation rights are allocated, each parent should incur the legal obligation to "foster the love, respect and affection of the child toward the other parent."

In most jurisdictions, the law goes well beyond a simple prohibition against interference with an ex-spouse's parental relationship with his or her children. A neutral stance is insufficient, family courts have ruled; former mates must actively and diligently promote their children's ongoing contact and involvement with the other parent.

A recent Florida case illustrates this principle. . . .

About a year after Mr. and Mrs. L. were divorced, Mr. L. appeared before a family court judge with a serious complaint. His children hated him, Mr. L. said, and the source of their deep animosity was their mother, the former Mrs. L. Interviews with the children and psychological experts persuaded the court that Mr. L.'s grievance was valid. The court fined Mrs. L. and ordered her to "do everything in her power to create in the minds of the children a loving, caring feeling toward their father." When Mrs. L. flatly refused to comply with its order, the court cited her for contempt.

In appealing the court's ruling and the contempt citation, Mrs. L. claimed that the court's order violated her constitutional right to free speech by illegally restricting what she could say to her children about their father.

An appellate court upheld the original anti-alienation order, the financial sanction that accompanied the order, and the contempt citation, finding, somewhat forcefully, that "the cause of the blind, brainwashed, bigoted belligerence of the children toward the father grew from the soil nurtured, watered, and tilled by the mother. The court is thoroughly convinced that the mother breached every duty she owed as the custodial parent of instilling love, respect and feeling for the father. Worse, she slowly dripped poison into the minds of the children, maybe even beyond the power of this court to antidote. But the court will try."

As the Florida court's comments suggest, interference with the parent-child relationship often is difficult to repair. Remedies commonly tried are financial penalties and substantial revisions of visitation schedules. Occasionally, as in the following example, alienation is serious enough to warrant the transfer of custody to the parent whose relationship with the child has been damaged. . . .

When Edward and Sheila divorced, Sheila was awarded custody of the couple's son. Launching what was ultimately judged to be a "calculated scheme to destroy a parent-child relationship," Sheila positioned herself squarely between Edward and his son. She used an answering machine to prevent Edward from talking directly to his son on the telephone, and she refused to allow the son to return his father's phone calls. She frequently called the son during his visits with Edward to say: "Don't worry, honey, it's almost over. You'll be home soon."

Sheila's interference with Edward's visitation rights went far beyond disruptive phone calls. Before each of Edward's visits, she became extremely protective, worrying out loud and issuing warnings to her son about the dangerous experience he was about to endure. She also gave the son small gifts to be opened, one each day, during the visits. Sheila canceled Edward's visitations without reason on several occasions and claimed the child was seriously ill on numerous other visitation dates. A refusal to allow the son to be examined by a doctor always accompanied these claims.

Interference with visitation was only one tactic in Sheila's campaign to sever the bond between Edward and his son. She also enrolled the son in a private school (registering him under her maiden name), and then refused to give Edward any information about the school. She informed the son that, because of the divorce, Edward was no longer his father. The man she was planning to marry, Sheila said, would be the son's "new daddy." Sheila denigrated Edward whenever the opportunity arose, in a conscious and continuous effort to convince the child that Edward was a worthless and evil man.

Sheila's actions, a family court determined, were so hostile to Edward's relationship with his son that they "reached a level requiring a change in custody." The judgment that dissolved her marriage to Edward required Sheila to "use her best efforts to foster the respect, love and affection of the child" toward Edward, the court noted, a requirement that Sheila completely ignored. In fact, the court ruled, Sheila's behavior was a cold, vindictive attempt to end Edward's parental relationship with his son. Transferring custody of the child to Edward was, in the court's opinion, the only available means of restoring the reciprocal affection normally shared by a father and his son.

Support

Large, frequent doses of media attention, legislative scrutiny, and public outrage have made child support the most debated and least understood aspect of family law. The source of the controversy and concern generated by our existing support allocation standards and collection practices is easy to identify. The child support system is not working—not for parents, not for children, and not for society.

Social and political pressure is forcing a nationwide evolution in support statutes. In deference to this ongoing passion for reform, our discussion of the legal rights and obligations inherent in the child support process will not stray far from the basics. Meanwhile, be alert for changes, coming soon to a courtroom near you.

The moral and ethical basis for child support law is the universally accepted presumption that support is a primary parental imperative as old as civilization itself. This precept was reasserted recently by the New York State Supreme Court. "The duty of parents to provide shelter and sustenance to their dependents is," the court declared, "an obligation which is perhaps the most fundamental and necessitous known to society." (A government's promotion of child support as a sacred human quality is, of course, not entirely altruistic. If children's parents don't support them, the children become wards of the state.)

In the eyes of the law, both parents have an absolute legal obligation to provide financial support to their children. A mother and a father may love, hate, or not care at all about each other; the quality of the relationship between parents does not affect their joint obligation to their children in any way. Child support is, has been, and will be a primary parental responsibility whether a child's parents are rich or poor, sick or well, together or estranged.

The case of J. N. illustrates the scope and force of the law's conviction that parents must support their children—no matter what. In deciding a parentage claim against him, a domestic relations court ordered J. N. to contribute to the economic needs of his illegitimate son. The ruling was upheld on appeal, even though J. N. was only fifteen—a child himself—when his son was conceived.

When children's parents live together as a family, child support rarely becomes a concern of the courts. When parents separate or divorce (or have a child out of wedlock), a family court attempts to enforce children's rights to financial support by ordering parents (or a parent) to pay specific sums of money either to the children's other parent or to a third party (a school, a day-care center, an insurance company, a counselor, a trust fund manager, and so on). Parents often are also required to secure medical and/or dental benefits for their children. Child support obligations begin when children are born and continue until the children reach the legal equivalent of adulthood. Courts typically require parents to provide life insurance or some other funding vehicle to guarantee that support payments will continue after the death of the parents.

The law is clear in its insistence that *both* parents share financial responsibility for their children, although the enforcement of the law often places a greater burden on fathers due to gender bias. In cases where one parent has sole or primary custody of a couple's children, custody itself frequently satisfies all or part of the custodial parent's support obligation. Support funds contributed by the noncustodial parent, when combined with the custodial parent's day-to-day support, must be sufficient to cover all normal child-rearing expenses (housing, food, clothing, medical care, education, and recreation).

In most states, a child's support entitlement is not limited to the funds needed to meet basic needs. Almost all support statutes now mandate support awards large enough to maintain the "standard of living the child would have enjoyed had the marriage not been dissolved." When a divorcing couple's income and assets are substantial enough to make such awards feasible, it's customary for family courts to require parents to continue to pay for the same kinds of "luxury" items they gave their kids before the divorce (tennis lessons, pets, private-school tuition, summer camp, counseling, club memberships, and so on).

Most domestic relations courts are extremely vigilant in protecting the support rights of children. In fact, many family court judges believe that their court's most important function is to ensure that child support is sufficient, appropriate, and consistent with the law.

Support statutes always make "the interests of the children" the main component of court-ordered support allocations. In divorces ending in settlement, the courts carefully review the support provisions of the settlement agreement to ensure that children's needs and entitlements haven't been compromised. It is not unusual for a family court judge to summon independent financial experts to evaluate the adequacy of support arrangements. Countless court orders have overturned or modified support settlements deemed insufficient.

Courts rarely allow a parent to waive child support. This protective attitude prevents parents from "trading" a child's support rights for other benefits to themselves or to the child. Most family court judges quickly detect and disapprove the most commonly attempted "deals"—agreements using support and visitation as commodities in cynical exchanges that, when decoded, turn out to mean: "If you go away and leave me and the children alone, I won't ask for support." As one state's supreme court noted, "An agreement waiving child support in return for relinquishment of visitation rights is void, unenforceable, and against public policy."

While specific child support levels are generally set in a case-by-case review, most states have established minimum statutory guidelines. As the following chart illustrates, these standards are usually expressed as percentages of a supporting parent's net or gross income.

Family law's definition of "net income" is intentionally broad. Typically, total income from all sources minus specific deductions designated by statute is the calculation used. Total income includes

Number of Children	Percentage of Net Income for Support
1	20%
2	25%
3	32%
4	40%
5	45%
6 or more	50%

not only salary or wages but also earnings from investments, worker's compensation awards, commissions, lottery winnings, unemployment compensation, annuity and retirement benefits, insurance proceeds, profit-sharing payments, and/or "any form of periodic payment to an individual, regardless of source."

Deductions from total income usually allowed in determining net income include:

Federal, state, and local taxes actually paid.

Social Security (FICA) payments.

Mandatory retirement fund contributions required by law, by a bona fide union, or as a condition of employment.

Union or professional association dues.

Health and hospitalization insurance premiums (for the parent, or the dependent).

Prior court-ordered support or maintenance payments.

Medical expenses necessary to preserve one's life or health.

Reasonable expenditures incurred for the benefit of the child.

When ordering a support award that deviates significantly from the law's guidelines, the court usually is required to justify its departure from the statutory norm. A family court judge can base a "nonstandard" award on any combination of factors he or she deems relevant. The factors most commonly cited are examined briefly in the next few pages.

The Financial Resources of the Child. A court will require children to spend their own money only under unusual conditions. In one case where a family court was asked to "invade" a child's trust fund for private school tuition, the judge did so only because the child's parents were unable to afford the expense. In another case, a teenaged boy had received a large insurance settlement in an auto accident. The boy's father's monthly support obligation was reduced because the son's estate far exceeded the father's total income.

The Financial Resources of the Parents. Wealthy or high-income noncustodial parents may be able to meet all their children's needs with a support assessment well below the minimum statutory standard. If a noncustodial parent earns $300,000 net annually, for instance, many courts will find a child support award of $25,000 a year for one child to be adequate, even though this amount—about 8 percent of the parent's net income—is less than half the statutory standard. Similarly, down a bit on the salary scale, a noncustodial parent earning $15,000 net a year (and whose ex-spouse has only minimal resources) may be asked to contribute 30 to 40 percent of his net income for child support.

Each individual case demands an evaluation of the circumstances of custody and the relative economic position of each parent. For example, if a child's custodial parent earns $150,000 net annually and the noncustodial parent only $8,000 net, it's not an abuse of discretion for a family court to decide that no child support is needed from the noncustodial parent. Nor is it unusual for a court to allocate support based on a wide divergence in income between parents. If a father's income is six times higher than a mother's, a court will often distribute support assessments in acknowledgment of that ratio.

The Standard of Living the Child Would Have Enjoyed Had the Marriage Not Been Dissolved. A court's commitment to the maintenance of a child's standard of living is the consideration most often cited in unusual support awards. Often, this factor is also the issue most hotly contested by divorcing parents.

In a typical case illustrating how the "standard-of-living" principle sometimes overrides statutory guideline percentages, a bond trader who earned more than $120,000 a year disputed a family court's child support award of $1,000 monthly. The trader contended that he should be held responsible only for his share of his child's basic needs, needs that could be met with much less than $1,000 monthly—especially since the child's mother earned a better-than-average salary. The court disagreed, noting, "A child is not expected to live at a minimum level of comfort while the noncustodial parent is living in the lap of luxury."

In another case, in another court, common sense was used to find a reasonable compromise between a statutory child support formula and the standard-of-living principle. The divorcing couple in this example were both doctors. The father's net monthly income was $24,000; the mother's, $7,000. The divorcing doctors had one child. A trial court ordered the father to establish a trust fund for the child in the amount of $19,000, to pay $800 monthly in child support, and to maintain a large life insurance policy with the child as beneficiary. The father was also required to contribute to his child's trust fund monthly an amount equal to 20 percent of his net income—minus the cost of the life insurance and the $800 monthly support payment.

Both doctor mom and doctor dad found this support order unacceptable. Mom argued that the award was insufficient because it fell over 60 percent short of the statutory standard. Dad claimed that the award was excessive because it extended far beyond his child's needs. The appellate court agreed with doctor dad. Pointing out that the law's support guideline (20 percent of the father's net annual income) came to over $50,000 a year—much more than an average American earned annually—the court concluded that no four-year-old was entitled to such a "windfall."

Another method that courts sometimes use in applying the standard-of-living consideration to derive cash support awards is a recognition of benefits children receive from "pay directs"— funds paid to third parties on a child's behalf. These funds can be used to pay for tuition; music, dance, or martial arts lessons; counseling; therapy; athletic camps; cars; or anything else the court regards as beneficial.

The Physical, Emotional, and Mental Condition of the Child. Special needs of children beset with health, adjustment, or developmental problems are always considered in determining support obligations. Whenever possible, courts will try to ensure that children who need special education, psychological counseling, psychiatric care, physical therapy, orthodontia, or other professional services continue to receive appropriate treatment after their parents divorce. In many states, especially when it affects the ability of parents to earn a living, day care is considered to be an essential service.

Support awards well in excess of statutory standards are often ordered to meet the costs of these health, safety, and developmental expenses.

In joint custody situations, allocating support responsibilities requires a degree of creativity. Fortunately, courts have found that
joint custody, by its very nature, opens a wide range of options for
deciding who pays what. Approaches used successfully by family
courts include:

- Application of the statutory percentage guideline to the income
  of each parent to establish a "pooled" support award.

- Division or allocation of responsibility for certain expenses
  (such as college and medical), with the provision that each parent will be solely liable for day-to-day expenses incurred while
  having custody of the children.

- Development of a comprehensive budget covering all the children's expenses, with each parent required to contribute half (or
  some other portion based on income, or on how often the parent
  has custody) the funds needed to meet this budget.

- Acknowledgment that each parent's support obligations will be
  a "full offset," with no exchange of cash necessary because each
  parent will support the children in much the same way the children were supported when the parents were married.

Enforcement of Support Orders

If child support is not paid in compliance with family court rulings, a variety of collection mechanisms are used to attempt enforcement. The most common is the issuance of an Order of
Withholding, a form of wage garnishment through which the court
collects delinquent support directly from the responsible parent's
employer.

Failure to pay child support can also result in the seizure of a parent's property, interception of tax refunds, and confiscation of bank
accounts. Private collection agencies and locator services operated
by federal and state prosecutors will assist in the enforcement of
valid support orders.

In several states, parents owing child support are unable to obtain driver's licenses, business permits, or professional certifica-
tions. From time to time, highly publicized task forces are formed.
They launch campaigns to "round up" support "deadbeats." Often
these campaigns are designed to embarrass or humiliate parents

who are behind in their child support obligations. Publication of the parents' names in local newspapers and the distribution of mock "Wanted" posters featuring their pictures are popular "shame 'em into paying" techniques. (I have never seen such posters featuring women who interfere with visitation.)

Defaulting on a child support obligation often results in a contempt-of-court citation. In many jurisdictions contempt of court can—and does—lead directly to jail.

SUMMARY

Family law exists to protect the rights of parents and children involved in the legal dissolution of a family. While parents involved in the dissolution process also deserve and often need the court's protection, statutes governing custody, visitation, preservation of the parent-child relationship, and child support are ultimately structured to safeguard the welfare, safety, and normal development of children.

A man determined to remain his children's father throughout and after the dissolution process must understand the law's perspective and comply with its requirements.

The message is clear. In family law, parents' rights are subordinate to children's needs. Any attempt to assert or maintain a father's rights must be expressed in terms of a value to his children's well-being; any demand for father's justice must include acknowledgment and acceptance of fatherhood's obligations. The advice and strategies we'll discuss are all based on this premise.

2
Inexcusable Bias, Unacceptable Consequences

Not long ago, Rollo Norton, the president of a large insurance company, attended a "collaborative management" seminar on a secluded island near Vancouver. What Rollo learned (from inspirational speakers, slick videos, and team-building games in the woods) was that a corporate culture stressing teamwork and shared responsibility offered substantial benefits—happier customers, happier employees, and higher profits. Dictatorial leadership and crusty, inflexible policies, Rollo was told, bred stagnation and inefficiency in customer service, and created a surly, uncaring workforce.

Rollo returned to his office aglow with evangelical fervor. Believing in his heart and mind that collaborative management was indeed a wonderful thing, Rollo immediately launched an intensive campaign to transform his company's authoritarian "hit the mark or hit the street" style into an open, cooperative culture in which employees would be treated as valuable partners, not disposable-wage slaves.

Memos flew. Happy, hyperkinetic meetings that employees soon labeled "love-ins" were held in every department of the company. Workers felt the spirit. Hundreds of fine ideas poured forth from every level of the organization. Rollo beamed.

Six months later, the company commissioned a climate survey to measure the improvements that the new culture surely had wrought. Minutes after digesting the survey's results, Rollo called together his senior executives.

"Nothing has changed," Rollo said. "In fact, in our employees' opinion, we've gotten worse."

"I don't understand," said the vice president of human resources. "We've spent sixty thousand dollars explaining and promoting the new culture."

The puzzle was solved the next day, when the consultant who had conducted the climate survey came across this anonymous comment from someone in accounting:

"Our managers came to us with open arms and smiling faces. They promised us empowerment, involvement and respect, but nothing happens. They talk the talk, but they don't walk the walk."

It's important for a father who must rely on the family court system to protect and preserve his paternal rights to recognize and accept the central message of this modest parable:

Policies, rules, procedures, clear directives in black and white, are not easily converted to meaningful action. Chapter 1 offered a review of what family law *says*. Now it's time for fathers to learn what family court judges *do*. Sadly, there's often a troublesome variance between a legislature's instructions (the talk) and a judiciary's actions (the walk).

Tony

Our first glimpse of a judge's possible baffling disregard for the basic tenets of family law comes through the eyes of Tony, a divorced father who lives in New Jersey. Here, in Tony's own words, is what happened to him and to his children. (Tony's story is adapted from *Fathers and Grandfathers Under Siege* by Sal Fariello and Jerome A. Wisselman.)

"My wife walked out on me and the kids. I had sole custody for six years. I raised those kids from diapers. My wife was a drunk, she slept around, she had a criminal record. She couldn't have cared less about the kids.

"Then one day she got religion. She joined some bogus church and started going to Alcoholics Anonymous meetings. After a couple of weeks, she decides she's saved, she's sober, she's a new woman. So she petitions the court for custody of the kids.

"When I show up to fight her petition, the judge comes after me. What's the matter with me, he wants to know. Why do I want to keep the kids from their mother?

"I can't believe I'm hearing this. Keep them from their mother? Where the hell has she been for six years? In a goddamn stupor, that's where. I'm surprised she remembers she has kids. I told the judge that maybe some visits would be okay if the ex proves she's really off the sauce, but custody? No way.

"The judge didn't like me suggesting what he might want to think about doing. He got real superior, and real nasty. He told me that deciding what was best for the kids was his call, not mine. In other words, he was in control, not me.

"So now I'm steamed. I ask him why the courts are all of a sudden so interested in my kids. I wanted to know where the court was when I was raising them. The courts gave me no money, no help, nothing.

"You don't know me or my kids, I told the judge. I'm their father, I said, I should have some say in what happens to them.

"Now the judge is pissed. He tells me I'm being selfish and that young children need their mother. Then he says I'm no prize as a father, anyway.

"I'm so mad now I can hardly see straight, but I manage to ask him what he's talking about. He says he's got a social worker's report that says I'm no more than 'adequate' as a parent. I admit I'm no father-of-the-year candidate, but I take care of my kids. They've got a house, food, clothes, toys, whatever. I make sure they do their schoolwork and stay out of trouble. I have to work a lot, but I'm with them as much as I can be.

"Near the end of the trial, when I realized that this judge was calling me a lousy father and when I saw he was about to turn the kids over to their mother, I went completely nuts. I called the judge an idiot and told him he could go fuck himself. He cited me for contempt and had the bailiff handcuff me.

"I spent the night in jail still fuming. About three A.M. I realized that no matter what I said or did, this asshole in his black robes would always have more of a right to decide how my kids would grow up than their own father."

Like many of his family court colleagues, Tony's judge actually believed that Tony's children "belonged" with their mother, that she was the children's "real parent." The tender years doctrine was banished from domestic relations law long ago, but, as I see it,, the notion that a mother is a child's "real" parent remains alive and kicking in this judge's mind. Most states now have laws specifically excluding even the suggestion that a parent's gender will be given any weight in custody, support, or access decisions. It doesn't seem to matter. The pure, clear equity promised by family law statutes filters through a thick labyrinth of deep-seated and widely held prejudices before delivery of real-life "justice" occurs. Often enough to trigger valid outrage, certain family court decisions plainly indicate that the influences of outdated cultural stereotypes and social presumptions can overwhelm reasonable and gender-neutral application of the law—and, in some cases, defy simple common sense.

A number of studies have found that although fathers are generally granted statutory equality by domestic relations law, they do not always receive fair treatment from family courts. Legislative inquiries in several states throughout the 1990s overwhelmingly support the conclusion of the Colorado Supreme Court Task Force on Gender Bias. This task force examined hundreds of family court rulings and found "a clear preference for the mother." In fact, the study team wrote, a mother had to be "nearly dysfunctional" not to win custody of her children.

The foundation of the pro-female bias that permeates too many domestic relations courtrooms is part myth, part social history.

During the first one hundred or so years of American history, a father was, by law and in practice, both head of the family and his children's primary caregiver. Fathers were actively involved in every aspect of their children's growth, education, development, and well-being. Fathers taught life skills, both through formal instruction and by example. Fathers decided who their children would marry and managed their children's entry into the world outside the home. The United States was a patriarchy, and when divorce occurred, courts almost always awarded full custody of children to fathers.

Early in the nineteenth century, the Industrial Revolution forced a dramatic change in family structure and a radical shift in parental roles and responsibilities. The family home became the mother's domain, and child care became a mother's primary responsibility. Fathers spent much of their time (an average of more than fifty hours a week) working outside the home. By the end of the nineteenth century, society had imposed gender-based identities and expectations on both mothers and fathers, assigning to each parent qualities and capacities based on his or her day-to-day duties within the family unit. Parental roles and capabilities were considered to be mutually exclusive. Women were seen as "natural" caretakers of children, endowed with special nurturing skills—an array of inherent instincts and talents that men simply did not possess. The aggressive, competitive, and analytical elements of a man's "nature," on the other hand, equipped fathers to fulfill their destinies as breadwinners, financial managers, protectors, and disciplinarians.

As these social stereotypes took root and hardened, the notion that mothers were superior parents—biologically programmed to love, care for, and nurture children—became a widely held belief, then accepted fact, and, ultimately, a tenet of law. Custody statutes across the United States mandated strict adherence to the "tender years" doctrine, a family court rule requiring that when divorce occurred, mothers were always to be presumptively awarded custody of children "of tender years" (age five and under). The presumption leading to establishment of the tender years doctrine—that mothers were children's "real" parents—effectively widened the rule's scope to the point that, in divorces involving children of any age, mothers (unless proven clearly unfit) were routinely awarded custody. In 1938, in a decision explaining his belief that "no child should be deprived of that maternal influence," a Missouri judge wrote: "There is but a twilight zone between a mother's love and the atmosphere of heaven."

Decades passed without a serious challenge to the tender years doctrine. Then, in the early 1970s, a somewhat odd, certainly ironic, convergence of civil rights and gender-equity activism (which included efforts of the feminist movement) led to the rule's demise.

In a 1973 ruling typical of this era, a New York court noted: "Apart from the question of legality, the tender years presumption should be discarded because it is based on outdated social stereotypes rather than a rational and up to date consideration of the welfare of the children involved. The simple fact of being a mother does not, by itself, indicate a capacity or willingness to render a quality of care different than that which a father can provide."

Abolishment of the tender years doctrine forced revision of custody laws in most states. New family court rules required each parent to be given equal consideration in custody cases, and legislators installed "the best interests of the children" as the single most important aspect of custody decisions.

Unfortunately for divorcing fathers, all the noble judicial talk and all the "gender-neutral" custody statutes enacted by suddenly caring, suddenly sensitive legislatures have had almost no consistent impact on family court policies and practices throughout America.

The belief that women are blessed with a "maternal instinct" is still widely held and rarely questioned—despite the fact that no scientist has ever been able to confirm its existence. A century of reverence for the traditional roles and trappings of motherhood have become embedded in our culture, continuing to influence judges, lawyers, and the general public long after women's roles in the family, and in society, have changed dramatically.

A brief return to a time when the tender years doctrine governed custody decisions provides disturbing but useful insights into the size and strength of the maternal preference.

Remember, the tender years presumption—a concept formally incorporated into family law in 1839—*required* that custody of young children be presumptively awarded to their mothers. Only a mother, the law stated, was capable of providing the nurturance and love children needed. The doctrine, although purged from most states' custody laws in the 1970s, lives on in the minds of many family court judges. But courts today must disguise their preference for mothers; they can't blatantly ignore the law's demand for gender equity. Current decisions are careful to cite some element of the child's best interests when a mother wins custody.

When adherence to the tender years doctrine *was* legal, judges freely expressed their respect and admiration for motherhood. A Wisconsin court declared that "nothing can be an adequate substitute for mother love . . . a nurture that only a mother can give because in her alone is service expressed in terms of love." In Washington State, a family court judge found "mother love" to be a "dominant trait in even the weakest of women, surpassing the paternal affection for the common offspring." The same judge suggested: "A child needs a mother's care much more than a father's." In Iowa, motherhood was described as "God's own institution for the rearing and upbringing of the child." A North Dakota court decided that no judiciary should ever "rend the most sacred ties of nature which bind a mother to her children."

Since most states have outlawed gender bias in custody cases, eloquent essays on the celestial nature of motherhood no longer clutter family court transcripts. That doesn't mean, however, that pro-female bias has been eliminated.

A brief examination of the outcomes in several recent cases from all over the United States reveals how family courts manage to bend, stretch, and twist the law to deny fathers the equitable treatment they deserve.

Tony (cont.)

Flip back a page or two and review Tony's encounter with a New Jersey judge. It would seem, to most objective observers, that Tony began his custody battle with several significant advantages. Stability is supposed to be a paramount consideration in determining the best interests of children; Tony had been his children's sole caretaker for six years and had established a comfortable home and secure routine for them. While by his own admission not a "superdad," Tony was at least a competent, caring parent.

Tony's former spouse, on the other hand, came to the custody hearing with a well-documented history of alcoholism and sexual promiscuity. Prior to her magical religious reawakening, Tony's ex-wife had expressed no interest in seeing her children, let alone a desire to care for them.

As Tony soon discovered, none of these facts probably mattered. The judge believed that the children belonged with their mother, so that's where he put them. When Tony, understandably incredulous, objected to the ruling, the judge chastised the angry father for attempting to "keep a mother from her children," cited him for contempt, and threw him in jail.

It's interesting to note that the New Jersey judge's written summary of the custody award makes no reference to the maternal preference one might perceive in the judge's heated exchange with Tony. The formal ruling in the case justified the custody order by praising the "remarkable recovery" Tony's ex-wife had undergone and the "overwhelmingly positive effects" of the woman's "hard won redemption." Other decisive factors, the judge claimed, were Tony's "undistinguished" rating as a parent and his display of temper at the hearing. (The social worker who spoke to Tony for about an hour described Tony as an "adequate" parent. Anger is probably an emotion most parents would experience in similar circumstances.)

Most attorneys familiar with Tony's case probably find the results incomprehensible. "A blatant abuse of discretion," one colleague told me. "The judge was hypnotized by some old

World War Two values, the flag, mom, and apple pie. How could he not notice that this case was about mom, casual sex, and tequila?"

A more sensitive, more logical, and certainly more equitable resolution of Tony's custody dispute might have been the establishment of a maternal visitation arrangement, perhaps with supervision. Tony's former wife could then, over time, demonstrate to the court (and to Tony and the children) that her recovery was permanent and her interest in the children genuine. Once the mother's integration into the family had succeeded—or failed—the issue of custody could have been reexamined.

Alex and Nell

At the time of their divorce, custody of Alex and Nell's fifteen-year-old son, Jon, was awarded to Nell. A year later, Alex asked a Minnesota court to reverse that decision. The reason for this request, Alex's petition stated, was that Jon was "not adjusting well to living with his mother. He has become withdrawn and depressed, and has demonstrated impulsive behavior, angry outbursts and insensitivity. He has expressed a strong desire to live with his father and has indicated that he might run away from home if that request cannot be granted."

During the evidentiary hearing held in response to Alex's petition, a psychologist testified that Jon's emotional development did indeed appear to be in jeopardy. The expert also told the court that Jon believed Alex was a better parent for him than Nell. Alex, Jon said, was much more able to provide support, understanding, and pleasant family activities. The psychologist concluded by expressing the opinion that Jon's "best interests would be most effectively served by granting Alex primary physical custody of the child, with an award of liberal visitation rights to Nell." A court-appointed therapist agreed with this recommendation.

The court listened, nodded, and decided that Jon would remain with his mother. In explaining its decision, the court acknowledged that Jon's "present home environment" (with Nell) was "not as suitable as the proposed environment" (with Alex), and that Jon would probably benefit from a change in custody. But there would be no change, the court ruled, because although a potential danger to Jon's emotional health had been demonstrated, the risk shown wasn't severe enough to warrant taking Jon from his mother.

In other words, while Jon obviously would be better off living with his father, nobody had proved that life with Mom would kill Jon or drive him crazy. Here again we see a family court judge possibly disregarding the law to honor a mother's request—and, in the process, rejecting the recommendations of two child-care professionals and ignoring the wishes of the child himself.

Brian and Darla

When Brian and Darla's marriage was dissolved, a two-week trial was necessary to decide which parent would be awarded custody of the couple's seven-year-old daughter, Amy.

The only evidence offered against Brian during the extended proceedings was that, as a partner in a New York City law firm, he often worked long hours. Testimony questioning Darla's fitness to be Amy's custodial parent, on the other hand, lasted for days.

The primary cause of his decision to divorce Darla, Brian said, was Darla's "constant and pathological lying." Often, Darla asked Amy to corroborate her lies. When the child refused, Darla punished Amy, or screamed at her. More than once, in the presence of witnesses, Darla called Amy "a fucking little monster" and a "fucking little brat."

Darla's psychiatrist told the court that Darla had developed a "histrionic personality." A concurring opinion used shorter, simpler words to characterize Darla's disorder. "She's a bald-faced liar," a court-appointed expert reported.

When Darla registered Amy for kindergarten, Darla told school officials that Amy spoke French, that the child showed signs of genius as an infant, and that Amy had been tested by pediatric specialists at several Ivy League universities. None of this was true.

When Amy encountered reading difficulties in first grade and was given special attention and assistance, Darla told Brian that their daughter had been placed in an accelerated program for gifted students. When informed by school counselors that Amy had a developmental disability, Darla claimed that Amy was in psychotherapy, trying to deal with the recent death of her grandparents and a two-year-old cousin. Darla also told Amy's teachers that the child was recovering from the effects of an automobile accident. All these statements were false, as was Darla's declaration to Brian (shortly before the couple separated) insisting she was pregnant.

Second to nonstop lying on Darla's list of favorite pastimes was the senseless squandering of money—lots of money. Darla admitted that she had systematically spent $135,000 (most of the family's savings) during a three-year-long spending spree. When Brian demanded an explanation for Darla's spending, Darla "ran from window to window threatening to jump, then she ran into the kitchen and tried to slash her wrists."

The trial record made it clear that Darla's psychological problems were numerous and that the disorders had existed for years. "She has lived in a fantasy world throughout her adult life," one expert testified.

At the conclusion of the trial, the court found both Brian and Darla to be equally fit as parents. Sole custody of Amy, however, was awarded to Darla because, in the court's words, "the intense acrimony between the parties makes joint custody inappropriate."

The severe shock and disbelief Brian experienced when the custody award was read quickly deepened into a surreal coma as more orders were handed down, one by one. In addition to custody of Amy, the court decided that Darla would receive: 25 percent of the couple's property (only $22,000—Darla had spent the rest), $250 a week in maintenance, $1,000 a month for rent, $100 a week for her therapist, $6,000 to pay her outstanding therapy charges, and $35,000 for her legal fees. Brian was also responsible for $50,000 in marital debt, most of which had been incurred by Darla.

The outcome of this case is an astonishing miscarriage of justice. The financial settlement imposed by the court seems ludicrous, and the custody ruling is a shameful display of maternal bias. In no way does the evidence in this case support the court's finding that Amy's best interests were served.

I can find no rational explanation for the judge's decisions—unless, perhaps, the judge was unconsciously rewarding his late mother whom he loved very much. Only God (and Freud) knows for sure.

Mike and Lila

When the marriage of Mike and Lila ended, a Wyoming court granted Lila custody of the couple's three children. Within two years of their divorce, both Mike and Lila remarried.

Lila left the children with Mike for an extended visit one summer. Mike was to return the kids before school resumed in August. He didn't. Instead, Mike filed a petition to modify the original custody decree, asking the court to make him the children's custodial parent.

While Mike's petition was pending, the children were returned to Lila. She and the children moved to Colorado. Because Lila failed to appear at the custody hearing, a default judgment awarded custody of the children to Mike. Three years passed before Lila and the kids moved back to Wyoming. (By then Lila had divorced her second husband.) Lila asked the Wyoming courts to return custody of the children to her.

When the custody matter finally came to trial, Mike produced evidence that Nate, a man who had been living with Lila and the children, had pled guilty to sexually molesting Mike and Lila's eleven-year-old daughter. Testimony revealed that the abuse occurred over a nine-month period. The child asked a teacher for help, and it was this contact that led to Nate's arrest and incarceration for second-degree sexual assault.

In addition to citing the dangers posed to his children by Lila's choice of companions, Mike complained that Lila's "nomadic" lifestyle deprived the children of stability and security. He also offered proof that while in their mother's care, the children's school performance had deteriorated to the point where they were all held back a year.

Lila responded that she had been unaware of Nate's deviant behavior and that Mike had expressed no interest in the children's lives, contacting them only once during the three years she and the children lived in Colorado.

In announcing its decision, the court noted that, while Lila's association with Nate was "unfortunate and deplorable," there was "no excuse for Mike ignoring the children and leaving the mother alone to raise them." Ruling that Lila would be awarded custody of the children, the court said, "She gave birth to them. She was there for all those years alone. I can't forget that. No evidence has been shown that she isn't a good and loving mother."

What?

Remarkably, the state's supreme court affirmed the trial court's decision. A dissenting opinion, apparently unmoved by the apparent maternal bias of the majority, called the lower court's ruling "a clear and grave abuse of discretion." The award of custody to Lila was contrary to the "great weight of the evidence," the dissent declared. Lila had continued to see Nate *after* his sexual assault conviction, the dissent noted, and she had allowed her children (except for the daughter Nate had molested) to be alone with him. Lila's conduct and lifestyle were "clearly detrimental to the welfare and best interests of the children," the dissent noted, and the children should have been "the trial court's paramount concern."

The experiences of Tony, Alex, Brian, and Mike are unusual only because the pro-mother bias that these men encountered was so extreme. In most jurisdictions across the United States, a predisposition favoring mothers in custody issues exists quietly, an integral element of business as usual. Raw numbers demonstrate the depth and breadth of the judicial prejudice facing fathers expecting equal treatment from family courts: Mothers win 85 percent of all custody disputes.

A strong pro-female bias is also evident in the courts' allocation of support obligations. A noncustodial father is almost always ordered to pay child support; judges rarely ask a noncustodial mother to contribute to the economic support of her children. A recent week in domestic relations court offers examples of this distorted principle in action.

On Tuesday of this sample week, a family court judge ordered a father to pay his former spouse child support in the amount of $1,200 a month—about half the father's income. Three days later, in the same courtroom, the same judge ruled that a noncustodial mother was not required to pay child support, even though she owned and operated a successful business.

Another clear indicator of the overpowering influence of gender discrimination in family court policies can be seen by examining the system's enforcement practices. Courts typically deal swiftly and harshly with fathers who violate orders and decrees. In many jurisdictions, a father who returns his child two hours late after visitation will often have his visitation rights suspended or revoked. And, of course, most family court judges deal swiftly and harshly with fathers who fail to meet their child support obligations. Wage garnishment, seizure of assets, criminal prosecution, and jail time are freely and frequently employed to enforce support orders.

A mother needing help to collect child support can rely on an extensive enforcement structure built and operated at taxpayer expense. On the other side of the aisle, a father seeking a court's help in protecting or preserving his parental rights too often spends a lot of money and a lot of time securing the judicial equivalent of a smile and a shrug.

Paul's case provides an example of how a judge's pro-mother favoritism can overrule a statutory duty to protect the parent-child bond.

Paul and Susan

In several discussions leading to the dissolution of their marriage, Paul and Susan agreed to assume joint custody of their son, Teddy. Susan was given primary physical custody of Teddy, but Paul saw his son frequently and was actively involved in the boy's upbringing.

The divorced couple treated each other courteously, and their joint custody arrangement seemed to be working well—until Paul remarried. The appearance of a "new woman" in her ex-husband's life triggered in Susan a course of conduct that a judge later described (accurately, I believe) as "appalling."

Consumed with jealousy, Susan appeared to mount a cold, vicious campaign to destroy Paul's relationship with Teddy. In fact, Susan decided, Teddy would be her primary weapon in the shameful, pathetic attack.

Susan's covert operation began slowly. After sabotaging a number of Paul's visitations, Susan suggested to Teddy that his father no longer cared for him. "He loves his new family now," Susan told Teddy. Within weeks, Susan managed to convince Teddy that Paul was possessed by the devil and that Paul's new wife was probably a devil herself. Repeated reinforcement of this bizarre programming left Teddy believing that he and his mom were the only people in the world who could save Paul from an eternity in hell.

At this point, Susan prompted Teddy to call his father and leave messages on Paul's telephone answering machine. On one occasion, Teddy called Paul's new wife a "whore." On another, Teddy begged Paul to "divorce that slut and come home." In another recorded message, Teddy told Paul, "Dad, I never want to see you again unless you get rid of her."

Paul believed that Susan's illegal interference seriously endangered his parental relationship with Teddy. He asked a family court for primary custody of his son, citing Susan's "outrageous" violations of a state law forbidding parental alienation as his justification.

There was no controversy during the custody hearing. Susan admitted that her behavior had been irrational, unlawful, and indefensible. She also said she was sorry.

The court agreed that Susan's conduct was "deeply disturbing." Nevertheless, Paul's petition for custody was denied. The judge, court records indicate, was "moved" by Susan's "dramatic plea from the witness stand." (What Susan said was, "I realize now that Paul is never coming back to me. I know what I did was wrong, and I apologize.")

In essence, Susan was allowed to pay for an "outrageous" and "appalling" crime with an apology. Compare the court's refusal to uphold a deserving father's valid complaint with the sledgehammer sanctions typically imposed when a father's support payments are late or when a father commits a minor violation of a visitation decree. The pro-mother influence on enforcement practices is crystal clear, and darkly disturbing.

The Ultimate Old Wives' Tale

The ingrained presumption that femininity and parental ability are "naturally" intertwined is a hardy, durable myth, apparently immune to the forces of science, social reality, political pressure, and public opinion.

Numerous studies of single-parent households have reached similar conclusions: There is no correlation between gender and child-rearing competence. While several differences in parenting styles were noted by researchers, both mothers and fathers were found to be equally capable as caregivers. (Parental competence, in all the studies cited, was measured through comprehensive evaluation of children's behavior, attitudes, school performance, and social skills.)

The results of these academic investigations are validated every day, in homes all over the country. Mothers and fathers are sharing child-care duties, often not because they want to but mainly because that's the way it has to be. That reality leads us to the aspect of the bias evident in many family courts that fathers, their attorneys, and social scientists find most unbelievable: Many judges continue to decide children's fates based on narrow, sexist stereotypes that no longer exist.

The fact is that the family roles assumed by both men and women have been changing for decades. Current Census Bureau statistics indicate that 68 percent of U.S. mothers with children under eighteen work outside the home. The "typical" postwar nuclear family is almost extinct. Ward and June Cleaver live on only in television reruns. Their pristine black-and-white family world has evolved into an unruly mélange of inventive family lifestyles.

June Cleaver's days were spent in an eternal marathon of housework, baking, and beauty shop visits. Today, women have made substantial advances in industry, government, the arts, and the professions. Inescapable economic forces, coupled with a wide range of personal fulfillment needs, have swept mothers out of the kitchen into the business world. While complete equality in the workplace has not been achieved, a woman's right to demand respect, status, and compensation based solely on job performance is no longer seriously questioned.

Ward Cleaver spent his days at the office, his evenings in the den. His parental duties consisted solely of delivering serious but amiable lectures nudging Wally and the Beaver back toward the straight and narrow. Men today routinely attend prenatal classes, assist in the births of their children, and take an active role in all facets of child rearing. Self-worth for men is no longer simply a function of success at work. Millions of fathers have discovered the joys and satisfactions of parenting. The following observation, from an essay on fatherhood by newspaper editor David Blasco, conveys an attitude now shared by countless fathers. Blasco, several months after arranging his work schedule to be able to spend his days caring for his young children, wrote this:

"I am the breadwinner. It's an old pattern, perhaps one of the oldest on earth. My father would be familiar with it. But my father never had the chance to know what it was like to be with his child much of the day. I've been lucky. I've had all that time in the park."

Teacher and historian Michael Kort is another father who found time for both full-time parenting and a traditional career.

"I'd be the first to admit that raising children is not easy," Kort wrote. "It takes much of my time and most of my patience. But in return, aside from happiness, pride and love, my daughters have given me some simple pleasures . . . appreciating a butterfly, watching with fascination a perfectly ordinary bird in flight, playing Wiffle Ball, riding a bike, building a sand castle at the beach . . . They've given me, in short, . . . a remarkable gift which could have come from nowhere else, [a gift] worth far more than it cost."

An accurate distillation of the feelings many fathers experience as they shift focus from career to family was offered by David Riley, a lobbyist from Washington, D.C.

"I never knew how much you could get by giving," Riley wrote. "Jake [Riley's infant son] takes a lot of my time, but he gives back a dimension to my life that I cherish. And I've come to think that the world might be a very different place if its workaholics had more of this dimension in their lives."

In most homes today, mothers and fathers share child-care duties and the daily labors necessary to operate a family (cooking, cleaning, shopping, feeding and bathing the kids, helping with homework, and so forth). With both parents working in so many modern families, child rearing often involves day care, baby-sitters, or an infinite array of creative scheduling choices. Both mothers and fathers have become, in the words of one pediatric psychologist, "executive parents"—more parental care managers than direct caregivers. In other words, families today are a lot like small businesses, with dads, moms, relatives, and hired help doing whatever must be done, with little regard for titles or status.

Over the past thirty years, women have made remarkable progress in areas of society that had been dominated by men for centuries. The women's movement was responsible for much of this advancement, and it was feminists who first pointed out that traditional gender roles were oppressive and demeaning to both men and women. Interestingly, only half of feminism's message has made a meaningful impression on our collective consciousness. Women are now viewed as being capable of success in the workplace. Men, however, are not yet seen as being capable of providing competent, attentive child care— at least not in the eyes of many family court judges.

In a recent *USA Today* poll, 88 percent of the eleven thousand Americans surveyed believed that mothers and fathers should share equally in all child-rearing activities. Because local judiciaries usually are in tune with prevailing public opinion, many political experts find the invincibility of the maternal presumption in family law to be remarkable. As one veteran analyst commented, "Walking into some of these courtrooms is like traveling back in time."

Years of experience and research have convinced me that to understand the gender bias condoned by many family courts, we must recognize the interaction of all elements of the phenomenon. An inappropriate reverence for a long extinct ideal of motherhood is certainly one important piece of the puzzle. The belief that fathers can't handle the rigors of child care is another. The conviction that children need a father's money much more than the father himself also plays a part. The final key might be the perception—widely held within the judiciary and shared by many "civilians"—that fathers don't really want, or need, parental rights or responsibilities.

Society's lack of respect for fatherhood and the inaccurate assumption that fathers are not truly interested in parenting combine to perpetuate a comfortable rationalization, a judicial delusion that plays out something like this: Mothers and children need each other. Fathers and children don't, or at least not as much. Accept that dubious premise and gender bias, although illegal and unfair, doesn't seem all that harmful. It's not like real bigotry. There's no violence, no blatant oppression. No one is lynching anyone; no flaming crosses are showing up on fathers' lawns.

The insensitivity and inaccuracy of the notion that divorced or otherwise estranged fathers really don't want or need continuing involvement with their children immediately became clear to me within days after my decision to represent fathers in family court. A client I'll call Jim sat in my tiny office weeping uncontrollably. He had only one request: an hour or two with his six-year-old son. "His mother has my kid believing that his dad hates him," Jim said. "I need to tell him that's not true."

Since that day, I've become too familiar with the very real pain and overpowering sense of loss suffered by fathers excluded from their children's lives. All kinds of fathers from all walks of life find separation from their children to be a torturous, devastating experience. The father might be a glib advertising exec or a quiet factory foreman. The agony is the same.

"The silence I thought would be so welcome turned out to be the most oppressive experience of my life," an estranged father told author Howard Irving.

"When my boy was with me, I felt whole," said another divorced dad. "When he was gone, I felt empty. This is the writhing in the soul divorced men feel. When he goes back to his mom, a part of you dies. Something in your manhood suffers a profound assault that you're powerless against."

Divorced novelist C. W. Smith's reflections on the loss of his children are particularly relevant. Like many fathers pushed to the periphery of their children's lives, Smith didn't appreciate the ines- timable value of what he had—until it was gone.

"I read the kids Curious George and Dr. Seuss books," Smith wrote. "Once, when a heavy snowfall closed the schools, we made an igloo in the yard. . . . Giving them a hug, or an off to school scuff on the head . . . making cheese toast, cheering while running behind my cycling novice son with one hand clutching the waistband of his jeans—these humble pleasures vanished the moment I decided to leave. To provide, to protect, and to guide . . . these had constituted the dogma of fathering I had learned as a son, and I didn't know that performing these ritual duties was such good spiritual nutrition."

The close involvement and deep affection for their children that so many modern fathers feel free to express has, of course, always existed, as has the realization that fatherhood is as precious to fa- thers as it is to children. More than two hundred years ago, Jean- Jacques Rousseau wrote that "paternal love" was the source of one of the "sweetest sentiments known to man." A century later, philosopher Lafcadio Hearn declared, "No man can possibly know what life means, what the world means, what anything means, un- til he has a child and loves it. And then the whole universe changes and nothing will ever again seem exactly as it seemed before."

I'm certain that most fathers know exactly the feelings that Rousseau and Hearn described. The belief that destruction of the father-child bond is a victimless crime is an utterly appalling, in- credibly cruel fallacy.

Consequences

The personal and societal damages directly attributable to current family court policies and practices are so extensive it's difficult to decide where to begin an assessment of the carnage.

For fathers and children, the pain, upheaval, and trauma often begin immediately. In about nine of ten divorce and dissolution cases involving children, the mother is awarded sole or primary custody. The father leaves the family and the family home; and a familiar environment disintegrates into a tenuous, artificial, often unworkable access arrangement. The father is awarded visitation rights. Typically, he'll be allowed to see his children about fifty days a year.

Most fathers quickly recognize that it is difficult, often impossible, for a visitor to be an effective parent. The loss of normal day-to-day interaction and the absence of shared living creates an uncomfortable, strained relationship between fathers and children. Most estranged fathers loathe visitation—both the term and the experience.

Sam, a supermarket manager, found visitation to be unnatural and insulting. "The only person in the world who's told how much time he can spend with my kids is me!" Sam complained. "Aunts, uncles, anybody in the neighborhood can drop by whenever they want—except me, their father. That has to be some kind of sacrilege."

A visiting father often feels like a stranger, an impostor. Visits become self-conscious, high-pressure interruptions of the children's "normal" lives. Fathers feel the need to entertain their kids or load them up with gifts. There doesn't seem to be enough time for the ordinary activities that "normal" dads and kids share—fixing a bike, taking a quiet walk, watching cartoons, painting the garage door. Time, most parents know, is an essential component of child rearing. Parents and children who don't spend a great deal of time together never become at ease with each other. Building trust and establishing effective communication become virtually impossible.

Unless a father and his children have an unusually strong relationship, visits become what one expert calls "the keenest torture that divorce has to offer."

Kip Eastman, a California teacher, wrote an essay recounting his experiences as a visitor/father, a role in which Eastman found himself to be "not quite useless, not quite needed. . . . It is this feeling that washes over me nearly every visitation. (I hate that word—like being in prison, or a psychiatric institution.) Am I still Chelsea's father when she's not here? . . . When we're together, none can mistake the relationship. But we are together so little. Every two weeks we make the transition from estranged correspondents to father and daughter. There is a brittleness about the first few hours; there is a melancholy about the last few. It leaves a painfully sweet day or two in between."

In addition to imposing a unique form of agony, a parental relationship constrained by the visitation process usually deprives a father of the moral authority he needs to offer guidance, exert leadership, and instill discipline. Children who view their father as an outsider, an entertainment director, or an eager-to-please supplicant are unlikely to extend the deference and respect that a "real" parent inspires. Typically, the children's failure to learn how to accept and respond to parental authority triggers a predictable chain reaction. First, the father's authority is challenged; soon after, the children become discipline problems for mothers, teachers, counselors, and coaches. Later in life, a chronic inability to respect the authority of employers, the police, and the courts is common.

"If you undermine the authority of a father, you plant the seeds of antisocial behavior in children," an East Coast social worker told a researcher. "Kids who turn on their fathers ultimately turn on their mothers. It may take some time, but it almost always happens. And many of these same kids come back to us later as juvenile delinquents."

In many instances, the daily access inherent in sole custody allows a mother to control, manipulate, and, if she wishes, destroy the father-child relationship. Many custodial mothers can (and do) use children as spies, as weapons of retribution, as instruments of extortion, and as commodities. In many households headed by divorced mothers, visitation rights are brokered like soybean futures; child support funds are spent in any way the custodial mother sees fit; and children are taught to fear and despise their fathers. Largely because of pro-mother bias, legal protection against these offenses is expensive and ineffective.

Beginning in the late 1980s author-psychiatrist Richard Gardner began documenting an epidemic of sorts—a unique disorder exhibited by children who had been involved in custody conflicts. Gardner called this emotional disorder "the parental alienation syndrome," and traced its cause to "conscious, unconscious, and subconscious programming orchestrated by one parent and directed at the other." The programming that Gardner identified was built on subtle but constant criticism, exaggeration of minor faults and weaknesses, and outright deception. Decimation or total destruction of a child's relationship with the "target" parent was the "programming" parent's objective. Given sufficient time, the programming parent was frequently able to induce in the child a frightening level of animosity for the other parent. Gardner found that while both fathers and mothers attempted these amateur brainwashing campaigns, custodial mothers were the source of 90 percent of the alienation disorders found in the children studied.

The programming techniques that Dr. Gardner examines in his book, *The Parental Alienation Syndrome,* are important ingredients in the assembly of the most powerful, and most despicable, weapon employed by vengeful, angry mothers: false child-abuse allegations.

Some matrimonial attorneys call abuse charges "the nuclear option." In many cases, the accusation itself ends all conflict between estranged spouses. Any hope for an equitable, compassionate resolution of the estranged couple's disagreements vanishes. The father, usually the target of these allegations, often surrenders unconditionally rather than face the public humiliation and personal trauma that inevitably arise from abuse charges—even if the accusations are untrue.

A father who chooses to fight back must overcome the custodial mother's considerable influence on the child, as well as the unlimited programming opportunities inherent in the free access a mother receives with sole or primary custody.

Dr. Domeena Renshaw, director of the Sexual Dysfunction Clinic at Loyola University in Chicago, acknowledged in a recent article that when custody issues are in question, abuse charges must be viewed skeptically. "It must be kept in mind that children are suggestible and compliant, especially with a parent they seek to please," Renshaw wrote. "Inducement or coercion of a child to falsify charges may be in the form of deception, rewards, or threats."

According to the National Committee for the Prevention of Child Abuse, less than 10 percent of abuse charges are false—unless the abuse allegation is part of divorce or custody litigation. In those situations, the incidence of unsubstantiated claims rises dramatically, as high as the 70-percent level in some jurisdictions.

Assisting predatory mothers in these shameful, defamatory attacks are assorted vermin from the dark periphery of the divorce "industry." If the family court system were a city, these residents would live in its sewers.

In a particularly disturbing case I handled not long ago, a custodial mother accused my client of abusing his three-year-old son. She claimed that my client forced pencils into the boy's rectum, that he beat the boy frequently, and that he had attempted to involve the boy in several deviant sexual activities—including intercourse with a dog. The mother needed medical confirmation of these charges, but corroboration was difficult to establish because

the charges were false. Even so, after visiting more than thirty doctors, the mother finally found one willing to say that, yes, the boy
had been abused, and the father (in this "professional's" opinion)
was the abuser. Luckily, it was clear to the judge in the case that the
mother had serious psychological problems and that, if the money
were right, the doctor would swear the child had been atomized by
space aliens.

In another case of mine, a mother asked a private detective to testify that my client had abused his children on several occasions.
Fortunately, when the detective took the witness stand, he was
trapped in a number of contradictions and inconsistencies. He became rattled and eventually admitted in court that he had been
asked to lie. Unfortunately, the name of the wrongfully accused father had already been published in the local newspapers. No penalties were ever assessed against either the mother or the detective.

Obviously, the devastation that befalls fathers victimized by untrue abuse allegations is severe, and frequently irreparable. Equally
disturbing are the profound effects that these reprehensible tactics
have on children and the father-child relationship. For many children purposely deceived into believing that they have been abused
by their fathers, fact and fiction eventually converge in terrible
memories of incidents that never occurred. The children's ability to
distinguish between fantasy and reality is lost forever. It's not unreasonable to suggest that thousands of American children are
growing up convinced that their fathers are child abusers, and hat-
ing their fathers for crimes they did not commit.

A Wider View

There is no question that the intense suffering and toxic trauma inflicted on fathers and children by judicial bias and incompetence is
serious, widespread, and shameful. For an evaluation of the cumulative, long-term consequences of family court failures, however, we
must step away from the personal chaos for a moment. By broaden-
ing our perspective, we can see how our court system's inequities
and deficiencies affect our society, and our nation's future.

No other country in the world has a higher divorce rate than the
United States. Over the past decade, an average of one million divorces
have occurred each year, involving 1.2 million children annually.

According to the Census Bureau, 18 million U.S. children now
live in single-parent homes. Only 3.5 percent of these kids live

with their dads. Unless my calculator is broken, that means we have 17.4 million children growing up fatherless.

Admittedly, in accordance with visitation agreements, some of these kids do see their fathers from time to time. As we've noted previously, the average visitation order gives a father fifty days a year with his children. Because 20 percent of custodial mothers see no value in maintaining the father-child relationship, visitation interference is common. That fifty-day allotment quickly evaporates. Only one in six divorced fathers sees his children once a week or more. Almost 40 percent of children who live with their mothers haven't seen their fathers in at least a year. The bottom line is, fathers are vanishing from the social landscape, and, as the following facts compiled by the National Fatherhood Initiative demonstrate, father absence has dramatic and extremely serious effects on us all:

- Seventy-two percent of all teenaged murderers grew up without fathers.

- Sixty percent of rapists were raised in fatherless homes.

- Seventy percent of the kids now incarcerated in juvenile corrections facilities grew up in a single-parent environment.

- Fatherless children are twice as likely to drop out of school as their classmates who live with two parents.

- Fatherless children are eleven times more likely than are children from intact families to exhibit violent behavior.

- Children whose fathers are absent consistently score lower than the norm in reading and math tests.

- Three of four teen suicides occur in single-parent families.

- Children who live apart from their fathers experience more accidents and a higher rate of chronic asthma, headaches, and speech defects.

- Eighty percent of the adolescents in psychiatric hospitals come from fatherless homes.

- Compared to girls raised in homes where both parents are present, the daughters of single parents are 164 percent more likely to become pregnant before marriage, 53 percent more likely to marry as teenagers, and 92 percent more likely to dissolve their own marriages.

- A growing body of evidence establishes a high correlation between fatherlessness and violence among young men (especially violence against women).

- The absence of a biological father increases by 900 percent a daughter's vulnerability to rape and sexual abuse (often these assaults are committed by stepfathers or the boyfriends of custodial mothers).

In the opinion of social critic David Blankenhorn, author of *Fatherless America,* "Fatherlessness is the most destructive trend of our generation." Vice President Al Gore concurred, declaring in a recent speech that "absent fathers are behind most social woes."

Knowledgeable social scientists have linked fatherlessness to a wide range of social nightmares and developmental deficiencies. Among these problems, judging by the results of numerous studies, are substantial increases in juvenile crime, drug and alcohol abuse, teenage pregnancy, promiscuity, truancy, and vandalism. Strong connections have also been established between a father's absence and a child's likelihood of becoming a dropout, jobless, a suicide victim, or a target of sexual abuse. A study of state prison populations found that only 41 percent of the inmates grew up with two parents. FBI statistics indicate that a missing father is a more reliable predictor of criminal activity than race, environment, or poverty.

U.S. News & World Report recently described the frightening reality faced daily by residents of fatherless city neighborhoods this way: "There are places in America where fathers—usually the best hope to socialize boys—are so rare that bedlam engulfs the community. Teachers, ministers, cops and other substitute authority figures fight losing battles in these places to present role models to pre-teen and teenage boys. The result is often an astonishing level of violence and incomprehensible incidents of brutality."

Two years ago, the National Center for Health Statistics reported that a child living with a divorced mother is almost twice as likely as a child living with both parents to repeat a grade of school, contract anemia, and suffer from intestinal distress, bed-wetting, and stuttering.

Several psychologists have documented the developmental difficulties endured by fatherless children. Low self-esteem, poor school performance, hyperactivity, lack of discipline, rejection of authority, depression, withdrawal, and several degrees of paranoia were among the disorders identified. As a group, these emotional and behavioral symptoms form what one researcher calls "the adolescent reactive adjustment syndrome." For years after childhood, hundreds of thousands of the fatherless continue to encounter educational, career, and relationship failures far more often than their peers from intact families.

The Economics of Father Absence

About half the fatherless families in the United States live below the poverty line. Children of these families are five times more likely to grow up poor than children who live with both parents. Children who are raised by a father and a mother usually climb higher on the socioeconomic ladder than their parents did; fatherless children generally slip lower on the scale.

The evil monster responsible for this deplorable psychosocial devastation is, in the eyes of the public, the deadbeat dad. Hated by all good Americans, this selfish weasel is arrogantly avoiding his legal and moral obligations to his children. Slipping, sliding, dodging, and hiding, the villainous scoundrel thumbs his nose at the formidable enforcement arsenal aligned against him.

"Get tougher on the bastards," the public demands.

Harsh no-nonsense legislation becomes even more punitive. Local law-enforcement officials form special task forces. The hammer comes down.

The cumulative costs of our decade-long war on deadbeat dads are staggering; yet there has been no measurable reduction in child support delinquencies.

Why not?

For openers, more than half of the delinquent fathers are dead, or in prison, or disabled, or seriously ill, or unemployed. Of the delinquent dads who do have jobs, 52 percent earn less than $6,200 a year (not enough to support one person).

Spending taxpayer money and government manpower trying to force men to ante up cash they simply don't have is ludicrous. An infinitely more productive use of public resources would target fathers able to pay child support but unwilling to do so *because they have been excluded from the lives of their children.* Reconnecting these fathers with their kids would reduce our alleged "child support crisis" to a nonissue.

Census Bureau data indicate that more than 90 percent of fathers with joint custody pay child support on time and in full. So do 80 percent of fathers who are satisfied with their visitation arrangements. On the other side of the coin, so to speak, we find that over 50 percent of fathers whose involvement with their children is minimal or nonexistent do not meet their child support obligations. I think it's safe to say that a clear pattern of cause and effect is apparent here.

A father's refusal to live up to his child support responsibilities cannot be defended, condoned, or rationalized. In many cases, however, a father's emotions, and not his character, rule his actions.

Many estranged fathers believe that withholding of child support is the only weapon they have to counteract the banishment, visitation obstruction, harassment, and alienation suffered at the hands of former spouses. Unable to obtain relief for legitimate grievances from biased or uncaring family courts, these fathers, essentially, are trying to use support funds to buy parenting time. It's a desperate measure by desperate men.

Other noncustodial fathers, frustrated and defeated by vindictive ex-wives and a useless judicial system, simply drift away from their children, overwhelmed by intolerable feelings of anger, failure, hatred, and loss. They stop paying child support because their children, their children's mothers, and the courts have stripped them of fatherhood. They retaliate by refusing to acknowledge the obligations of fatherhood. It's illegal, and morally wrong, but as one fathers' rights advocate explained, "To a father denied the sight of his daughter's piano recital, or his son's jump shot at the buzzer, child support is the modern equivalent of taxation without representation."

Our legal system's definition of "support," it seems to me, must be expanded—to include the love, nurturance, discipline, guidance, and companionship a child needs from both parents. Financial support is only one contribution parents can make to a child's well-being, and, it turns out, the money is not nearly as important as we've been led to believe. In academics and in tests of social competence, children from low-income two-parent families consistently outperform kids from wealthy single-parent homes. A recent study of 273,000 children identified thirty requirements vital to a child's successful growth and development. Financial support didn't make the cut. Parental availability, approachability, communicativeness, and involvement were at the top of the list. Please note that all these qualities rely on frequent parent-child interaction. Apparently, the most valuable support a parent can provide isn't payable in cash.

SUMMARY

Our discussions to this point have been about context. We've reviewed the rules, practices, and policies of the family court system, and I've tried to convey the bias, rage, and chaos that so often distort and disrupt what should be careful, compassionate deliberations.

The cases we examined in chapter 1 displayed our domestic relations courts at their best. Judges conscientiously weighed the evidence before them, then rendered decisions based on facts, legal standards, and sincere concern for children. In the cases in this chapter, there seemed to be no sign of respect for justice or the rights and needs of fathers and children. In these rulings, family court judges appear to have allowed ingrained prejudices and outdated presumptions to overwhelm objectivity, the dictates of the law, and, in many instances, common sense.

Which set of examples more accurately portrays the real-life workings of our judiciaries?

That depends. In some jurisdictions, fathers rarely encounter gender bias. Decisions determining custody, access, and support are rendered fairly and sympathetically. In other courts, the maternal presumption is so strong that, for a father to win custody, a mother must be proven to be completely unfit.

Frankly, domestic relations proceedings often resemble a midnight walk through unfamiliar countryside. The legal terrain a man must traverse to remain his children's father is tangled with thick underbrush and dangerous canyons, but it's not always a landscape composed entirely of rocks and hard places.

Largely due to the efforts of men's rights groups, the message that fathers, mothers, children, and society itself are all better off when fathers and children stay together is finally beginning to be heard in the halls and courtrooms of our judiciaries. Social scientists, child-care professionals, and legislators are all becoming aware of the importance of the father-child relationship and the disturbing, sometimes horrifying, effects of father absence.

Change is coming slowly, but it is coming. The antiquated cultural myths that cling to the walls in many family courts won't fade away completely until the judiciary becomes younger or more closely attuned to modern family life. Meanwhile, fathers seeking equitable treatment must assume that the playing field is not yet completely level and act accordingly.

In a nutshell, acting accordingly is what the rest of this book is about. Preserving fatherhood after divorce should not be such a challenge, but it is. Fathers must recognize that asserting their parental rights will require substantial reserves of self-control, patience, resolve, tenacity, and flexibility. Hardship, frustration, and stress must be endured because, as we've seen, the stakes are high. The lives, and futures, of millions of children are at risk, and so is the basic fabric of our society.

As every father knows, preservation of the father-child bond is not without its rewards. This book is about fathers' rights, but as psychologist Thomas Oakland reminded us, "Being a father is an exciting privilege." Fathers play an irreplaceable role in their children's lives—providing, protecting, guiding, shaping values, instilling discipline, and encouraging growth. Children repay these paternal investments tenfold, renewing a father's vitality, enriching a father's existence, and brightening a father's soul.

3
Basic
Training

A man who wants to remain a father despite the end of his marriage must survive a difficult passage from one life to another. To do so, more often than not, the divorcing father must conquer an arduous, demeaning, and frequently maddening process.

Typically, the full range of this dissolution process has four distinct stages (reminiscent of Dr. Elizabeth Kubler-Ross's theories on facing death):

Preseparation. *The couple is still living together, but their marriage is dead. Unhappiness, anger, disillusionment, and constant conflict are common.*

Separation. *The couple agrees to end the marriage and both partners experience feelings of depression, rage, guilt, and relief.*

Bargaining. *The former mates accept the end of their marriage, mourn its loss, and begin to rebuild their lives, addressing the myriad personal, economic, social, and parental changes that must occur.*

Starting Over. *This stage, the ultimate goal of the adjustment process, is characterized by recovery and reconnection—the successful reconstruction of one's life.*

For now, we'll follow the many twists and turns of the preseparation cycle, up to the point where custody issues become either a matter of compromise between two edgy but still civilized adults or the cause of all-out war.

The Final Days

It's over. The decision is final, irrevocable. The damage to the union is severe, beyond repair, and permanent. Life together has become unbearable. The dissolution of the relationship, you are about to discover, is no walk on the beach either.

The gap between accepting things the way they are and wishing them to be otherwise is the tenth of an inch that separates heaven and hell.

"If we rage and resist, our angry, fearful minds have trouble quieting down sufficiently to allow us to act in the most beneficial way for ourselves and others." Phil Jackson, head coach of the Chicago Bulls, four-time champions of the National Basketball Association, said that. Jackson's observation accurately describes the emotional state of many divorcing fathers as they begin to realize that an important and intimate relationship is ending.

In the early stages of the passage from the end of marriage to the beginning of the formal divorce process, it's not unusual to feel terrible most of the time. You are likely to experience some overpowering, frequently painful emotions: rage, grief, loneliness, depression, anxiety, confusion, self-pity, guilt, feelings of worthlessness, a sense of failure. You may also be vulnerable to sharp, sudden mood swings—exhilaration or profound relief one moment, despair and self-hatred the next. You may not be able to sleep, eat, or concentrate on your work.

Although divorce can vaporize an unstable psyche (divorced men are eight times more likely to be hospitalized for mental illness than married men), you probably are not going crazy. You are reacting normally to intense situational stress. Countless fathers have endured and survived the same emotional chaos. This is how some of them initially responded to the disintegration of their marriages. . . .

> "My only thought was to get from day to day without cracking up."
>
> *(Phil, 32)*

> "I had a tough time waking up in the morning because I was restless and having nightmares all night. I felt broken, physically and emotionally."
>
> *(Mickey, 29)*

> "I was in shock. I stared out the window all day, for weeks."
>
> *(Brent, 44)*

"I felt despondent, a failure to myself and my kids."

(Al, 37)

"My feelings were frozen. I didn't care about anything."

(Vince, 28)

"I felt awful, horrible. Betrayed and deserted. Fucked over and fucked up. It almost destroyed me."

(Leo, 46)

"I felt like I had a sign around my neck that read 'This man has left his wife and children. He couldn't keep his family together.' I felt like a loser. It made me sick to see myself in the bathroom mirror."

(Darryl, 41)

"I felt burned out, crushed by the weight of all the things I felt I had to do right away—deciding where to live, what to do about the kids, the house, all the financial and legal crap. I couldn't stand it."

(George, 31)

"I drank, I cried, I thought about suicide."

(Ed, 42)

What these men are recalling is the extreme psychological agitation that almost always accompanies divorce—mental and physical upheaval worse than the stress of losing a job or going to prison. Only the death of a loved one creates more inner turmoil.

"Nothing is more painful than the edges of a broken dream," author Persia Woolley observed. It doesn't matter why a marriage shatters or who decides that the relationship must end. There is no easy way out. Even when both partners agree to part with no apparent hard feelings, some degree of sorrow and animosity usually lies just below the surface.

Recovering from the emotional beating is a divorcing father's first challenge. Psychologists tell us that the return to emotional equilibrium and functional rationality can occur quickly, slowly, or not at all, depending on a number of fairly obvious factors: the causes of the marriage's erosion, the individual father's need—or reluctance—to see the relationship end, the degree of financial hardship involved, self-image and inner resources, and the degree of support provided by family, friends, and professionals.

As a father seeking custody rights, it's important for you to deal with the emotional upheaval of the early stages of divorce as quickly and as effectively as you can. I know that the beginning of the end is often a volatile time, a debilitating marathon of anger, pain, disappointment, and bitterness. Legitimate and imagined grievances are hurled back and forth. Vicious accusations and righteous countercharges fly in a knock-down drag-out free-for-all that ends with both you and your wife absolutely certain that the other person exists only to make life as miserable as possible.

My advice to fathers in this situation may seem harsh, but here it is: Move on. It's over. Whatever feelings brought you and your spouse together are gone. It no longer matters who is responsible for the breakup. An endless replay of what went wrong, and why, is pointless. It's not important who changed or who refused to change, or who was caught with his pants down or her skirt up, or who's a bitch and who's a prick. Fault is irrelevant now. The marriage is broken and it can't be fixed. It's time to redirect your energies and efforts toward your children—who, by the way, will probably be more devastated by the end of your marriage than you are.

I have represented thousands of divorcing fathers. Some of these poor guys were so overcome by trauma they were barely able to function. If they had been cartoons, their heads would have exploded. I recognize that the emotional disarray triggered by divorce is incredibly powerful and frequently unmanageable. Nevertheless, a divorcing father must do whatever needs to be done to gain control of his feelings and actions. There are at least four compelling reasons why.

1: *Everything you say, or do, or threaten to do can be held against you in a court of law.* Remember that many family courts are governed at least as much by cultural stereotype as they are by statute. The stereotype at work in this instance allows a mother to be irrational. She can scream, rant, weep, rave, throw dinnerware, pour paint in the pockets of your best suit, sell your custom-made golf clubs for two dollars, and fill your toothpaste tube with Preparation H. Because she's a woman, many judges feel, her erratic behavior is simply a natural reaction to a terrible personal tragedy.

The other side of this badly out-of-balance scale dictates that fathers, regardless of provocation, justification, or basic human wiring, must remain calm, wise, conciliatory, and rational. Courts are reluctant to place children with a father who seems unable to control himself.

I suggest that divorcing fathers borrow a strategy that has been proven successful in presidential politics. Typically, the incumbent in a national election uses his position to create in the minds of voters an image of cool competence. When his opponent attacks, the incumbent counters by signing a treaty, or visiting the scene of some natural disaster, or welcoming the Olympic volleyball team to the White House. These scenes of the veteran chief executive effortlessly discharging the duties of his office are designed to show the incumbent "being presidential." The opponent is the hungry, desperate politician, these tactics imply, while the incumbent is obviously a statesman, a leader, above the petty skirmishes of electoral combat.

Numerous presidents have retained the office by "being presidential." Divorcing fathers can improve their chances of retaining their parental status by "being fatherly." Respond to screaming and wailing and foaming at the mouth with composure. Meet insults with quiet resolve.

2: *The sights, sounds, and psychic debris of marital discord are harmful to children.* Hearing parents berate each other and seeing parents' faces twisted with rage and loathing are deeply disturbing to children of all ages. For younger children, parents' fights are terrifying. Little kids are extremely self-centered. They find it easy to convince themselves that they are to blame for their parents' fights and that neither parent really wants or loves them. Their world is ending, or so it seems. "Who will take care of me?" children of divorce wonder. Often, anxiety and uncertainty supply the answer to this question in the form of frightening fantasies.

When parents denigrate each other, it hurts kids badly, even when what is said is true. A mother and father may despise each other, but their children love them both.

Parents who have the good sense to move hostilities to a private battlefield may keep open conflict from their children's view, but the parental love and support the children need to survive divorce are still missing. Parents absorbed in their own troubles cannot provide the care and concern children require.

3: *Conflict feeds upon itself.* Experts in the dynamics of interpersonal communication have found that retaliating in kind to strident, irrational expressions of rage, pain, and animosity usually deepens conflict and pushes the dissenting parties farther apart. This insight into the obvious can be illustrated quickly via a trip to a local playground, where two twelve-year-olds have pooled resources to buy candy:

MACK: Hey, you said we were gonna split those Milk Duds.

ZACK: We did.

MACK: No, you got six; I only got four.

ZACK: Quit whining, you little baby.

MACK: Bite me, cheater.

ZACK: You're a stupid raisin-face whiny butt baby. And you're ugly.

MACK: Not as ugly as you, fat ass. You're a slimy cheating ferret and you smell bad.

ZACK: You're a baby, you eat baby shit, and your mother sucks elephant dicks.

Can we see where this self-perpetuating dispute is headed, and why? I think we can.

The emotional agitation of marital discord is never going to level off if both you and your spouse insist on fueling the fire at every opportunity. As the lovely story of Mack and Zack teaches us, your conflict will escalate. If you think Mack's fight with Zack is stupid, think about this: The differences between you and your soon-to-be ex-wife are irreparable (that's why you're ending the marriage, isn't it?). So what is the point of continuing to tear yourselves up clawing through the ashes of a bond that no longer exists? Disengage. While there's no guarantee that your refusal to participate will end any given conflagration, you can at least reduce its volatility by half.

4: *Decisions made in the midst of emotional turmoil can adversely affect you and your children for years, or forever.* Resolution of custody, support, and other financial issues requires careful planning, objective thought, and rational discussion. None of these is likely to occur until you and your spouse have regained your emotional stability. Impulsive behavior related to psychological trauma has caused countless fathers to give up or lose parental prerogatives. Giving in to the urge to escape an unbearable relationship no matter what or overreacting to feelings of guilt or worthlessness could bring serious, and irreversible, consequences.

The problem with advising fathers to adjust as quickly as possible to the internal chaos inherent in divorce is that there are no step-by-step, by-the-numbers instructions to offer. Each father must take his own path to recovery and control.

Fortunately, in most parts of the United States, help in finding that path is readily available. Because divorce has become so common, a variety of assistance options exist.

Almost every divorcing father now has friends who have been through the dissolution process. These friends can supply valuable emotional support and, sometimes, useful guidance. At least the divorce novice will learn what has worked and what hasn't.

A number of excellent books offering survival advice for the newly divorced are available. Several of the best are listed in the Appendix.

Most metropolitan areas have at least one volunteer-staffed divorce organization. The first and largest of these not-for-profit groups is Parents Without Partners (PWP). Founded in 1957, PWP has well over a thousand chapters in the United States and Canada, and membership of over two hundred thousand. Countless smaller divorce organizations also exist, most of them regional and much smaller than PWP. These groups usually can be found through the community calendar published in most local newspapers.

While many of these support organizations are basically social clubs, most of them also offer regular discussion groups, classes, and lectures on divorce issues, including information about how to cope with the trauma of the initial phase of the dissolution process.

Another potential source of meaningful assistance is a relatively new service offered by many family therapists: divorce counseling. The purpose of divorce counseling is not reconciliation. The advice and guidance provided are geared to help divorcing couples fashion a clean break. Some divorce counselors are private practitioners; others are associated with large marriage-counseling centers. Some of these centers are operated on a not-for-profit basis by family-service and mental-health organizations associated with local governments or volunteer agencies. Others are private counseling services with higher fees.

A divorcing father's best choice for access to emotional support may be a local fathers' rights organization. These groups work diligently on behalf of disenfranchised fathers, and most are excellent sources of vital information and well-informed guidance.

While research on the value of support groups and divorce counseling is scarce, several small-scale studies have found that newly divorced or separated subjects made quicker emotional adjustments and, overall, experienced less stress than survey participants who remained isolated. Two-thirds of the men who sought professional or peer-group counseling found the experience helpful.

Keep in mind that the goal of internal trauma management is not total mastery of your feelings or some mystical all-encompassing inner serenity. What you need is a level of self-control sufficient to allow you to function rationally and effectively in dealing with the legal and practical aspects of the dissolution process.

Home Rule

As a troubled relationship speeds toward its ending, the influences of toxic emotions often lead to perhaps the most common mistake made by fathers in the early phase of the dissolution process: leaving the family home.

No matter how uncomfortable or hostile the home becomes, the father generally must stay. Leaving often radically reduces his chances for custody. If litigation becomes necessary to resolve custody issues, he might be portrayed as a father who turned his back on his children. Once out of the family home, he'll likely face great difficulties getting back in. By leaving, the father is allowing the children's mother to become the (de facto) primary custodial parent. He is giving her the opportunity to create for the children the "familiar, stable environment" that courts are so reluctant to disrupt.

So stay. And stay under control. Avoid confrontations, violence, threats of violence, and even defensive violence at all costs. If your spouse provokes you, verbally or physically, withdraw to the bathroom and lock the door. Or go for a walk until tensions ease. If you feel endangered by your wife's conduct (she brandishes a butcher knife, for instance), call the police and report a domestic dispute.

Sometimes, mothers attempt to use "kick-out" orders (ex-parte orders for protection or exclusive possession) to obtain a tactical advantage in future custody disputes. If you have engaged in violence or threatening behavior of any kind, your defense against these ploys will be severely undermined.

Another strategy that spouses sometimes employ unfolds like this:

> WIFE: Our marriage is in serious trouble. We're at each other's throats every minute. I'm a wreck. Maybe we should give each other some space, some time to think.
> HUSBAND: What are you suggesting?
> WIFE: Why don't you stay at a hotel (or with your brother, or your mother, or a friend) for a week or so? Maybe we'll be able

to actually talk calmly if we get away from each other for a while.

HUSBAND: You might be right. I know I could use some peace and quiet.

The husband leaves. Just for a week, he believes. Three days later, here comes a process server. The father is being sued for divorce, his wife has established herself as the children's custodian, the locks have been changed, and the father is on the outside looking in.

I'll say it again: Don't give in to the often overpowering need to escape; don't overreact to emotional forces. Stay in your home with your children.

If your spouse says that living with you is intolerable, suggest that she should move out, and leave the children in your care. In fact, if you can afford it, offer to help finance her relocation.

Choosing an Attorney

It is a standard scene familiar to all viewers of the gritty, life-in-the-urban-jungle police drama. . . .

A suspect is arrested and hustled into the interrogation room. Down the hall, detectives huddle, concocting a strategy to coerce, cajole, or trick the suspect into confessing before he "lawyers up." A competent attorney, the detectives know, will force them to honor the suspect's right to avoid self-incrimination and block their attempts to use the suspect's fears and ignorance of the law against him. The early involvement of a lawyer moves the issue of the suspect's guilt or innocence out of the volatile pressure cooker of the interrogation room into the highly structured rules-oriented arena of the judiciary—where it belongs.

Divorce is not a criminal matter, but there is an important lesson for divorcing fathers at the core of the "lawyering-up" concept. Instead of making commitments you will deeply regret later, "lawyer up" before you agree to anything. Early consultation with a competent matrimonial attorney is vital to the protection of a father's rights. Knowledgeable legal advice can save a divorcing father years of frustration and thousands of dollars.

Although some marriages shatter suddenly, with literally no warning, the end of most troubled unions comes only after a grueling, arduous ordeal spanning months, or years. Don't wait for the death rattle. Don't become a target looking for an arrow. As soon as you realize that your marriage is in danger of coming apart, find an attorney.

There is no foolproof method for locating and choosing an attorney, so plan to spend some time in research and interviews. Because it is an important decision, very likely to shape your future as a father, be thorough, and careful.

One of the most common methods for finding qualified counsel is the use of personal referrals. Ask divorced friends to rate their attorney's capabilities and performance, especially in custody matters. Ask these friends about their spouse's attorneys, too. Find out who seemed to have the upper hand in court and in negotiations.

A lawyer who currently represents you personally or in your business, or a friend who is an attorney, may be able to offer useful recommendations. Be aware, however, that a social or business relationship between the recommender and the recommendee may provide the impetus for the referral.

The Martindale-Hubbell Law Directory, available at many public and courthouse libraries, attempts to list every attorney currently practicing in the United States. The directory's listings are regionalized by state and city. Each attorney's listing includes age, year of admission to the bar, and codes indicating the college and law school attended. A triangular symbol before the attorney's name tells you that he or she is a member of the American Bar Association. (Membership in the ABA is not, by itself, evidence of professional skill.) Attorney listings include a rating. The "a v" rating is the highest available, and is awarded only if the attorney has at least ten years' experience. For attorneys who have practiced for at least five years but less than ten, a "b" is the highest rating given. An attorney's rating is determined by his peers and applies only to a specific locale.

The bulk of each volume of this comprehensive directory consists of professional "cards." These cards can be inserted only by a law firm or an individual attorney having the "a v" rating. An attorney's card includes some useful information: a biographical sketch, the legal areas the lawyer believes to be his specialties, and a summary of what he's done and who he has represented.

Most local, county, and state bar associations operate a lawyer referral service. Generally, these services will provide you with the names of several attorneys who consider themselves family law specialists. (Some states certify specialists in domestic relations law; others do not. For example, Illinois does not, and it is unethical for an Illinois lawyer to represent himself as a family-law or custody specialist.) Usually, these referral services are not allowed to rate lawyers or comment at all on an attorney's competence.

About thirty years ago, the American Academy of Matrimonial Lawyers was founded to "encourage the study, improve the practice, elevate the standards and advance the cause of matrimonial law, to the end that the welfare of the family and society be preserved." This group of domestic relations attorneys, which now includes several thousand members across the United States, publishes a list of Certified Fellows in each region. While membership in the AAML is no guarantee of proficiency, it is an indication that family law is an important element of a member lawyer's practice. At the very least, an AAML fellow has continuing access to a wealth of current information on custody legislation and judicial trends.

Parents Without Partners and similar organizations are also sources of informed referral information, particularly if individual members are canvassed. Fathers' rights organizations provide another excellent option. (You will certainly learn immediately which attorneys *not* to retain.)

Lawyers no longer view advertising as crass or tacky, so check your local newspapers for divorce specialists. Use the yellow pages only to find a lawyer's phone number; obtain the attorney's name from a better informed source.

Take as long as you need for your search. Don't stop looking until you have compiled a list of at least three possibilities. Schedule an interview with each attorney on your list. Some attorneys charge their normal hourly rate for the initial consultation; others, a reduced fee. Many charge nothing at all for the first meeting. Don't drop an attorney from your list of potential advocates based on the cost of the initial consultation. Bargain hunting at this early stage may cause you to exclude an attorney exactly suited to your needs.

As you prepare for these initial interviews, remember that you are the consumer, the lawyer's services the product. It's up to you to evaluate the experience and lawyering skills of each attorney you'll meet. It's up to the attorney to furnish the information required to make that evaluation.

In order for you to gain the knowledge you need to make an informed decision, your first interview with each potential advocate must be a two-way exchange of information and philosophies. All your discussions with prospective attorneys, no matter how brief, are, under the law, privileged conversations. Whatever you divulge will generally remain confidential, so don't be reluctant to be open and honest. However, exceptions do apply. In Illinois, for example, the privilege does not apply if you communicate your intent to participate in a future crime or if your lawyer sues you for fees.

The lawyer will probably ask you to describe your marriage briefly—its length, number of children (and their ages), the state of the family finances, your job, your wife's job, and so forth. Then the attorney will want a concise history of the events and feelings that led to the decision to divorce. He'll want to know what both you and your spouse have contributed to the breakup. It's important that you answer the attorney's questions as completely and as frankly as possible. To accurately assess the strengths and weaknesses of what will become your case, the lawyer needs to know *all* the facts, favorable and unfavorable. The natural tendency to "rewrite" the past must be avoided. Your self-delusion will distort the attorney's perception of what needs to be done and how easy or difficult it will be to do it.

Be sure to tell the attorney something about your spouse's character and personality. (In divorce cases, psychological profiles are almost as important as facts.) Also, discuss the children's personalities, and how you think the divorce will affect them. Make your desire for custody or meaningful parental contact known.

Financial aspects of the impending dissolution must also be examined briefly in the initial interview. Be prepared to answer questions about your income, pension, profit sharing, stock options, property, and other assets.

Be aware of the lawyer's reactions to your story, but don't allow yourself to be taken in by a skilled suck-up.

All competent attorneys are attentive and responsive listeners. Unfortunately, many not-so-competent lawyers are good listeners, too. Don't evaluate a potential advocate on his listening skills—unless he has none. If the attorney you are interviewing cuts you off in midsentence to launch a heavy-handed lecture about what you and your children really need, cross him off your list immediately.

Believe me when I tell you that you don't want a lawyer who decides unilaterally what to do and then pushes you into doing it. You'll be much better off with an attorney who understands your goals and offers all feasible legal options for reaching them. Also be wary of lawyers who react to your narrative by not reacting at all. You want an advocate capable of at least professional empathy for your situation. Heed this advice from the comic strip *B.C.*: "Don't hire a lawyer who says 'whatever' a lot."

After the attorney has a basic understanding of your situation, it's your turn to ask some questions. Your objective is to find out all you can about the attorney's competence, style, knowledge of the local family courts, availability, and success rate. Ask what percentage of the lawyer's practice involves domestic relations. Be wary if the total is less than half. Ask what percentage of the lawyer's cases are settled out of court. If the number is less than 80 percent, it's possible that the attorney is a bit too fond of combat—and the fees that accrue during prolonged litigation. Conversely, if *none* of the lawyer's cases are ever decided at trial, the attorney may be prone to bargaining away your rights rather than asserting them in court.

A lawyer's availability and accessibility are vital elements of the attorney-client relationship. Try to gauge the size of the lawyer's workload and determine how frequently the attorney anticipates communicating with you. Because most domestic crises occur late at night or during weekends, find out if the lawyer offers twenty-four-hour availability for emergencies.

Obviously, as a father intent on remaining a parent, you must learn all you can about the attorney's philosophy and attitudes about custody matters. As I warned earlier, many family law specialists, *including lawyers who represent fathers,* still believe deep in their hearts that mothers want and need custody rights, while fathers really don't.

Reject instantly any attorney who gives you the impression that your children should be a low-priority issue. On the other hand, look favorably on a lawyer who has been successful in winning primary custody for fathers or who has participated in fashioning effective joint custody agreements.

Near the end of the interview, ask the attorney for a preliminary evaluation of your situation. Beware of the lawyer who assures swift and total victory on all fronts, who declares you doomed as doomed can be, or who has no opinion at all about potential outcomes. Prefer a lawyer who is willing to offer you realistic estimates of your chances of prevailing in the resolution of the various issues expected to be in dispute. These initial impressions will necessarily be general, but they should reflect an understanding of your case and an informed prediction of how local court policies, practices, and attitudes will affect your goals.

You need a lawyer who is competent, trustworthy, and reliable. Be alert for comments, facial expressions, or body language that indicate the lawyers you are meeting lack one or more of these qualities. Supplement your impressions by speaking to former clients of each attorney you interview. If you haven't been referred by a past client, ask the lawyer for some names. Or do your own research—divorce actions are matters of public record.

Consolidate the information you've gathered from your interviews and recommendations into an evaluation checklist that you can use to compare the attorneys you've met.

A sample checklist follows. Use it as a base, and add whatever other considerations you feel are important to your individual needs. (The checklist is also a good source of material for your interview questions.)

COMPARISON CHECKLIST
General

- Percentage of practice devoted to family law?
- Certified Domestic Relations Specialist (if applicable in your state)?
- Years of family law experience in this jurisdiction?
- Does he/she seem familiar with the attitudes and predispositions of local judges?
- Is he/she aware of the expectations, standards, and personal quirks of local custody evaluators?
- Does he/she recommend the inclusion of a divorce counselor or family therapist in custody discussions?
- How does he/she feel about the parental capabilities of fathers?
- How does he/she feel about joint custody?
- How many options for resolution of custody disputes did he/she offer?
- Did he/she explain the advantages and disadvantages of mediation and arbitration?
- What percentage of cases does he/she settle out of court?
- How many divorce or custody trials lasted more than a year?
- How many trials decided in his/her client's favor?
- Is he/she a divorced parent?
- If so, does he/she have custody of the children?

- If not, why not?
- If so, how was custody obtained?
- How often will he/she supply status reports?
- How often does he/she anticipate meeting with me?
- Does he/she offer twenty-four-hour availability for emergencies?

Interview Notes

- Did he/she give me his/her undivided attention?
- Did he/she rush me, or was I allowed to fully explain my situation, needs, and goals?
- Did he/she ask relevant questions and allow me to answer them completely?
- Did he/she paraphrase what I said accurately?
- Did he/she moralize?
- Did he/she offer what seemed to be a realistic appraisal of my situation?
- Did he/she explain what had to be done and how?
- Did he/she say or do anything that indicated a lack of interest in my case?
- Were we frequently interrupted?
- Did his/her overall demeanor inspire confidence?

Former Client's Evaluation

- Was client satisfied with his/her representation?
- Did he/she keep the client well informed?
- What did the client like best about him/her?
- What did the client like least?
- Did the attorney help or hinder communications with the ex-spouse?
- How promptly did he/she return former client's calls?
- How close to estimate was his/her final bill?

Fees

- Amount of retainer?
- Hourly rate?
- Estimate for this case?
- What constitutes complications?

- Will he/she send a monthly statement?
- Payment arrangements he/she requests?

If none of the attorneys you interview seem to meet your requirements, resume the search. (You really have no choice.) Unless you live in a remote area, numerous skilled professionals are available. Keep looking until you find one you feel comfortable in retaining.

If more than one of the attorneys you visit seem equally acceptable, base your decision on rapport. Admittedly, rapport is a vague term, encompassing instinctual feelings of trust, harmony, accord, and affinity. It is a personal reaction difficult to define but immediately recognized when it appears.

Working with Your Attorney

When you believe you have found a competent professional advocate, a wonderful feeling of relief may wash over your battered psyche. You will be tempted to relax, secure in the belief that having a lawyer will solve all your problems. Instead of evaluating the attorney's advice, you allow your lawyer to do whatever he or she thinks is best. You immediately take your counsel's every suggestion without reflection. Before long, it's not your case anymore. You have given up control.

Don't do it. Never give up control of your life to anyone—not your lawyer, not your spouse, not your children. Establish reasonable, realistic goals, and ask your attorney to advise you in achieving them. Your lawyer's role should be to explain your legal options and offer an objective, informed analysis of the benefits and dangers of each course of action. Your role is to decide what to do. You should respect your attorney's advice, but the final word should always be yours. After all, it's your life (and your children's) at stake.

Regular contact with your attorney is essential. You must be kept up-to-date on the status of your case and the activities of the other side. If your lawyer doesn't provide regular status reports and seems unable or unwilling to return your calls promptly, you may have to consider finding a different attorney.

On the other hand, don't call your advocate every time you have an anxiety attack. It's not unusual for a divorcing father to feel the need to contact his lawyer incessantly—especially during the emotionally charged initial stages of the dissolution process. Each and every interaction with his ex, no matter how casual, triggers a phone call. Every change he sees, or thinks he sees, in his children must be discussed with counsel immediately and at length, as must every custody case he reads about in the newspaper or hears about on talk radio. Mostly, the divorcing father calls his attorney when he is feeling down, or angry, or confused, or overwhelmed. Most experienced matrimonial lawyers understand and sympathize with the emotional trauma their clients are experiencing. Many will suggest peer-group support or professional counseling, and recommend providers of these services. Other attorneys, because they see themselves either consciously or unconsciously as the father's savior (or hero, or champion), will attempt a form of counseling themselves. Some lawyers will serve as semipro psychologists because their years in family law have left them familiar with, and responsive to, the divorcing father's pain. And a small number of divorce attorneys welcome frequent contact because they are being paid for these little gabfests. An even smaller number want to know everything about everything that happens to their clients. They are as emotionally involved in the case as the client. (That's not always a good thing. The dissolution process is a long, slippery road. Either the client or the lawyer has to be the designated driver.)

Early in your conferences with your attorney, reach an understanding about what information is important to your case and what isn't. Keep a case journal to record these data. (Don't call these notes a diary. In many jurisdictions, diaries are subject to discovery. A case journal, on the other hand, might be viewed as a client/attorney work product and, as such, privileged.) Use this journal to keep track of significant events and behavior. Your attorney will provide an exact definition of what is and isn't significant, but generally your journal should focus on parenting activities and communications between you and your spouse.

Once you and your attorney agree on the kind of information he/she needs from you, keep subsequent discussions within these parameters. If you need someone to talk to about your feelings, don't call your lawyer. Find a friend, join a divorced men's organization, or see a divorce counselor. You'll save a great deal of money and receive more useful support.

I have tried to emphasize that your attorney works for you. Ultimately, you are in charge. Your lawyer is required by law and professional ethics to zealously represent your best interests and carry out your instructions (unless they're illegal). There will be times, however, when you should defer to your attorney. It makes no sense to hire a professional advocate and then reject or ignore that professional's advice. When your lawyer tells you not to harass your ex-spouse, or not to overextend visitations, or not to squander marital assets, it's because the attorney knows these actions will damage your case. Listen to these instructions and comply. If your lawyer tells you that a settlement offer is as good, or better, than what you would get if your case were to go to court, recognize that most seasoned matrimonial attorneys are aware of the tendencies of the courts in which they work. They know a good deal when they see one. Factor your lawyer's experience into your decision. Unless you detect a fatal flaw in a settlement offer that your attorney favors, give the offer serious consideration.

As your case progresses (or fails to progress), you may find yourself dissatisfied with your attorney's performance. If your dissatisfaction reaches the point where you feel a change must be made, I suggest you analyze your motives before taking that step. If your lawyer isn't offering the emotional support you feel you need, or if a personality conflict has developed, remember that in your situation you need a professional advocate, not a friend. The fact that you find your attorney to be rude, or aloof, or just plain annoying is not a valid reason to make a change. That decision should be based on an honest, objective answer to one simple question: Is he or she representing you competently and aggressively?

I recommend that you consider looking for new counsel only if one or more of the following criteria applies:

- You are spending a lot of money and seeing no activity or results.

- Your attorney does not understand or agree with your custody objectives.

- There is no communication from your attorney except requests for money.

- The attorney ignores your instructions without reasonable explanations.

- The attorney seems to be much too friendly with your spouse's counsel.

- The attorney is too busy (or not interested enough) to devote the time your case requires.

If it does become necessary to change attorneys, don't do so until you are confident that you have found an able and willing replacement. Severing your relationship with a lawyer you find unsatisfactory requires no explanation; a simple one-sentence notice is sufficient. You must, however, be prepared to pay off any reasonable outstanding fees. Most jurisdictions recognize that a lawyer has a lien on his or her case files, and some lawyers won't release the file until they are paid in full.

Although a change in representation may be necessary and beneficial in the long run, don't make a habit of it. Each time you make a change, it will take time for your new attorney to assimilate and understand the details of your case, which will be yet another hurdle to overcome.

We've already demonstrated that family court judges (and most humans) are strongly influenced by ingrained attitudes and perceptions. Here's another potentially damaging predisposition you may encounter if you replace your attorney more than once: Many judges feel that litigants who frequently change lawyers are probably unstable and/or unreasonable. If you appear before him with your fourth or fifth lawyer at your side, a judge may have already decided that the problem with your case is you.

Temporary Custody

The place has been your home for years, but now the surroundings seem alien—like a barren, sun-scalded asteroid in another universe.

There you are. There she is. Both lawyered to the gills. Your attorney has advised you not to move out; her attorney has given her the same warning. The first stage of the dissolution process has reached critical mass. Unless somebody does something, one or both of you will ignite or melt away.

The advice "Don't blink first" is another of those easy-to-dispense, difficult-to-follow nuggets of wisdom we lawyers are so fond of. Nevertheless, it is often the only realistic option for a divorcing man who wants to continue to be a father.

Too frequently, the need to escape an intolerable home environment, a spouse's offer to reduce child support demands, the lure of a new love, or some other enticement pushes a divorcing father into a "temporary" custody agreement that effectively prevents him from having any meaningful role in the lives of his children. When the father attempts to modify the temporary pact's unacceptable terms, a nasty jolt awaits down at the courthouse. The phrase "temporary custody," it turns out, has a special definition in the minds of many family court judges. It means, "I'm not changing a thing unless you show me some damn good reasons why I have to."

Although the language of the law states that temporary custody orders are indeed "provisional," many courts are reluctant to alter the status quo. It's true that, on paper, the legal standards for modifying a temporary custody order are much less stringent than the level of proof required to alter a permanent custody award. In real life, however, courts rarely uproot children from what seems to be a stable environment. (And, of course, if the parent asking for a change in the temporary order is the father, there may be gender bias to overcome as well.)

Early in the dissolution process, you and your lawyer must reach a clear understanding of the custody rights you need to retain your parental status. Unless these rights are included in a temporary custody order, reject it. Ignore the argument that "It's only temporary, let's see how it goes. We can always modify it later."

Hopefully, your firm commitment to your children will convince your spouse that she will never get you out of her life until she becomes serious about an equitable custody arrangement.

Shielding the Children

You're struggling with the emotional upheaval that always comes with the end of an intimate relationship. You are trying to cope with a hostile environment and the irritating demands of a lumbering, insensitive legal process. Your time, energy, and inner resources are stretched to their limits. You don't need another live grenade to juggle, but here comes one: You have children.

As a parent, you must fight to protect them from the carnage and confusion that always reigns when the family structure crumbles.

Psychologists and other family scientists have made children of divorce one of the most thoroughly studied groups in the history of social research. The results of these comprehensive investigations will not surprise divorced parents. Children, regardless of age, are terrified of divorce. Almost without exception, children want their parents to stay together. Even after a divorce becomes final, most kids fantasize that their parents will reconcile.

As you might expect, children's specific reactions to divorce vary by age. Toddlers (two to three years old) often become bewildered and cranky, likely to cling fiercely to any adult family member.

Preschoolers (ages four to five) seem to blame themselves for their parent's breakup; they suffer a decline in self-image and a loss of self-esteem. Kids of grade-school age commonly become extremely sad and frightened. Older preteens often feel lonely, ashamed, and angry. About half of the children in this age group exhibit physical symptoms (such as headaches, clumsiness, and stuttering). Depression, difficulties at school, and problems with other kids also surface frequently. For adolescents, their parents' divorce more often than not triggers pain, anger, depression, and resentment, sometimes resulting in hostile behavior, substance abuse, withdrawal from peers, promiscuity, and suicide.

The damage inflicted on children by their parents' divorce is severe, and, psychologists have found, the injuries linger. Five years after their parents' divorce, most children still show signs of trauma. About a third develop several social and personal problems. Fifteen years after their parents' divorce, more than half the children studied remained troubled.

Many of the same studies that have chronicled the debilitating effects of divorce on children have found that divorce's impact can be lessened substantially *if the divorced father remains closely involved in the children's lives.*

The message is clear: Despite the almost unbearable stress of divorce, you must not neglect your responsibility to help your children cope with the devastation that they are suffering.

Presumably, when you and your spouse decided to end your marriage, you were careful to consider what the decision would do to your children. You determined you were not breaking up in response to some new-age fascination with "self-actualization" or as an overreaction to normal marital crises. Preferably with the help of a qualified marriage counselor, you have tried reconciliation or rededication. Now you are certain that your marriage is over.

Tell the children as soon as possible. The best time to break the news is after basic child-care arrangements have been agreed upon (or ordered by a court) but before one of you leaves the family home. You should give the children enough time, while both of you are still around, to weather the severe shock kids usually feel when a family is dismantled. To absorb the impact and begin to adapt, the children need a period of emotional convalescence. But don't tell them about your decision so far in advance of the actual breakup that the continued presence of both parents keeps alive false hope that the marriage will be repaired.

Explain to your children that you and their mother tried to work out your problems but that the differences between you are simply too great. You need not go into the harrowing details of the breakup. Simply say that the conflict between you and their mother has made everyone in the home miserable and that it will be better for everyone if you and your spouse live apart. This is certainly true. One of the few family situations more damaging to children than divorce is growing up with the cold, relentless hostility that permeates a dead marriage. A union that operates on artificial life support "for the sake of the children" does everyone a disservice. It often is helpful to consult with a skilled divorce counselor or pediatric psychologist before discussing your divorce with your children. If it's possible, both parents, together, should explain the impending separation. Whatever truce needs to be negotiated to bring this joint effort about is worth the trouble. Learning about your decision from both of you will ease the children's fears of abandonment somewhat and hasten their adjustment to the changes about to occur in their lives.

Telling your children about your divorce will not be easy, but children are tougher than you think. And they are not stupid. Don't say that Daddy's going on a long trip or that Mommy will be at Grandma's for a while. Tell the truth.

It will be hard for them to hear, but easier to bear than the vague fears and disturbing fantasies kids suffer with when they know something bad is happening but not exactly what. Be honest with them; they need to know where they stand. Use simple, direct language. Don't confuse the children or mislead them into thinking reconciliation is possible.

Do everything you can to emphasize to the children that your decision to divorce is not their fault. Make certain that they understand that the breakup will not affect your love for them. Assure your kids that, while moms and dads sometimes fall out of love with each other, parents love their children forever. Explain that a dad can never divorce his kids and that, while they may not see you every day anymore, you'll always be close by and you'll always be their father.

Children whose parents are divorcing want to know what to expect. Tell them everything you can about what their everyday routine will be like after the separation. Be specific about where they will live, where they will go to school, where their parents will live, how often each of you will see them.

Help the children understand that, whatever the separation arrangement, both parents will always be in touch with them and that both of you will continue loving them and taking care of them. Encourage them to ask questions and to talk about their feelings. Be prepared for tearful or angry responses. Offer comfort and support—admittedly not an easy task at a time when you probably need a little comforting yourself.

When it's necessary for a father to tell his children the bad news (or his "side of the story") alone, the temptation to blame his spouse for the breakup is often powerful. Resist. Children need to respect both parents to develop normally, so for the children's sake, keep your opinions to yourself. Kids usually become very upset by criticisms of their mother, even if the criticism is valid, even if the critic is their father. They resent being encouraged to take sides in their parents' conflicts. (Judges are not fond of these attacks, either.)

Unless the mother of his children abandons the family completely, or an extremely creative joint custody agreement is implemented, divorce means that a father and his children will be separated for days, possibly weeks, at a time. Stay in touch with your children during these absences, especially in the first few months after the separation, when children need proof that you will still be there for them. Use the phone, E-mail, greeting cards, or letters. Whatever it takes, let the children know that they are on your mind. Give them your telephone number and your picture. Whenever you, or they, must go away for more than a day or two, be sure the children know when you'll all be together again. Your kids need reassurance that your divorce won't drive you out of their lives. The more contact you keep, the more secure they will feel.

Children are amazingly adaptable. Given sufficient time, care, attention, and support, most kids can adjust successfully to their parents' divorce. If your children exhibit chronic symptoms of anger, depression, destructive tendencies, disruptive behavior, or extreme withdrawal, recognize that they may need professional counseling to come to terms with their new lives.

Strengthening the Father-Child Bond

When his relationship with his children's mother ends, there are only two ways for a father to (legally) ensure that he will remain an active, involved parent: a negotiated custody settlement or successful litigation. In either situation, a divorcing father must be prepared to demonstrate the competence, character, and commitment mandated by the law's standards of parental fitness.

No court will approve a sole or joint custody agreement unless the custodial parent provides a clean, safe home and effective, attentive child care. If the father is the primary custodian, these standards apply even if the children's mother runs off with a saxophone player, or joins the circus, or journeys to the Himalayas to "find herself." While a mother's desertion of her family may leave a father with sole custody of the couple's children by default, the gender bias so prevalent in many family courts makes modification or vacation of these custody rights a very real possibility if the mother suddenly reappears. Revisit Tony in chapter 2 if you find this disclaimer farfetched or paranoid. Tony's wife, you may recall, wandered off one night in an alcoholic haze, leaving Tony to raise the kids. Years later, Tony's wife experienced a religious awakening, went to a couple of AA meetings, captivated a family court judge, and ended up with custody of the couple's children.

Despite the emotional chaos and legal wrangling that surrounds him, a divorcing father must find the time and energy to maintain or strengthen his relationship with his children. There are at least two reasons why the quality and depth of this bond is important. First, evidence that a strong link exists between a father and his children carries significant weight in family court proceedings and settlement discussions. Second, once divorced, a father is without a child-care "partner." He may need to provide evidence that he has acquired (or always had) the necessary skills to effectively perform duties that, before the split, were the mother's exclusive domain.

For many divorcing fathers, the advice to become more active in child rearing is unnecessary. These dads have been significantly involved in every aspect of their children's growth and development. Unfortunately, economic forces, misplaced priorities, or the vestiges of obsolete cultural expectations have kept other soon-to-be divorced fathers from developing or demonstrating parental competence.

Determining parental fitness is obviously a subjective undertaking. A thousand family court judges and a thousand social service professionals use dozens of often dissimilar criteria to measure a parent's capabilities. The following summary, compiled from experience and research, lists parental attributes, behaviors, and attitudes known to have influenced family court evaluations of parental competence.

To be recognized as a good parent, a father is expected to:

- Exhibit genuine love and concern for his children.
- Take an active interest in the children's physical, social, emotional, and academic development.
- Arrange regular visits to doctors and dentists.
- Attend the children's athletic events, music and dance recitals, school plays, debates, science fairs, and so on.
- Meet with the children's teachers regularly.
- Impose and enforce (but not with corporal punishment) reasonable rules of behavior.
- Shop for the children's food and clothing.
- Encourage involvement in school and after-school activities, and participate in those activities with the children.
- Foster church or synagogue attendance and moral development.
- Ensure that children are bathed and properly dressed.
- Be trustworthy, reliable, and of good character.
- Help with homework and school projects.
- Spend time with the children.
- Assist children in solving problems.
- Be emotionally stable.
- Encourage and support children's creative tendencies.

Regardless of overall parenting capabilities, a father will generally be judged *unfit* if:

- He abuses drugs, alcohol, women, or children.
- He gambles compulsively.
- He exhibits violent tendencies.
- He exhibits symptoms of mental illness.
- He neglects the safety, nutrition, or educational needs of his children.
- He interferes with the children's relationship with their mother.

"I look for a positive role model," an experienced custody evaluator told me. "A parent who teaches solid values by word and example. A good parent spends a lot of time with the kids, and knows how to discipline them constructively. Love is important, but let's face it, most parents love their kids. If you're a lousy parent, that love doesn't do much for your children. I want to see some indication that the parent is helping the child learn and grow."

The strategy for divorcing dads seems obvious. If you have been hovering at the edges of your children's lives, it's time to get down on the floor or out in the park with them. Meet their friends and their friends' parents. Take the kids biking, to the zoo, to ball games, to plays. Read to them, play Monopoly and Scrabble, fly a kite, go sledding. Reinforce a sense of belonging together. To the extent possible, share your hobbies with the kids and become involved in activities that interest them. Adjust your schedule to spend more time with your children. Talk, and listen, to them.

Remember, however, that you are the children's father, not their buddy. Don't allow emotional fallout from your impending divorce to affect your parental status. You must retain your position as disciplinarian, provider, protector, and mentor. Take part in school functions and attend PTA meetings. Get to know the children's teachers, coaches, counselors, doctors, and dentists. See to it that the children's religious training isn't interrupted.

If you believe in spanking or other forms of corporal punishment, recognize that most family court judges do not.

Find less physical ways to impose discipline. Control your temper. Correct your children's unacceptable behavior without screaming in their faces.

Prepare for single fatherhood well in advance of the separation. Improve (or develop) your performance of child-care chores. You need to know the basics of cooking, laundry, housework, and grocery and clothes shopping. Learn by doing, or enroll in one of the numerous parenting classes now available at community colleges and adult education centers.

As separation draws near, put together an independent child-care plan. This plan should include a detailed schedule indicating who will be supervising the children for every minute they are in your custody (you, a relative, a baby-sitter, a day-care worker, and so on). Identify the changes you will make in work and leisure patterns to clear time for parenting activities.

If your custody agreement will require that you leave the family home, look for a residence nearby, preferably in the same school district. To preserve custody rights later, your new home should be in a safe, quiet residential neighborhood and be big enough to accommodate you and your children. (Many custody evaluators prefer separate bedrooms for children of different sexes.)

The work and responsibilities of solo parenthood sometimes cause a divorcing father to cringe. He doubts himself and his parenting capabilities. Often, these anxieties lead to his acceptance of custody terms that minimize his parenting time (and, in effect, his meaningful involvement with his children).

A significant body of research suggests that divorcing fathers concerned about their parental competence need not worry. Several studies comparing the child-rearing skills of single fathers with those of single mothers found no difference between the two groups. If you think you can't be an effective, successful single parent because you are a man, think again.

Many divorcing fathers will find that the transition from married dad to single dad can be accomplished with only a minor increase in effort and commitment. For others, a major realignment of priorities and lifestyle. In either case, when compared with the value of fatherhood to children, to fathers, and to society, the price is small.

SUMMARY

The "preseparation" stage of the dissolution process is a turbulent, demanding time. A divorcing father must overcome his own emotional turmoil, find reliable, effective legal representation, minimize the trauma suffered by his children, validate his parental fitness, and begin planning a new life. All this chaos must be met head-on and, for the most part, all at once.

Fortunately, help is available. With professional assistance and careful deployment of his inner resources, a divorcing father can position himself squarely near the center of his children's lives. If he thinks clearly and acts wisely, a divorcing father will be well armored for the next challenge in the dissolution gauntlet—securing an honorable peace, or winning a nasty war.

4
An Honorable Peace

LAW PROFESSOR: How often should a lawyer attempt to negotiate a custody dispute?
LAW STUDENT: Always.
LAW PROFESSOR: Always?
LAW STUDENT: Yes sir. A bad deal is better than a good trial.
LAW PROFESSOR: Generally, I detest those little rules of thumb. In this instance, however, I am forced to concede that you are 99 percent correct. Remember, though, there is no "always" in family law . . . and precious few "nevers."

A simple, real-world cost/benefit analysis clarifies why a father is wise to try negotiation before committing to an all-out war.

Costs and Benefits

BENEFITS OF LITIGATION

If a divorcing father has competent representation, he will probably know his rights and understand the full range of the legal remedies available for their assertion and protection. Ignorance, frustration, confusion, stress, or guilt will not cause him to make harmful, unnecessary concessions or uninformed decisions. The father's case will be presented aggressively and professionally. An impartial (we hope) arbiter will have all the evidence needed to render a wise and compassionate decision. Legitimate grievances will be redressed. A vindictive spouse's unreasonable demands will be rejected.

The interests of the divorcing couple's children will be served, not the selfish desires of either parent. In fact, acrimonious litigation between unruly, contentious parents will usually result in the appointment of an attorney or guardian *ad litem* to represent the children.

Often, the built-in delays and postponements inherent in the litigation continuum will impose a useful cooling-off period—or simply exhaust the warring parties. Outrageous positions taken by either side may soften to the point that meaningful settlement discussions become possible.

COSTS OF LITIGATION

Adversarial custody proceedings can last two or three years—or much longer if appeals are necessary. The expenses incurred can range from $5,000 up to . . . well, up to whatever you've got. The discovery, depositions, motions, petitions, briefs, interviews with experts, investigation of witnesses, and all the miscellaneous bickering that defines—and fuels—the litigation process often guarantee total depletion of a father's resources.

Money that should be going into the kids' college fund finds its way into the pockets of lawyers, detectives, psychologists, and court reporters. Energy and focus that should be channeled into rebuilding a life are expended on strategy, posturing, attack, and self-defense.

The litigation process magnifies the rancor and bitterness of divorce, prolonging and deepening the emotional wounds of everyone involved. Children are deployed as weapons or spies, and frequently used as bargaining chips. Their adjustment to their parents' breakup is severely retarded. Often, the kids become emotional refugees—confused, saddened, embittered, or disgusted by the hostilities.

As we've seen, divorcing fathers are not always treated fairly by family courts. As a Connecticut matrimonial attorney once observed, "A father who stands on his rights stands on quicksand." An excellent, well-prepared case may not ensure victory at trial. While there are many superb judges in the family court system, there are also hacks—average or below-average civil servants worn down by years of case overload and inadequate support personnel. A divorcing father expecting attention and fair play from these burnouts might be living in a fantasy world.

In many custody cases, a family court renders a decision that neither parent finds acceptable. These orders are usually based on assembly-line standards; the judge really doesn't know anything about the litigants or their children. Routine orders dispose of routine matters. The fact that these decisions radically alter the lives of fathers, mothers, and children doesn't really concern many of these judicial claims processors. They go home to their families at the end of the day.

A serious, rarely anticipated disadvantage of custody litigation surfaces when one side or the other comes away from trial with a decisive victory. Some fathers, reamed and ravaged by a court order combining inadequate parental status with a crushing child support burden, simply vanish. The children and their "victorious" mother find themselves on welfare. Some mothers, enraged by verdicts against them, retaliate by sabotaging the father-child relationship— the same bond the court's decision was supposed to safeguard.

If a court order deprives either parent of all meaningful contact with his or her children, parental kidnapping immediately becomes a significant danger. (Fifty thousand American parents kidnap their own children every year.) Veterans of the domestic relations system know that any decision viewed as grossly unfair by either litigant might have little practical value. An order was issued, but the dispute was never really resolved. The loser in these one-sided contests immediately launches another round of litigation to reverse the original trial's outcome, or simply refuses to comply.

BENEFITS OF NEGOTIATIONS

Compared to litigation, a carefully crafted settlement of custody issues can get you more of what you want—months or years sooner, and at a much lower cost. Voluntary agreements generally are more humane and more practical than litigation edicts. This higher "quality" level probably explains why compliance rates for custody orders are dramatically higher when the rulings come as the product of negotiations rather than as an arbitrary decision of the court.

While preparations for successful negotiations often require the same discovery and investigation expenditures as the early stages of litigation, pretrial and trial costs are avoided. In an average case, these savings will amount to thousands of dollars. If a complex, viciously fought court battle can be averted, a small fortune can be saved.

Another important advantage of negotiation is that your needs and desires actually have some impact. What you want is rarely a consideration when a judge decides your fate. Also, creative solutions to custody problems can be offered and discussed. Parents aren't restricted by the bored letter-of-the-law rulings that are the trademark of many family courts.

When conducted properly, custody negotiations become an educational process. Each parent becomes aware of the other's opinions and feelings, and each learns what obstacles must be overcome to shift focus to the children's best interests.

Although settlement discussions are not exactly warm fuzzy chatfests (and often not even civil interactions), they are usually less intimidating than custody trials. Wounded feelings can be expressed and sometimes soothed. Significant issues that would never see the light of day in a courtroom can be surfaced and dealt with in negotiations.

Tactically, information gleaned in settlement discussions can be helpful in preparing for litigation or in reshaping future talks. And, persuasive strategies not generally allowed in court proceedings (including flattery, threats, emotional appeals, and unorthodox bargaining) are fair game in negotiations.

Most important, settlement benefits the children of divorce. Parents can stop fighting over the kids and go back to caring for them. A negotiated truce means that children will be able to begin adjusting to their new routines and relationships sooner and, usually, more smoothly. The danger of losing one parent's support, guidance, and love is substantially reduced.

Finally, settlement of divorce issues allows divorcing fathers and mothers to move on into the final stage of the dissolution process. An agreement acceptable to both parents "closes the book gently" on a traumatic and disappointing experience. Reconstruction, rebirth, reconnection—whatever we choose to call it—cannot really begin until this closure occurs.

COSTS OF NEGOTIATIONS

If you are being advised by an able advocate, there are few disadvantages in attempting to negotiate settlement of your custody dispute. Some serious pitfalls do exist for the poorly represented. Early settlement may preclude the discovery of evidence that would have strengthened your bargaining position or improved your chances of prevailing at trial. Emotional factors (such as guilt about the children, a desire to be done with the dissolution process, and the illusion that reconciliation is possible) may cause a divorcing father to "give away the store." The other side, having no desire to bargain seriously, may use settlement discussions to stall or to assess your strategy. Attempting to negotiate with an unreasonable, intractable ex-spouse is, of course, a waste of time and money better spent in trial preparation. The truly unacceptable costs of negotiation are incurred when an incompetent lawyer botches the bargaining effort or when a greedy, devious attorney (on either side) prolongs or sabotages settlement attempts to generate fees.

In summary, negotiation should be your first choice to resolve all child-related disputes. If you have competent representation, there is little to lose. The litigation option remains available if settlement efforts fail, and preparation for trial is almost identical with the planning and evidence-gathering tasks that must be completed to establish a workable negotiating position.

A REASONABLE GOAL

Before your attorney can begin negotiation of custody issues in your behalf, he or she needs to know what the goal of these efforts should be. In short: What do you want? The question isn't as easy to answer as it seems to be.

Let's start by clarifying what you *don't* want. If you are at all committed to remaining an active, involved father, you cannot accept the traditional custody arrangement in which your children's mother gets sole custody of the kids, with you relegated to the humiliating role of "ghost dad"—the pitiful visitor/banker. Your children need a real father: a caring, concerned, fully functional parent. To achieve that status, you must have meaningful authority in all major decisions affecting your children's lives, and you must have all the parenting time necessary for the establishment and maintenance of the respect, trust, warmth, communication, and closeness that characterizes a healthy, successful parent-child relationship.

What you may think you don't want anywhere near your children's lives is their mother. But unless she is truly an unfit parent, you're wrong. Face the fact that children need two parents. Besides, a goal that requires revocation of your ex's parental rights is generally both unrealistic and ethically indefensible. If it's cruel and reprehensible and harmful to exclude a father from his children's lives, wouldn't banishment of the children's mother be equally outrageous? Of course. And if you set intelligent, reasonable negotiation goals, it shouldn't be necessary.

If you accept the premise that a divorcing man's primary goal should be the preservation of his fatherhood, you and your lawyer can begin exploring the legal options available for reaching that goal.

Obviously, sole custody would give you all you want. Your ex would become the visiting parent; you would become your children's primary caretaker. You would see them daily and be there for all the important moments of their lives. You would have complete control of all decisions affecting their growth, development, discipline, education, and socialization. You would also be responsible for every aspect of their care and protection.

A joint legal custody agreement designating your home as your children's primary residence would also bring the frequent close contact you need to be an effective parent, but you would likely make important decisions about your children's lives in partnership with the children's mother.

Under a joint legal and physical custody order directing that children must spend the same amount of time with each parent, both decision making and the children's companionship are shared equally by you and your ex.

A joint legal custody agreement designating the children's mother as their primary custodian may be acceptable—if you retain parental authority and if the children will be spending at least two days a week and part of their school vacations living with you.

The custody option you choose to pursue should depend on several factors that you must weigh carefully. Child rearing is a demanding, time-consuming activity. Only you can determine how much parenting you can realistically handle. Calculate the hours you need to devote to making a living and the energy you'll have to expend to rebuild your own postdivorce life. Being a father is an important role, perhaps the most important part of being a man— but fatherhood cannot, and must not, become an all-consuming passion. Keep part of yourself for yourself and for the grown-up world.

Generally, if the logistics can be worked out, an equitable shared-parenting agreement offers fathers, children, and mothers the best opportunity for successful postdivorce adjustment. The marriage ends but a family endures (albeit in a new, sometimes radically altered form).

Later in this chapter, we'll explore shared parenting in detail. For now, let's just say it's a concept worth considering.

Negotiation has been called "the art of the possible." What you want, need, or deserve aren't the only factors you must wrestle with in establishing your custody goals. You must also recognize what you can reasonably expect to get. This side of the goal-setting equation has several variables. It's a complex problem that you will need your attorney to help you solve.

In fashioning attainable settlement goals, you and your attorney must be able to predict realistically, and with a high degree of accuracy, the answers to dozens of questions like these:

- How strong is your case? In other words, how close to what you want are you likely to get if your custody dispute goes to trial? What were the results of home visits by family-services personnel? Are your medical and psychiatric experts good witnesses? Will you be a good witness? Is there enough meaningful evidence to demonstrate your parental competence? Is there anything in your past that might suggest you are not a good parent?

- How strong is your spouse's position? Is there conclusive evidence of neglect, abuse, inappropriate behavior, mental instability, drug or alcohol usage, and so forth? How will she react on the witness stand? Are her witnesses credible? Can her experts be impeached during cross-examination?

- What does she really want? Money? The house? Security? Revenge? Retribution? Is there anything you can negotiate for custody rights?

- Does she have a boyfriend? Is she hoping to remarry soon?

- Can you honestly say that you are a better parent than she is? Does she consider you a good father?

- Would your assumption of child-care duties help her in her career? Socially?

- Is she acting rationally and practically?

- What is her opinion of joint custody? If the case goes to trial, can joint custody be imposed over her objections? (In several states, the answer is "yes.")

- Does the local judge or custody evaluator have a record of pro-mother bias?

- Is her attorney experienced? A seasoned negotiator?

- Is yours? Will her attorney give her an objective analysis of her position?

- Can she be convinced to focus on the children's needs and well-being?

After discussing and weighing all the relevant information available, you and your attorney should be able to reach accord on settlement goals that seem both realistic and acceptable. A negotiation strategy can then be formulated.

Negotiation Strategy

Divorce settlements normally focus on four major issues: custody, child support, the classification and division of marital property, and spousal maintenance. The successful resolution of custody questions almost always influences the disposition of other issues. Child support awards are based on custody allocations. (A visitor/banker dad pays much more than a father who has primary custody or some form of joint physical custody.) Spousal maintenance, if paid at all, is usually viewed as compensation for the divorced parent who forgoes wage-earning opportunities to stay home with the children. Where the kids will live obviously affects what happens to the house, the cars, and the home furnishings. Most veteran attorneys apply a standard strategy to divorce cases involving minor children: Settle custody issues and everything else falls into place.

From this time-tested formula comes the first element of your negotiation strategy. Profess a willingness to be reasonable (even liberal, if you can afford it) in money matters if your ex will be reasonable in custody discussions.

Am I suggesting that you should offer to "buy" custody of your own children? Of course not (at least not yet). I'm simply advising you to put first things first. Screw the house and the pile of stuff you and she used to own together. Make it clear that your primary concern is your relationship with your children. Take the position that a rational, humane solution to the custody issue will foster the practical cooperation needed to solve the other problems spawned by the divorce.

Yes, that includes the money problems. Theoretically, custody and the financial aspects of divorce are supposed to be separate. In real life, they often are not. Your stance simply acknowledges the link. Aside from focusing negotiations on the dissolution issue most important to you, your insistence that custody talks must precede discussions about other unresolved matters implicitly offers some settlement incentives to an ex-spouse worried about the economic impact of divorce. Specifically . . .

1. You are communicating to her that her financial uncertainty will continue until custody issues are stabilized and the children are out of harm's way.

2. She will know that her financial needs are more likely to be met if your custody goals are achieved and the children's best interests are protected.

3. Attorney's fees and other litigation costs would be saved if prompt settlement occurs, substantially improving the total financial picture for both of you and the children.

Ideally, custody negotiations are an exercise in problem solving. With the aid of your attorney, you and your children's mother identify concerns, needs, and goals. Then you explore all the available options for satisfying each parent's interests. Then you work out a custody plan that gives each of you what you want, and more important, provides for all the children's needs. Then a purple pig flies into the room, singing "Glory, glory, halleluja."

You're right. It is a fantasy. While some custody negotiations proceed amicably and smoothly, most do not. Anger, greed, hostility, distrust, contempt, vengeance, and other corrosive emotions often infect or distort the process. Settlement "conferences" sometimes degenerate into heated confrontations. Insults, threats, and personal attacks fill the meeting room. Rational thought and cooperation become impossible. The result is a ruinous stalemate recalling the words of Mahatma Gandhi: "An eye for an eye and we all go blind."

In some negotiations, the parties refuse to accept the fact that the purpose of settlement discussions is to create an agreement that both parents can live with. Mothers and fathers (and their lawyers) too often view negotiations as a competition, a dress rehearsal for the adversarial litigation the settlement discussions are supposed to avoid. Each side suspects the other of deceit, manipulation, and bad faith. Eventually, these suspicions become self-fulfilling prophecies. In the end, neither side will agree to anything less than complete surrender by the opponent.

In some custody negotiations, one of the attorneys is the most serious obstacle to a fair agreement. I've noticed that the more knowledgeable an attorney is about custody issues, the better the odds are for an equitable settlement. Some young, inexperienced lawyers are afraid to suggest acceptance of any settlement offer. These novices would rather let a judge decide custody questions than be a party to a settlement that may later come back to haunt them. Other domestic relations attorneys, as we warned earlier, are wedded to stupid, archaic, pro-mother "principles." They refuse to accept any agreement that doesn't give sole custody of children to their mother. Struggling with professional paranoia or some other self-image problem, some attorneys believe that any settlement offered by a more seasoned or better qualified colleague has some devious diabolical trapdoor hidden in it somewhere. Because of these usually groundless fears, these lawyers, in effect, won't agree to anything. Other attorneys are fascinated by the sound of their own voices. They see settlement discussions as performance opportunities. Enamored by their own lawyering skills, they posture and preen and argue and object. But they don't negotiate. Finally, we have in our profession a number of attorneys who see custody negotiations as profit-making ventures. They show up. They listen. They mull. They talk. They are meticulous and deliberate. They analyze every element of every point. They talk in riddles, reason in circles. They really don't care about reaching a fair settlement; they're much more interested in keeping that fee-meter spinning full speed.

While there's no doubt that bad lawyers can subvert custody negotiations, in most cases the truly destructive influences are the estranged parents. One or both of these former mates cannot or will not set aside the pain, rage, and disappointment of the broken marriage to concentrate on the real issue at hand: the children.

If acrimony between you and your children's mother threatens the success of custody negotiations, you must do all you can to reduce the emotional intensity of settlement conferences. While no one expects you to control your former spouse's feelings or behavior, there are techniques you can use to moderate the impact of emotional distractions.

Changing your ex's confrontational attitude to a cooler, problem-solving mind-set is not an easy task, but considering what's at stake, it's certainly worth a try. The first step is learning to control your own feelings and behavior. When you are attacked, your instinctive reaction is to counterattack. As our little buddies Mack and Zack in the last chapter showed us, responding to insults or abuse in kind usually leads to a rapidly escalating cycle of conflict. Your custody goals are forgotten as you become involved in meaningless invective and name-calling. Your position becomes more extreme, more rigid. And so does hers. To end this unproductive spiral before it starts, you must . . . well, do nothing. Really. Don't react at all to your ex's emotional attacks. One of Newton's laws of physics tells us that "for every action there is an equal and opposite reaction." But that law applies to objects, not human beings. In custody negotiations, the rule to keep in mind is, "It takes two to tangle." You can choose not to react to nasty pokes and childish cheap shots, and that's a choice you must make. To keep negotiations on track (or at least headed for the track), you will have to resist your natural impulses and suppress your natural reactions. Admittedly, gaining this essential control is difficult—but it can be done. Follow the advice of the legendary samurai warrior Musashi; take "a distanced view of close things." Imagine that you are a law student watching these custody negotiations on videotape. The woman calls her ex-husband a "beer-swilling needle-dicked lump." The law student (while mildly amused by the woman's syntax) recognizes the comment as a stupid emotional outburst having nothing to do with the issues being discussed. This is the "distanced" view you must learn to adopt. Refuse to become involved in alley skirmishes even when the need to do so rages within you.

Your next step in the dispersion of hostile emotions requires the adoption of a conciliatory manner. Your ex may feel distrustful, angry, threatened, deeply hurt, or all of the above. You need to make an effort to help her regain her emotional balance. Until she does, rational dialogue will be impossible. To stabilize the settlement discussions, you are going to have to look at custody issues from her perspective. Adopting her perspective, even for a few minutes, may be the very last thing you feel like doing. Do it anyway. Your ex will not acknowledge your point of view until you recognize hers.

So, give her a hearing. Be willing to listen to her concerns. Listening is one of the cheapest concessions you'll ever make. Your ex (and each of us) feels a deep need to be understood. Simply by fulfilling that need, you may be able to substantially reduce the effects of disruptive emotions. And listening doesn't mean merely keeping your mouth shut. Real listening requires patience and self-discipline, but it's a valuable skill. Close attention to your ex's narrative provides insight into her position and often valuable indicators of her secret concerns and hidden agenda. As veteran diplomats learn early in their careers: Effective negotiators listen far more often than they talk.

If at any time during settlement discussions an issue arises that seems to make your ex angry, or suspicious, or upset, give her all the time she needs to express her concerns. Don't interrupt, even when what she's saying is completely inaccurate or deeply insulting. Maintain eye contact, nod or murmur, lean forward. In short, let her know that her recitation is making an impact—even if it's not. As any consumer relations manager can confirm, most people derive deep satisfaction from airing their grievances and resentments. Once you have heard her out, your ex may become less emotionally driven, more willing to listen to your viewpoint, and ultimately, more responsive to problem-solving activities.

Another negotiation strategy that is sometimes effective in moving settlement discussions away from emotion and into areas of substance is the acknowledgment of the validity of your ex's viewpoint and feelings. It's important to stress that accepting a position as "valid" does *not* mean that you must agree with it. It means only that you hear and understand what your ex is saying, and, yes, maybe it's something that should be discussed further. Acknowledging your ex's views and feelings can often create a neutral climate in which negotiations can proceed rationally. To offer acknowledgment of her position's validity, use phrases like "I understand what you're saying" and "I can see why you might feel that way."

Another way to provide recognition is to apologize. Whether or not you've done something that warrants an apology is pretty much irrelevant. Saying "I'm sorry" or (better) "I'm sorry you feel that way" or "I'm sorry things turned out the way they did" is not an acceptance of blame. What an outraged or disappointed former mate may want most is the recognition that she's been hurt and that she has the right to feel badly about it. A general expression of regret from you may satisfy that need.

Once settlement discussions advance beyond the my-turn-your-turn carousel of emotional monologues, actual custody negotiations may begin. Remember to approach these talks as problem-solving opportunities. Be flexible and creative. Seriously consider any custody plan that gives you the parental status and access that you need. Use the experience of both attorneys in the case, as well as the expertise of divorce counselors or family-services professionals who know your situation. Ask "Why not?" and "What if?" and "What would make this fair?" whenever the opportunity presents itself.

Be ready to explain your custody plans in terms of their benefits to the children and, especially, your ex. Remind your former spouse that your participation in child rearing will give her time for her career and a social life. Show her a custody timetable that allows both of you to maintain close contact with the children without becoming child-care slaves. Indicate how your plan will improve her financial situation and ensure your continued support of the children. In short, stress the elements of *your* plans that meet *her* needs. When you find some facet of her plan unpalatable, stress how her position doesn't meet the *children's* needs. Keep your needs out of the discussions as much as possible.

If you can't settle your custody differences based on what's best for the children, consider bringing other factors into the problem. Look for low-cost, high-benefit trades. One divorced father I know negotiated favorable custody terms because he was able to get his former wife a better job. Another father agreed to allow his ex to use his family's cabin in the mountains for a week each summer. Another offered to pay his wife's college tuition. You know your ex. Ask yourself what she wants that you can provide.

"What do you think will happen if we don't settle this?" That's an excellent question to pose to the other side if emphasizing the best interests of the children, accentuating the positive, or old-fashioned horse-trading don't seem to be getting you anywhere. The future, you should suggest, could be interesting. Ask her if she really wants a judge who doesn't know her or you (or the children) deciding who will see the kids—and when—for the next decade. Maybe that judge will feel that you are a better parent than she is. Perhaps something unsavory in her past will become public. Maybe child support or spousal maintenance ordered by the court will be less than you might offer if settlement occurs. Maybe you'd have to appeal an adverse decision and drag out divorce litigation for another two years.

No one really knows what will happen if you don't reach a settlement. That's the danger—and, in this context, the beauty of our goofy capricious court system. You can wonder out loud about all sorts of plausible scenarios that may threaten or unsettle your former spouse, and there is at least a chance that those idle musings will someday come to pass. Use of this approach requires a careful, subtle touch. Contrasting what your ex may lose in court with what she can gain in settlement mustn't be perceived as blackmail. So be cautious. Warn, don't threaten.

If you have an exceptionally strong case (your parental credentials are impeccable, hers suspect, and so on), use your power wisely. When exerting pressure, your purpose, to paraphrase William Ury of the Harvard Law School Program on Negotiation, should be "to bring her to her senses, not to her knees." In other words (mine, I think), educate, don't dominate. Steamroller tactics may strengthen her resolve. If you offer your ex no face-saving way to settle your custody dispute, she may feel that she has no choice but to fight on. And on. And on.

Some custody negotiations go smoothly. Most don't. The process is often tedious and frustrating, especially when you are dealing with an adversary with whom you share a history of conflict and bitterness. Expect impasses. Be ready to fall back, regroup, and try again. Remember that to be successful, you will often have to force yourself to do exactly the opposite of what you want to do. When insulted, you must not retaliate. When you want to talk, you must first listen. When you feel like fighting for your position, you must respect hers. You must teach yourself to view your former mate not as an enemy but as a necessary colleague in an important undertaking. You must replace the urge for victory in confrontation with a quest for a cooperative solution to a common problem.

Accept the fact that the negotiation process may be a rough ride. To bolster your spirits and replenish your resolve, remind yourself daily why you're doing what you're doing. Visualize your children's faces. Negotiation experts call this "keeping your eyes on the prize."

Mediation

In recent years, our family court system has become more crowded, more contentious, and more chaotic than ever before. Many judges, legislators, lawyers, and family-services professionals are now doing whatever they can to shift the settlement of divorce issues from an overburdened, understaffed judiciary to a number of alternative dispute mechanisms. Mediation is the out-of-court resolution process most commonly recommended for the settlement of custody disagreements.

In mediation, a knowledgeable, neutral third party helps a divorcing couple solve their disputes themselves. When conducted competently, mediation is not an adversarial process. The purpose of the process is to assemble an agreement, not declare a winner and a loser. A mediator has no power to impose solutions or make decisions. In its ideal form, mediation identifies no guilt and finds no fault. The process is a cooperative search for reasonable and equitable solutions to divorce conflicts.

Mediation has a long and honorable history. The Beth Din, a Jewish mediation council, is thousands of years old. In China and Japan, the mediation process is the cornerstone of their entire legal systems. Restoration of "peace and tranquillity" is the goal of Japan's mediation-based judiciary. Japanese judges are not interested in who is right or wrong. A quest for harmony is a Japanese court's primary function—not the deliverance of retribution. (Interestingly, Japan has one lawyer for every twelve thousand citizens. In the United States there is a lawyer for every six hundred people.)

Most modern divorce mediation services are based on principles conceived by a Los Angeles County court in 1939. The stated goals of this prototype mediation project were "to protect the rights of children and preserve the public welfare by preserving, promoting, and protecting family life," and "to provide the means for amicable settlement of family controversies."

Rapidly rising divorce rates in the 1970s, coupled with the frustrations of judges forced to referee one hostile, bitter custody fight after another, led to a dramatic increase in the use of mediation by family courts and domestic relations attorneys. The success of conciliation programs in California, Wisconsin, and Minnesota spawned pro-mediation legislation in numerous other jurisdictions. Today, eleven states require mediation in all custody disputes, and nineteen more allow family courts to order mediation for the resolution of custody conflicts. The voluntary use of private or court-sanctioned mediation services is either encouraged or permitted in most other jurisdictions.

Mediation is conducted within a variety of similar formats. The mediator may be a lawyer, a retired judge (with or without psychological training), a psychotherapist, a psychologist (with or without a legal background), a family-services professional, a social worker, or even a clergyman. Some mediations last weeks or months; most are completed in from two to five sessions. Some mediators include the divorcing couple's children in some sessions; others simply encourage the parents to keep their children informed about the settlement discussions. In some jurisdictions, the couple's lawyers are included in the sessions. More typically, each parent consults with his or her lawyer before, after, and between mediation conferences.

In 1980, the American Association for Mediated Divorce (AAMD) was founded by Dr. Marilyn Ruman, a psychologist, and her husband, I. Richard Ruman, an attorney. The AAMD suggests that divorce mediation should be conducted by a team—an impartial lawyer to advise couples of their legal options and a therapist to help couples manage the emotional turmoil of the dissolution process. Expanding on this team principle, several local divorce-counseling agencies around the country have established mediation committees consisting of a legal expert, a communication facilitator, a family-science professional (usually a pediatric psychologist or a psychiatrist), and an educator. These committees strive to make available any and all information and assistance a divorcing couple needs to reach a custody agreement.

Several recent studies indicate that mediation works quite well. A Toronto court's research found that only 10 percent of mediated agreements later became issues for litigation—as opposed to 25 percent of nonmediated settlements. The Toronto surveys also discovered that couples who completed mediation were three times more likely to report better postdivorce relationships with their ex-spouses than "nonmediated couples." According to a study conducted by the Colorado Bar Association, 60 percent of couples who used mediation services were able to resolve their custody controversies. A Pennsylvania review of mediation results found that 70 percent of mediating couples agreed to joint custody. In Maine, only 25 percent of mediated custody cases move on to litigation. Virginia statistics revealed that mediation reduced custody litigation by 67 percent. Data from the same study indicated that joint custody was the solution of choice in almost 75 percent of mediated settlements. (By contrast, in 89 percent of custody disputes decided by Virginia's family courts in the same time period, mothers were awarded sole custody.) Almost every postmediation survey available suggests that, even when mediation is not completely successful, the process substantially reduces mistrust and acrimony.

As I suggested earlier, the mediation process is not a win/lose proposition. Mediation sessions are, in essence, triangular settlement conferences overseen and guided by a neutral facilitator. The mediator doesn't decide anything. His or her role is to help the divorcing couple become rational and responsible enough to reach mutually acceptable compromises. Rather than weigh the strength of one position against another, a mediator attempts to blend the best of each parent's custody plan to create a third option: a custody agreement that protects the rights of both parents and, more important, provides the best possible postdivorce life for the couple's children.

The interests and well-being of the children of divorce are the primary concerns of every truly dedicated custody mediator. The principles and philosophies of competent, caring custody mediation are clearly apparent in *The Children's Bill of Rights*. Devised by a Wisconsin court's mediation branch, this articulate and insightful declaration insists that children in divorce actions must be guaranteed:

I. The right to be treated as an interested and affected person and not as a pawn, possession, or chattel of either or both parents.

II. The right to grow to maturity as a competent, responsible citizen.

III. The right to the affection, care, discipline and protection of both parents.

IV. The right to know both parents, and to have the benefit of each parent's love and guidance.

V. The right to a positive and constructive relationship with both parents, with neither parent to be permitted to degrade or downgrade the other in the mind of the child.

VI. The right to have moral and ethical values developed by precept and practices and have limits set for behavior, so that the child, early in life, may develop self-discipline and self-control.

VII. The right to the most adequate level of economic support that can be provided by the best efforts of both parents.

VIII. The right to the same opportunities for education that the child would have had if the family unit had not been broken.

IX. The right to the periodic review of custodial arrangements and child support orders as the circumstances of the parents and the benefit of the child may require.

X. The right to the recognition that children involved in divorce are always disadvantaged parties, and that the law must take affirmative steps to preserve their welfare and protect their interests.

Unless divorcing parents seem intent on fashioning custody arrangements that clearly violate the rights of their children, a skilled mediator is to remain completely objective. He or she has long ago mastered the negotiation skills we outlined earlier in this chapter. If we were able to catch a glimpse of an experienced mediator's resume, we might see entries like these in the "Responsibilities" section:

- Assists in problem resolution.
- Helps divorcing parents set aside destructive emotions.

- Encourages compromise.
- Avoids placing blame or finding fault.
- Prevents name-calling, insults, recriminations.
- Is an advisor and a catalyst, not a dictator.
- Guides parents to creative solutions of mutual problems.
- Identifies areas of agreement and disagreement.
- Promotes personal responsibility, interpersonal recognition, and mutual respect.
- Manages communication between antagonists.
- Asks the right questions and allows parents to find the best answers.
- Disconnects parents from rigid positions and causes them to focus on legitimate issues.
- Invents options for mutual gain.
- Teaches parents how to listen and understand.
- Permits parents to make their own decisions, but controls the decision-making process.
- Helps parents learn new patterns of behavior, with each other and with their children.

While styles vary, most mediators (working as individuals or in teams) use a similar process. An exploration phase allows the mediator to get to know each parent. In individual premediation meetings, the mediator tries to understand what each parent wants and needs. Each parent's problems are identified; each parent's position is clarified. Honest expressions of emotion are tolerated in these individual conferences in hopes that hostilities vented early can be managed more effectively later.

Initial mediation sessions involving both parents form the educational phase of the process. The mediator makes it clear that both parents must set aside whatever feelings they have for each other and concentrate on working together in their children's best interests. Ground rules are set, and the mediator assures each parent that his or her concerns and ideas are important and will be respected.

Problem solving is the next stage. The mediator needs to know, very specifically, what each party is willing to accept. The mediator uses questions and paraphrasing to ensure that everyone in the room understands everyone else. The mediator attempts to clarify ambiguities, untie semantic knots, and decode strategic posturing. In short, the mediator tries to isolate the *real* obstacles to agreement.

Providing emotional support to both parties, the mediator elicits the information that the parents need to create possible solutions to their dispute. The mediator helps the parents evaluate proposed solutions and often offers options that neither side has considered. If an impasse occurs, the mediator intervenes, nudging parents to look beyond their own positions and goals to see the future through the eyes of their children.

When problem-solving sessions are fruitful, the mediator assists the divorcing couple in refining and retooling solutions. An agreement in principle becomes a highly structured plan, detailing how each parent will contribute to his or her children's care and development and giving each parent the access and authority to fulfill obligations. Living arrangements, educational and religious considerations, medical needs, vacation plans—anything the parents feel is important—are eventually incorporated into the mediated agreement, as is a clause indicating how future disagreements will be resolved.

A settlement reached through mediation (like a negotiated agreement devised without mediation) does not become legally binding until it is signed by the parents and approved by the court.

Harry and Ann

The following case history illustrates how a successful mediation works. I've compressed and simplified some of the issues involved in this particular case, but nothing essential to an understanding of what happens in mediation has been left out.

Harry and Ann have been separated for several months. They have two children, ages eight and ten. Divorce litigation is pending. Both parents have instructed their attorneys to file petitions seeking sole custody of the couple's children. Both lawyers have asked the couple to first try to settle their custody dispute through mediation. A mediator I'll call Roger has been selected and approved by both attorneys. Roger speaks to both Harry and Ann by telephone and schedules an orientation meeting.

As soon as the couple and the mediator are seated in Roger's conference room, Harry says: "I want you to know that I've got to have custody of my kids, or there's no use in us talking."

"No way," Ann chimes in. A loud, animated account of Harry's past parenting blunders follows. Harry returns fire.

Roger cuts the confrontation short with an authoritative announcement. "Quiet, please. You'll both be given every opportunity to explain your positions," Roger says. "For now, I want you to calm down. I need some information."

A prickly silence falls as Roger collects biographical facts, a current history of custody and visitation arrangements, an estimate of how much time the kids spend with each parent, school and day-care information, and some data about grandparents and extended family.

The need to answer Roger's innocuous questions forces both parents to talk to Roger, not to each other. The tension in the room dissipates slightly. Roger then explains his ground rules:

"I'll be controlling the mediation process, but that's all I'll be controlling. I won't be making any decisions. Any agreement that you reach will be of your own design. My management of these sessions doesn't mean that you won't be able to say whatever you feel needs to be said. It does mean that I won't allow you to interrupt each other. And I'm not going to let either of you turn these sessions into a forum for placing blame or venting hostility. We're not really concerned with your past in these meetings. We're here to deal with the *future* of your family. And there's no need to try to win me over. I won't be siding with either of you. I'm your children's advocate. My role is to help you see your dispute from their vantage point, which, in case you haven't noticed, is right in the middle of all this. I want you to feel safe in being open and honest. Let me assure you that everything we say here will stay here."

The couple listens attentively to Roger's words, and there are no objections.

"I'm sorry if I seemed upset before," Harry says. "All I was trying to say is that I want my kids."

"They're my kids, too," Ann says.

"What do you think is the most important reason you want sole custody?" Roger asks Harry.

"So I can see my children," Harry replies. "The way it is now, I'm lucky if I'm with them a couple of hours a week. Ann is giving me a lot of trouble every time I try to see them."

"His visits are very disruptive," Ann says.

"Only because you make everything such a huge hassle," Harry says.

Roger breaks in. "Ann, why do you feel you need sole custody?" he asks.

"Those kids are my whole life," Ann says. "I love them."

"Oh, and I don't?" Harry says.

"Okay. Fine. Let's agree right now that I'm dealing with two parents who love their children very much," Roger says.

Harry and Ann nod, almost in unison.

"Can we further agree that no matter what happens in this mediation, neither one of you will cause the other to be banished completely from the children's lives?" Roger asks.

Another pair of nods are Roger's reply. Harry has a hesitant "what's the catch?" look on his face.

"Neither one of you will lose your children," Roger says. "Are we all clear on that? I will not tolerate that kind of tragedy happening to either of you."

With Roger's guidance, Harry and Ann agree that since mediation is likely to take several weeks, a temporary parenting schedule is needed to indicate when the children will be with each parent. (Roger almost never uses terms like "temporary custody" or "visitation." Instead, he talks about "access" and "time with Dad." Harry's home isn't "the noncustodial parent's residence," it's "Dad's house.")

The second mediation takes place ten days later. Harry has had the children overnight twice during this period. Ann immediately indicates she is not happy about that. "It won't happen again," she vows. Harry can't understand why Ann feels as she does. Roger sees that both parents have retreated to their sole-custody stances.

Roger produces a large pad of graph paper. "I want each of you to tell me why you think you are the better sole parent," he says. Roger prints each parent's response on a separate chart. He permits no extraneous comments or challenges from either parent while he's recording this information. When Roger is finished, he posts both charts on his office wall and asks the parents to study them.

"Please don't say anything about these lists right now," Roger says. "I have some homework for you."

The homework is simple. Each parent is to make three lists:

• A summary of all the good things each parent can honestly say about the other's parental capabilities.

• What each parent is willing to give up for sole custody.

• What each parent would need in return for withdrawing his or her demand for sole custody.

When Harry and Ann return two weeks later with their homework completed, two important elements of the couple's custody dispute become apparent to mediator Roger.

First, Harry's demand for sole custody is really a demand for adequate access to his children. Second, Ann's real problem is Harry's girlfriend. Ann is reluctant to allow the children to spend time at Harry's home because Harry's girlfriend is frequently present.

After a few minutes of careful questioning, Roger determines that Ann is still angry about having been rejected by Harry. And she will not tolerate a substitute mother who might interfere with her relationship with the children.

Based on the results of their homework assignments, Roger concludes that neither Harry nor Ann has any misgivings about the other parent's child-care skills. Harry thinks Ann may be "a little too protective" but concedes that she is a loving, supportive mom. Ann believes that Harry's parenting style is probably too structured for kids of eight and ten, but she has no other criticisms. "Harry's a good father," Ann has written. "He just needs to let the boys have a little more fun."

As conversations triggered by the homework proceed, momentum for compromise begins to build. Roger contributes a suggestion. Since both Harry and Ann seem to be competent, caring parents, why not consider a shared-parenting agreement?

"How would that work?" Harry asks.

"Any way you two want it to," Roger says. "You need to come up with an arrangement that gives both of you equal responsibility for critical decisions about the children's upbringing and a parenting schedule you're both comfortable with."

After several more questions and answers, Harry and Ann seem ready to accept Roger's suggestion. A serious effort to work out the details of a shared-parenting pact begins. Roger produces calendars. Harry and Ann devise midweek, weekend, holiday, vacation, and special-event schedules. Harry agrees that when he has the children, his girlfriend won't stay overnight. Ann admits that based on the children's comments, Harry's girlfriend is no real threat to her maternal status. She says she will have no objection to the children occasionally spending time with Harry's girlfriend. Visitation for both sets of grandparents is also arranged.

Harry and Ann agree to cooperate in decisions affecting the children's education, medical care, religious training, and general well-being. They also agree to return to Roger's office for additional mediation if parenting disputes arise in the future.

Harry and Ann's mediation was successful primarily because mediator Roger identified the divorcing couple's real concerns and then guided the parents toward a fair, workable resolution of their dispute. The fact that Harry's and Ann's mutual animosity for each other did not seriously distort either parent's opinion of the other's parental skills was a great help to Roger and to the mediation process.

Few divorcing fathers will be surprised to learn that custody mediation rarely flows so smoothly. Often, one or both dueling parents disrupts or stonewalls the process at every opportunity. It's not unusual for a parent to cling to a completely unreasonable or totally inflexible position. Reviving the past, assessing blame, shouting, crying, and irrational outbursts are among the diversionary tactics frequently employed to slow or stop the problem-solving effort.

When obstacles are encountered, a skilled mediator will intervene. Among the intervention techniques mediators have found to be effective are these:

- The mediator will recess the proceedings to allow embattled parents to cool off.

- The mediator will remind the parents of the rules of the mediation: no blame assessment, no endless reexaminations of past injustices.

- The mediator will do something silly, like asking the skirmishing couple to slow down their angry exchanges so the mediator can keep an accurate tally of hits and misses. Or the mediator will don a hard hat, or wave a little white flag.

- The mediator will conduct a reality check to emphasize what will happen if the custody dispute goes to trial (the delays and monumental costs involved, the placement of the children squarely in the center of the battlefield, the likelihood that neither parent will be thrilled with the court's decision, the possibility of endless appeals, noncompliance, and so on).

- The mediator will express grave disappointment that two intelligent adults cannot conduct themselves in a constructive, civil manner. Combining flattery and disgust, the mediator hopes to embarrass the parents into more reasonable behavior.

- The mediator will place each parent in a separate room and talk to each individually. These conversations may be warnings or fact-finding missions. Isolation of the parents allows the mediator to practice a form of shuttle diplomacy. Moving back and forth between the parents, the mediator hopes to find a plot of common ground large enough for both parents to occupy.

- The mediator will refer one or both of the parents to a therapist (a psychiatrist, a psychologist, or a social worker) and suspend mediation until the emotional difficulties impeding the mediation process have been resolved.

When no combination of persuasion, intervention, or therapy is effective, the mediator is forced to terminate the process, either permanently or until the parents alter their positions or overcome their dysfunctional behavior.

THE PROS AND CONS OF MEDIATION

A summary of the benefits and disadvantages of mediation closely corresponds to the cost/benefit analysis we used to compare custody negotiations to litigation. Compared to going to trial, mediation is faster, cheaper, more humane, and more likely to result in an equitable outcome. Compliance rates for mediated agreements are also much higher than compliance rates for trial orders.

Mediation offers some benefits not always found in settlement negotiations conducted by the parents and their attorneys, but there are also some potential pitfalls in the use of mediation.

Whether or not a divorcing father should submit to mediation to reach his custody goals depends on a number of interrelated variables. . . .

Positive

A skilled, objective mediator is a valuable catalyst for problem solving. Having no allegiance to either side, the mediator may be able to find potential solutions not apparent to the parties or their lawyers.

Negative

A pro-mother mediator places the divorcing father on the wrong side of a two-on-one rush to judgment.

Positive
Divorcing parents tend to behave more rationally in mediations than in negotiations. An experienced mediator manages conflict better than most divorcing parents and most divorce attorneys.

Negative
A divorcing father may not be able to articulate his position effectively without his attorney's assistance.

Positive
A divorcing mother may not be able to articulate her position effectively without her attorney's assistance.

Positive
A number of studies indicate that divorcing fathers generally achieve "more satisfactory" custody outcomes in mediation than they do in litigation. (I realize that this is not earth-shaking news, considering the beatings fathers take in pro-female courtrooms.)

Negative
If mandatory mediation takes place before the divorcing parents are psychologically ready to talk to each other, the process may become more traumatic than litigation. Often, the snail's pace of court proceedings gives the parties time to collect themselves and prepare their psyches for negotiations.

Positive
A conscientious, dedicated mediator vigorously represents the children's interests. While a court will sometimes appoint a lawyer for children trapped in acrimonious divorce litigation, an attorney rarely represents the children in party-to-party negotiations.

While analysis of these pluses and minuses may help you gauge the usefulness of the mediation process, the real key to a successful mediation is the mediator.

An experienced domestic relations attorney—especially if he or she practices in an area where mediation is commonplace—should know which mediators are acceptable and which mediators could be trouble.

Most mediators will provide detailed summaries of their qualifications, training, and experience. You should be interested in what percentage of the mediator's cases have remained settled and if the mediator's record includes any evidence of pro-mother bias. (If there seems to be a pro-father or joint custody predisposition in the mediator's past performance summary, cross your fingers and hope that your ex's lawyer doesn't notice.)

If you submit to mediation, have your lawyer prepare you carefully and thoroughly before sessions begin. And always consult with your lawyer between and after sessions. While some mediators allow attorneys to sit in on mediation conferences, very few will permit lawyers to participate in the process.

Before mediation begins, obtain a signed confidentiality agreement from the mediator. It is imperative to ensure that the mediator cannot be called as a witness should litigation become necessary.

Be ready to present your own custody case as clearly and as unemotionally as you can. The same self-control techniques we discussed for use in negotiations will be effective in mediation. Reread the Children's Bill of Rights presented earlier in this chapter. Offer your custody goals in terms of your children's needs and best interests.

If you feel you aren't being heard or understood, or if you believe that the process is futile, or if you mistrust or simply don't like the mediator, remember that you can withdraw from mediation at any time if it is not court ordered. You need not give a reason. I doubt that I need to tell you this, but I will, just to be safe: Don't sign anything until your attorney sees it.

Arbitration

Arbitration is similar to litigation, except it's faster, usually cheaper, and a shade less intimidating.

Unlike mediation, arbitration is an adversarial process. There will be a winner and a loser. The mechanics of arbitration are straightforward. The divorcing couple submits their custody dispute to an arbitrator (or an arbitration panel). Each side agrees, in advance, to comply with the arbitrator's decisions.

Arbitration hearings are less formal than court trials. The proceedings take place in the arbitrator's office or conference room. The arbitrator listens to evidence presented by both sides, examines witnesses, and then renders a decision.

Generally, arbitration is used when only a small number of divorce issues remain unresolved or when both parties in a divorce want their disputes disposed of quickly.

Obviously, submission to arbitration should never occur unless both sides respect and trust the arbitrator. Typically, when divorcing parents can't agree on an arbitrator, each side selects their own. These two arbitrators then choose a third to hear the case.

Even more so than when he's involved in mediation, a divorcing father who uses arbitration services must do his homework. The father will be the arbitrator's prime source of information, not the father's attorney.

Some arbitrators are also mediators. These professionals offer a combination of mediation and arbitration called "med arb"—one-stop shopping for dispute resolution. If a divorcing couple uses the med arb process, any differences they are unable to settle in mediation are resolved in an arbitration hearing.

Divorcing fathers may wish to consider arbitration of custody issues if:

- The judge likely to hear the father's court case is blatantly biased toward mothers and the arbitrator is not; or,

- the father has a very strong case *and* an effective presentation style *and* a serious need to have custody issues resolved immediately.

Shared Parenting

The reason I helped draft the Illinois joint custody statute—and worked diligently for its passage—is that I truly believe that shared parenting is the best available antidote for the family devastation caused by divorce. The presumption that joint custody is the most equitable, most effective, and most humane way to serve the best interests of children is a philosophy shared by family courts in forty-six other states. While shared parenting is by no means a panacea for all the problems children and parents encounter during and after divorce, it is far more often than not the only fair, workable, and compassionate solution available. Admittedly, shared parenting is not feasible for every divorcing couple. There are mothers and fathers out there who shouldn't be allowed anywhere near their children (or anyone's children). And shared parenting won't succeed unless both parents are committed to making it work.

An effective shared-parenting agreement requires parents to place children's interests above their own. Acceptance of parental responsibilities must supersede personal feelings. Careful planning is also essential. The parents must live close enough to each other to provide children easy access to either parent's home. Parents cannot undermine each other's authority, and they must participate equally in all major decisions affecting their children's lives. Child-rearing conflicts must be settled by compromise, counseling, or mediation. While success in shared parenting doesn't require that former spouses like each other, mothers and fathers must be able to act as partners in parenting. Affection between parents isn't essential. Respect and cooperation are.

In short, shared parenting is hard work. The Rube Goldberg routines and complex logistics necessary to establish and maintain a viable parental partnership are often tedious and frequently annoying. Fortunately, the rewards are bountiful.

When shared parenting succeeds, the emotional bond children share with both parents remains intact. Kids are not forced to choose one parent and lose the other. Mothers and fathers share the responsibilities and satisfactions of parenting. The emotional and financial inequities imposed by traditional sole custody awards are eliminated. Neither parent becomes a pathetic outsider; neither parent must work all day and most of the night to raise children alone. Despite their divorce, parents don't have to assume artificial, uncomfortable roles. They can go on being Mom and Dad, reinforcing in the minds of children the natural truth that parents are forever. Children know that both parents still love them and will care for them. They see grandparents and members of both parents' extended families as often as they did before the divorce. Both parents shoulder a lighter economic burden, and both are granted the time and space they need to rebuild their lives.

Shared parenting has been called "the best gift a divorcing couple can give their children." By maintaining a family structure (functioning differently, perhaps, but still fundamentally intact), parents are protecting their children from many of the influences that twist and disturb children raised by single parents.

Except in cases where a mother poses a serious danger to her children, a divorcing father concerned that he will lose his children in the dissolution process must give some version of shared parenting serious consideration. Joint custody is sometimes viewed as an easy but unattractive compromise—a necessary strategy to end divorce litigation. And of course, joint custody *is* a compromise—but, if the parties involved are both concerned, stable, and competent parents, shared parenting is also the right thing to do.

Skeptics within the domestic relations industry raise two major objections to the shared-parenting concept. The first involves parental conflict. According to shared parenting's critics, parents who could not resolve their differences when they lived together are even less likely to cooperate with each other after divorce. In some extremely bitter, relentlessly antagonistic divorces, that's a valid observation. Divorcing parents obsessed with inflicting pain or gaining revenge typically will not cooperate in raising their children. They don't care about their kids; they're on a mission. What they want, need, and must have at all costs is the total destruction of their former mates. If children are wounded in the crossfire, that's tragic, but war is hell.

Fortunately, most divorcing parents regain their emotional balance at some point in the dissolution process. Aided by friends and family, a wise attorney, a competent therapist, and rational introspection, these men and women are able to isolate their marital conflicts from their parental roles and responsibilities. It's not uncommon for joint custody couples to admit that although they can't stand each other, they refuse to allow the animosity between them to disturb their children's lives. As one joint custody father wrote, "The best interests of the kids is to cut down on your anger and aggression, and act in a much cooler, more compassionate way."

Several studies of joint custody families have found that shared parenting, rather than extending or widening conflict, tends to reduce postdivorce friction. "Cooperative behavior 'staged' for the children's benefit oftentimes becomes real," one researcher noted.

Comments from the parents interviewed in the joint custody studies provide some valuable insights:

"Sharing custody is like working at the office or the plant with someone you don't particularly like," said a father with joint custody. "You can't let your feelings affect your ability to get the job done."

"My conflicts with my ex are smaller and less frequent now," said another joint custody dad. "We're almost friends. Now that I don't have to deal with her every day, she's not hard to get along with at all."

"We're learning to trust each other with the kids," said a third father. "The more time that passes, the easier it seems to be."

"If I had known he was going to become such a good father, I probably wouldn't have divorced him," said a joint custody mother.

In general, child-rearing differences that arise in shared-parenting situations are no more serious than parental disagreements that occur in intact families. Conflict between joint custody parents is undeniably less extreme—and less frequent—than the vicious and unending free-for-alls that infest so many sole custody arrangements.

The second concern that critics voice when attempting to analyze the value of shared parenting is often called "the yo-yo effect." Theoretically, children of joint custody families are supposed to feel like yo-yos, shuttling back and forth between Dad's home and Mom's, living under two different sets of rules and two different parenting styles, frustrated and confused by divided loyalties.

While this objection to shared parenting sounds plausible, most available evidence suggests that the yo-yo theory is an inaccurate generalization. Numerous investigations of coparenting arrangements found that an overwhelming majority of children growing up in joint custody families feel completely at home with either parent. Children, we must remember, are masters of adaptation. (Isn't growing up the process of dealing with constant change?)

Usually, in shared-parenting situations, a practical living arrangement evolves through trial and error, planning and refining, and replanning. Problems with scheduling and conflicting priorities surface, just as they do in traditional family units. Joint custody families deal with these difficulties in much the same manner as intact families do: Dads, moms, and kids work them out as best they can.

Once a stable routine is established (no matter how unusual that routine is), most children adjust rapidly and successfully. The emotional and logistical adjustments shared parenting imposes are certainly far less damaging to children than the trauma of growing up without one parent or the other.

If negotiation, mediation, arbitration, or some combination of each results in a shared-parenting agreement, divorcing fathers should not be disappointed. While it may not be immediately apparent, your cup is much closer to full than to empty. With careful planning, creative scheduling, and a reasonable degree of cooperation from your ex, you will probably find yourself fully (and wonderfully) immersed in your children's lives.

Be open-minded, thorough, and practical in finalizing a shared-parenting agreement. Remember that there's no sure-fire guaranteed-or-your-money-back joint custody approach. There are almost as many shared-parenting arrangements as there are divorced parents sharing child-raising responsibilities.

Focus on the needs of your children first. Accommodate their school and day-care schedules, their extracurricular activities, and their social lives. To the extent possible, customize your working hours and residential choices to complement your availability for child-care duties and parenting time. The younger your children are, the more structured your shared parenting routines need to be. Little kids will accept almost any living arrangements you and your ex agree on. You can be as unconventional as is necessary, as long as the same unconventional events occur regularly and predictably. Older children don't require as much structure. Preadolescents and teens can be as flexible as you are. In fact, if older children are mature enough, allow them to participate in assembling the shared-parenting living arrangements.

The legalities of shared parenting must be addressed carefully. To validate your joint custody agreement—and to change or enforce its provisions should the need arise—a formal Joint Parenting Agreement must be devised, executed, and approved by the court.

The joint parenting document must be detailed and specific. The rights, privileges, and duties of each parent must be spelled out clearly. Don't sign on the dotted line until you and your attorney are satisfied that the agreement ensures you the access and authority you need to be an effective parent. You want rights as well as obligations.

The parenting contract should include a clause indicating that changes to the agreement will be negotiated as necessary to accommodate the children's future growth and any meaningful change in circumstances experienced by you or your ex. A commitment to submit future parenting disputes to mediation or arbitration is also essential.

The sample Joint Parenting Agreement that follows is offered only to suggest the scope and level of detail found in shared-parenting contracts. Your attorney is a better source for joint custody advice applicable to your unique needs and circumstances.

Sample Joint Parenting Agreement

John Doe, and Jane Doe, this ___ day of ___, 1996, enter into this agreement with respect to the custody of their minor children, Amy, age 10, and James, age 7.

A. General Intention

As parents, John and Jane wish to secure the maximum involvement of both of themselves in the physical, mental, moral, and emotional well-being of their children. This involvement and cooperation, they agree, is in the best interests of the children. They wish to share in decisions, and by this agreement produce an understanding of their rights and responsibilities concerning the personal care of their children. In so doing, John and Jane wish to continue to develop in the minds of their children the feelings of comfort, security, love, warmth, and affection that arise in their children's realization that both parents are participating in their upbringing. The parents wish to give their children the clear message that they are loved and wanted by each parent, and that they retain a sense of importance in a family now reconstituted in two households.

John and Jane want their children to have the knowledge that their parents will use their best efforts to jointly care for the children, and that the children will have frequent physical access to both parents.

John and Jane each acknowledge that the other is a fit and proper parent to assume the care, custody, control, and education of their minor children, but they acknowledge that the primary residence of the children shall be with John.

B. Purposes

John and Jane both acknowledge that: (1) Amy and James shall have a continuing need for close, frequent, and continuing contact with both parents in order to minimize, to the greatest extent possible, the effects of the termination of their parents' marriage; and, (2) the circumstances of John and Jane and the children are likely to change over the time this agreement is in effect, and have, accordingly, specified herein certain methods of resolving disputes and reviewing these terms; and, (3) the on-going relationship between the parents and the minor children will require flexibility, so that the spirit of this agreement is more important than exact compliance with each word. Accordingly, the parties will continue to share responsibility for the children's care, fully participate in major decisions affecting the children, but with the least disruption of the children's life patterns as possible.

C. Residence

The children's primary physical residence shall be in the home of John, but the children shall be with Jane as often as is practicable in view of Jane's work schedule. At the present time, the children will be with Jane:

—Every other weekend from Friday at 3:00 p.m. until Monday morning. Jane will be responsible for ensuring that the children arrive at school on time Monday morning.

—Tuesday and Thursday evenings from 3:00 p.m. until 7:00 p.m.

—For four weeks during each summer vacation.

—On Mother's Day and on Jane's birthday.

—Christmas Eve from 10:00 a.m. until 6:00 p.m., Christmas Day from 3:00 p.m. until 9:00 p.m., New Year's Day and Easter from 3:00 p.m. until 8:00 p.m., Thanksgiving Day from 3:00 p.m. until 8:00 p.m., July 3 in odd years and July 4 in even years, Labor Day and alternating school holidays including but not limited to, Veterans' Day, Columbus Day, Good Friday, Martin Luther King's birthday, and Presidents' Day.

—During spring break in alternating years.

If John or Jane is unavailable for their agreed-upon parenting times, he or she shall first request that the other parent take care of the children before making other arrangements. The other parent retains the option of declining such a request without any specific reason or obligation.

D. Communication and Information

To enable both parents to actively participate in raising and guiding their children, John and Jane shall share all important information concerning the children's medical, dental, psychological, and educational status. Each parent shall be notified of and invited to consultations with teachers, counselors, or medical professionals involved in the children's education or health care.

The parent having the children in his or her home shall at all times allow reasonably open access by telephone to the other parent. Each parent shall inform the other in writing of the location and duration of any trip taken with the children. Each parent shall at all times keep the other apprised of their current address and telephone number, and/or a telephone number where they can be reached at all times.

E. Decision Making

The residential parent shall have the power to make minor, routine, day-to-day decisions concerning the children's well-being. However, both parents shall share the joint legal custody of the children so that they together shall reach major decisions concerning, but not limited to, education, religious training, extraordinary medical care, or extracurricular activities. Without limiting the generality of the foregoing, the parents shall attempt to agree on health-care professionals, religious schooling, attendance at religious activities, and choice of schools. In an emergency where time will not allow consultation with the other parent, the parent with physical possession of the children shall take whatever emergency action is necessary and appropriate to meet the immediate need.

F. Modifications

Either party wishing to modify this agreement shall submit their modification proposal in writing to the other parent prior to any action being taken in accordance with paragraph H.

G. Review

The parties shall confer from time to time to review this agreement as to its adequacy, feasibility, and appropriateness in view of the children's age and developmental progress. Unless otherwise agreed, these conferences will take place annually within a week of the youngest child's birthday. Such conferences will also be scheduled if either parent changes employment, moves more than two miles, or remarries.

H. Dispute Resolution

If the parties cannot agree as to any vital nonemergency major decision affecting the children's welfare, or if either party wishes to change the terms of this agreement in a manner to which the other party does not agree, or if any other dispute arises about the meaning of this agreement or anything else concerning the children, the parties will attempt to avoid the expense and acrimony of formal court proceedings. Accordingly, any such disputes shall first be submitted to mediation by any mediator on whom both parties agree. If they cannot agree on a mediator, the parents shall seek the services of the family court to provide the names of three qualified mediators and select one of these three by lottery. Both parties will participate in the mediation process before seeking relief from a court. The parties will also consider (but are not required) to submit their dispute to binding arbitration if mediation fails.

I. Medical and Health Care

Each parent shall promptly inform the other of any serious illness of the children requiring medical attention. In no event shall notification exceed twenty-four hours from the date of illness. Elective surgery shall only be performed after consultation between both parents. Both parents shall inform each other of any medical or health problems that arose while they had physical custody of the children. Both parents shall provide each other with any medications the children are taking at the time custody is transferred, along with sufficient information to allow the parent assuming custody to obtain refills of those medications.

J. Rules for Sharing Parenting Time

The parents agree to share parenting time and to adhere to the following rules:

—Each parent shall refrain from discussing the conduct of the other parent in the presence of the children except in a laudatory or complimentary way;

—Neither parent shall threaten to withhold the other's parenting time, or delay the return of the children after the conclusion of his or her scheduled parenting time;

—Each parent shall prepare the children both physically and mentally for the time scheduled with the other parent;

—Each parent shall advise the other as soon as possible if they are unable to meet their parenting time commitments;

—Neither parent shall question the children about the other parent's activities or personal relationships;

—Neither parent shall expose the children to immoral conduct;

—Neither parent shall drink alcoholic beverages to excess in the presence of the children;

—Neither parent shall attempt to visit the children at unreasonable hours when the children are in the other parent's custody;

—Each parent shall work with the other to arrange parenting schedules which take into account the children's educational, athletic, and social activities, and either or both parents shall attend appropriately planned activities;

—Either parent may temporarily take the children to another state for vacation or other good reason, as long as the other parent has been appropriately informed in writing and in advance of these travel plans with contact informastion;

—Both parents shall at all times conduct themselves in a manner that promotes the beneficial effect on their minor children of this shared-parenting agreement.

K. Merger into an Order of the Court

The parties agree that the terms of this agreement shall be merged into and become part of any final judgment entered in Case No. ____.

Divorcing fathers who found the task of plowing through our sample parenting agreement pretty much intolerable may find the following list of guidelines for shared parenting agreements helpful:

Checklist of Joint Parenting Considerations

1. Prefatory language
   a. a declaration of the fitness of both parents
   b. an acknowledgment that children need close, continuing, and frequent contact with both parents
   c. a declaration of the joint custody rights the parents will share
   d. rules of conduct
2. Physical custody details (who will have the kids when)
   a. weekly parenting time schedules
   b. holidays, birthdays, other special events
   c. vacations
   d. provisions for variances
   e. telephone contact
   f. transportation between homes
   g. child care while parents are at work
   h. financial responsibilities (daily expenses)
3. Major parenting decisions
   a. day care
   b. schools
   c. extracurricular activities
   d. summer camp
   e. selection of health-care professionals
   f. handling of medical emergencies
   g. elective surgery
   h. extraordinary treatment
   i. religious training and practice
4. Dispute resolution
   a. mediation (agreement to submit, and how a mediator will be chosen)
   b. arbitration
   c. a declaration that litigation and acrimony will be avoided if at all possible
5. Adjusting to growth and change

a. annual review of children's needs and parents' circumstances
b. a modification procedure
c. exchanging educational, medical data
d. employment, residential, and marital changes.

SUMMARY

Many divorcing fathers, embittered or enraged by a former mate's marital misconduct or attitudes, view any settlement of custody issues as a form of surrender. Even though a significant number of these men are unquestionably better parents than their children's mothers, this ask-no-quarter-and-give-none stance can cost certain fathers negotiated custody arrangements that are far more favorable than rolling the dice in court. A divorcing father who truly cares about his children must fully explore and seriously consider every opportunity for a compromise that will bring an end to parental hostilities and a beginning to the healing process that must occur before family members can get on with the rest of their lives.

If your spouse is resisting settlement of custody issues, you and your attorney must do everything in your power to promote resumption of negotiations. If you are the parent steadfastly opposing settlement, read the next chapter and then reexamine your position. Ask yourself if you really want to spend the equivalent of your child's college tuition in unpredictable litigation. Then revisit your custody goals to determine if there's any way to become more flexible and creative. Strangely enough, an observation made thirty-some years ago by Mick Jagger and the Rolling Stones may prove helpful in this exercise. "You can't always get what you want," Jagger reminded us. "But if you try sometime, you just might find you get what you [and your children] need."

5
Going to War

Win or lose, custody litigation is an expensive, life-consuming process—a usually frustrating, often infuriating, frequently brutal experience that no one should have to endure. But when counseling, negotiation, and mediation prove fruitless, a divorcing father determined to remain an active, involved parent really has no choice: He must take his case to court.

When it becomes clear that a father's rights cannot be preserved without a fight, a father must commit himself and all his resources to the fray.

If litigation is necessary for resolution of his custody dispute, a divorcing father must prepare himself for a grueling, soul-numbing ordeal. Unlike the courtroom dramas you've seen on television or at the movies, real-life litigation involves very little real action. Forget the swift pace and entertaining eloquence of fictional law. Steel yourself for months, or years, of skull-crushing tedium, interrupted every now and then by moments of incendiary rage and pitch-black despair.

To keep some semblance of sanity, realize and accept right now that almost nothing will happen quickly or decisively. Assemble a large pile of money and a deep reservoir of patience and determination. Expect delays, setbacks, pain, confusion, and anxiety. Be prepared to defend every minute of your married life against an opponent who probably knows more about you than anyone in the world. Anticipate judicial bias and tedium. View institutional incompetence as a given. Recognize that what lies ahead could very well be one of the worst experiences of your life. Devise a way to keep your children out of the line of fire and resolve to prevail in spite of it all.

A divorcing father's decision to fight for his children in court raises hundreds of questions. Because no two custody disputes are identical, there aren't many one-size-fits-all answers to these queries. There is, however, a predictable structure to most custody cases. So, while I obviously can't address the specifics of an individual custody action, I can, based on my experience as the father's advocate in thousands of custody (and related) matters, offer some well-informed observations about the litigation process and its principal participants. In other words, I can tell you how this life- altering game is usually played, and I can introduce you to some of the key players. Hopefully, these insights will demystify the custody litigation process and provide an effective antidote to the intimidation and apprehension that the process often engenders.

Planning and Perspective

The first step down the steep, treacherous road to trial is a series of intense preparation and planning sessions. Your lawyer will explain what is likely to happen to you, and why.

I can pretty much guarantee that you will not like what you hear. You will learn, for instance, that a "bare-bones" custody fight will cost you (at the very least) $5,000. Complex, prolonged litigation, with its heavy discovery expenses, staggering trial costs, and sizable cash outlays for the services of private investigators, custody evaluators, other expert witnesses, and, possibly, an attorney for the children, can have a price tag of $50,000 or more.

In addition to emptying your bank account, a full-blown custody battle may also strip you of your privacy, blacken your reputation, eat away at your self-confidence, and scrape your nerve endings raw. You and your relationship with your children will likely be poked, prodded, inspected, dissected, insulted, and denigrated by your opponent's experts and family court personnel.

Once your lawyer has made clear what you are getting into, an objective review of your case's strengths and weaknesses will move to the top of the preparation agenda. The specter of gender bias often casts a thick gray shadow that must be acknowledged and dealt with in this analysis. Yes, pro-mother favoritism still taints too many family court decisions. I think we've established that. But I think we've also made it clear that the maternal presumption, though prevalent, is not insurmountable.

Turn back to chapter 1 for a moment. Study the case histories you'll find there. Notice two things:

1. The law, not a judge's personal prejudices, apparently formed the basis for the decision in each of these cases.
2. Fathers won.

As the chapter 1 cases demonstrate, fathers can, and have, overcome the gender bias that contaminates the family court system. Furthermore, these fathers and their attorneys didn't need miracles to prevail. Carefully planned, competently executed legal strategy got the job done. The playing field *can* be level, chapter 1 shows us. The assumption that the mother *always* has an insuperable edge in custody disputes is inaccurate. More and more fathers are fighting for custody every year—and succeeding.

Instead of hanging your head, wringing your hands, and whining like a wounded puppy, use the very real possibility that gender bias may affect the outcome of your case as motivational fuel. Recognize that you must go the extra mile to assemble a bulletproof strategy—a case strong enough to overcome whatever advantage bias may give the other side.

When your discussion turns to the specifics of your case, expect your attorney to be completely candid in assessing your position's strengths and deficiencies. And, as I advised in chapter 3's basic training, you, too, must be open and honest. To effectively neutralize any negatives in your past, your lawyer needs to know what they are.

Remember that the legal standard that generally governs all custody litigation awards is "the best interests of the children." Accordingly, you and your advocate must present compelling evidence that you, not the children's mother, can offer the most stable, most secure, and most nurturing child-rearing environment. Because many more custody cases are won by accentuating the positive than by exploiting the negative, prepare to demonstrate that your parental skills and capabilities are superior to those exhibited by your spouse. Unless dramatic, conclusive evidence that your spouse is thoroughly unfit to raise children can be developed and presented, plan to use facts damaging to her position sparingly, as effective contrast to your positive qualities.

Although a prominent divorce attorney's assertion that a mother's conduct will be held against her only if "she's a prostitute who services her clients in her children's presence" is an exaggeration, it is true that a mother's behavior must be blatantly inappropriate to attract the condemnation of most family court judges.

Factors that usually help fathers win custody cases are corporal punishment of the children by the mother (or her boyfriend, or a stepfather), proof of sexual molestation suffered by the children while in the mother's care, or evidence showing that while in the mother's custody the children have become distressed and have exhibited serious behavioral disorders (starting fires; skipping school; indulging in drugs, alcohol, or inappropriate sexual conduct; threatening suicide; running away from home; and so forth).

Divorcing fathers are always surprised that this list isn't longer. These dads raise numerous additional considerations that they believe should be crucial in a court's custody decisions. Typically, divorcing fathers will point out that their children's mother:

- Maintains a filthy home.
- Sends the kids to school dirty and poorly clothed.
- Makes them prepare their own meals.
- Is a lesbian.
- Doesn't help the children with homework.
- Has a gambling problem.
- Is openly living with another man.
- Does not promote religious training.

None of these factors alone is likely to carry much weight in custody litigation unless a harmful impact on the children can be shown. On the other hand, if a mother's parental history includes several of these negatives, a father's chances for custody improve substantially.

As I emphasized in chapter 3, the foundation of a father's custody case must be evidence that clearly and conclusively demonstrates his parental capabilities and commitment. Judges and custody evaluators consistently prefer the parent children turn to when they are sick or troubled; the parent who takes the children to the doctor and the dentist; the parent who attends and participates in school functions, talks with teachers, and helps with homework; the parent most involved in the children's sports, social, and cultural activities; the parent most active in the children's ethical and religious training. In short, most family courts take the position that the best interests of children are served when they live with the parent most qualified to enhance and enrich the child's development and well-being.

Chapter 3 outlined the behavior and attitudes that define effective parenthood in the eyes of the court. In custody litigation, unfortunately, being an accomplished parent is not enough. A divorcing father must prove his capabilities and offer meaningful support for his contention that he is a better parent than the children's mother.

Some evidence required to support a father's claim is uncovered through discovery, depositions, and a variety of investigative options. Other facts and informed opinions essential to a court's custody decision are presented by witnesses.

Discovery

Pretrial discovery is an important, often critical phase of custody litigation. If used effectively, the tools of discovery will yield valuable insights into your opponent's case and unearth vital information supporting your position. An early and aggressive discovery effort can severely restrict your spouse's ability to raise new allegations later. Also, the discovery phase may intimidate your opponent by making clear the size and shape of the ordeal that lies ahead. And the truckloads of paper rolling back and forth could cause the other side considerable expense.

INTERROGATORIES

Interrogatories are written questions that your attorney prepares and sends to your spouse's lawyer. (In most jurisdictions, interrogatories can be directed only to a legal action's principal litigants.) Your spouse is required to answer each of these questions in writing and under oath. Because her replies to your interrogatories are the equivalent of sworn testimony, any contradictions between these answers and your spouse's later statements for the record can be used to attack her credibility.

If your spouse's custody petition is vague or misleading, a well-crafted set of interrogatories can clarify and crystallize her complaints against you. Additionally, your lawyer will be able to ask for the names, addresses, and the "extent of knowledge" of every witness your spouse plans to call.

Answers to your interrogatories will usually provide your attorney with a valuable preview of your opponent's case—an essential understanding of what (and who) you are likely to encounter at trial. What you learn in this initial discovery stage will play a significant role in the formulation of your litigation strategy.

To expedite the receipt of replies to your interrogatories, your attorney will usually confine the questions posed to a manageable number (thirty or fewer in most jurisdictions) of specific—and pointed—queries that your spouse should be able to answer simply and directly. A court is much more likely to compel responses to straightforward, relevant interrogatories than to complex, multipart questions.

REQUESTS FOR PRODUCTION

Early in the pretrial phase, your attorney will send opposing counsel a formal notice requiring your spouse to produce all documents she has that are relevant to your custody dispute.

Typically, materials such as the following are specified in this request for production:

- Any documents or other physical evidence the other side plans to introduce at trial.

- Your spouse's diaries, address book, and any notated calendars.

- All available photos of the children with either parent.

- All available video- and audiotapes of the children and either parent.

- Medical records of the mother and the children.

- The children's school materials, including report cards, academic and attendance records, and any information regarding the children's classroom behavior, disciplinary action, or academic difficulties.

- The children's school papers, including drawings of the family, what-I-did-on-vacation essays, and so forth.

- Canceled checks, credit-card bills, and bank statements.

- All written reports of any investigators or experts retained by the opposition, as well as all test data supporting the experts' conclusions.

- Any correspondence between the parents, between the children and either parent, and between the children and their grandparents.

While the primary function of the request for production is to examine and analyze the documentary evidence your opponent has, you may find material useful to your case as well: a personalized Father's Day card, for instance, or a photo of you beaming proudly in the background as your child receives a school award. Because most state laws view the obligation to respond promptly and completely to production requests as a continuing responsibility, your opponent should not be able to suddenly offer "new evidence" you have never seen on the eve of trial.

DEPOSITIONS

A deposition is simply the questioning of a subject under oath. The purpose of a deposition is to discover what the subject knows and/or to accumulate evidence designed to impeach (discredit) his or her testimony at trial.

The subject of a deposition can be questioned in person or in writing. In a custody case, school personnel or other parties whose trial testimony is expected to be brief and limited are usually deposed in writing, if at all.

An oral deposition is sometimes called an examination before trial—and that's exactly what it is. Because of the substantial legal fees, court recorder payments, and transcription charges incurred by both parties, an oral deposition is the most expensive form of discovery. If conducted competently, it's also the most valuable discovery tool.

Generally, depositions are taken in a lawyer's office. Except for this relatively informal setting, giving a deposition is very much like being on the witness stand in a courtroom. In fact, because no judge is present and the rules of inquiry are much less stringent, a deposition can often be more traumatic then trial testimony.

In child custody cases, both parents are almost always directed to be deposed by the other side's lawyers. Obviously, the questions that litigating parents face will reflect the unresolved issues of each individual dispute, but, generally, inquiries similar to the following can be anticipated in your spouse's deposition, and in yours:

- Why are you seeking custody?
- Why do you believe that you would be a better custodian for the children than your spouse?
- What are your parenting strengths and weaknesses?

- What is your opinion of your spouse's parenting skills?

- What facts will you rely on to establish your custody claim? (Describe these events by recounting when and where they occurred and tell us what witnesses, if any, were present.)

- Do you believe that your spouse is an unfit or improper custodian for the children? If so, what is the basis for this belief?

- Name everyone who has knowledge of the facts and events you contend support your custody claims.

- Have the children ever been lost, injured, taken ill, frightened, or neglected while in your care? If so, provide all relevant details.

- Identify all professionals who have treated, counseled, or interviewed the children (physicians, mental health professionals, psychiatric social workers, school advisors, and so forth).

- Have you ever been diagnosed with a physical or mental illness?

- Have you ever been arrested?

- Have you ever been convicted of a crime?

- Identify all your expert witnesses and indicate what matters each will testify about.

- Provide your work schedule and a summary of the child-care arrangements you have made, or plan to make, if you are granted custody.

- What school do (or will) the children attend?

- Who are the children's best friends and most frequent playmates?

- Describe the cultural, educational, and recreational amenities that are (or will be) available to the children if they are placed in your home (playgrounds, parks, pools, libraries, theaters, social centers, and so forth).

- How much time do you spend with your children?

- What kinds of activities do you share with them?

- Describe your relationships with teachers, administrators, and counselors at your children's school.

- Describe your spouse's involvement with your children's education.

- What are the names of your children's teachers, guidance counselors, and coaches? Name last year's teachers.
- Describe your children's performance in school (grades, awards, special achievements, extracurriculars, incidents of discipline).
- Who else lives in your home?
- Are you currently involved in an intimate relationship?
- Describe your children's relationship with their grandparents.
- Do you have sexual relations in your home?
- Provide the names and addresses of all baby-sitters you employ.
- Have you ever denigrated or insulted your spouse in the children's presence? (Details, please.)
- Have you ever indulged in improper or ill-advised child-rearing behavior?
- Provide all particulars concerning any private investigators in your employ.

Prior to his spouse's deposition date, a divorcing father will participate actively in the preparation of questions. Tell your attorney all you know about your former mate's personality, parental history, blind spots, and vulnerabilities. During the mother's deposition, the father's role should be limited to assisting his lawyer in reacting to any new information that arises. The father's only other duty is to behave himself.

Prepare yourself in advance to listen silently and dispassionately to bitter attacks on your character and behavior. Remember that a court reporter is recording the proceedings. If your spouse says something vicious, false, or outrageous, do not blow up or come apart. Unless your spouse is its source, you don't want an abusive emotional outburst to become part of the case's record.

There is really no reason to become involved in any conversation with your spouse during her deposition. Allow your lawyer to conduct the examination without interruptions.

In child custody cases, the father's attorney should take the mother's deposition as early in the litigation process as possible. Some domestic relations lawyers prefer to accumulate every scrap of paper they can think of before deposing the mother. This obsession for documentary evidence can delay the mother's deposition for months and allow the mother's attorney far too much time to educate and rehearse the opposition's star witness.

An early, thorough, and aggressive deposition of the mother reveals exactly what claims the father must contend with. The strategy also prevents additional allegations from popping up later in the litigation process.

When the time comes to take the witness chair for your own deposition, the need for self-control and adrenaline management increases geometrically. Realize that your deposition is crucial to the success of your case. Don't allow the feelings raging within you to affect your presentation of your side of the custody dispute.

Don't be surprised if your spouse's attorney, a model of class and courtesy in all your previous meetings, suddenly comes after you like a shark on amphetamines. And don't allow yourself to be rattled. Some divorce lawyers become hostile, vitriolic, intimidating, or insulting during the deposition. Don't swallow this transparent bait. Refrain from angry rhetoric, and do not become overly defensive. Sarcasm and arrogance are also inappropriate. Remain calm and respectful throughout your testimony. If you prove yourself to be a strong witness, difficult to discredit or fluster, your spouse's lawyer may think twice about taking the custody battle to trial.

Well in advance of your deposition, your attorney will prepare you for your testimony. These sessions will include an extensive review of the questions you are likely to be asked, the identification of all key elements of your custody claims, and some basic advice like the following.

Answer only what is asked. Whenever you can, respond to questions with an unadorned "yes" or "no." If you don't know or don't recall some piece of information, don't be afraid to say so. While it's not a good idea to claim numerous memory lapses, no one expects you to remember every detail of every day of your married life with perfect clarity.

Be careful not to testify to inaccuracies or exaggerations. Tell the truth, or your attempts at deception will come back to haunt you at trial. Listen carefully to each question, and be sure that you understand each question before you answer. If you are uncertain about what you are being asked, require the examiner to repeat or rephrase the question.

Resist the temptation to help your spouse's attorney. This seems to be a goofy suggestion, but I've noticed that some peculiar inner force often compels a witness to assist a lawyer who is struggling to phrase a question correctly. Don't give in to a desire to help move the proceedings along. If the examiner can't put together concise, cogent questions, that's your spouse's problem, not yours.

During predeposition planning, your attorney will have warned you to expect embarrassing questions about the most intimate aspects of your personal life. There will almost certainly be moments during your deposition when you will be extremely uncomfortable. When a line of questioning offends you or strikes close to a weakness in your case, do not allow an emotional response to betray your discomfort to your spouse's attorney.

Regardless of how outrageous or inappropriate a question seems, you often have no right to refuse to answer—unless your attorney has objected to the question and instructed you not to reply. Courts grant lawyers considerable flexibility in conducting depositions, but, generally, you can't be asked the same question over and over again or be required to respond to irrelevant or argumentative inquiries. Before you answer a difficult question (or any question, for that matter), pause for a beat or two to allow your lawyer time to raise an objection, should one be appropriate.

Typically in a child custody dispute, the period immediately following the parents' depositions is a time of intense evaluation and strategic adjustment. You and your lawyer will reassess the other side's case in light of the sworn testimony now on record. Elements of your spouse's case that seem ripe for further investigation or exploitation will be identified, as will the actions necessary to shore up, patch, or camouflage gaps in your position.

Together, you and your advocate will critique your spouse's credibility and effectiveness as a witness. Your own performance center stage will also be dissected. This candid postmortem can greatly improve your presentation of testimony at trial.

For most divorcing parents, the exchange of depositions provides a first taste of eyeball-to-eyeball legal combat. Because very few humans enjoy being chewed on and clawed at—especially when they are paying hundreds of dollars an hour for the privilege—the deposition experience sometimes convinces one or both litigants that maybe voluntary settlement of custody issues isn't such an unacceptable idea after all.

If a mother has exaggerated a father's parental deficiencies in her original complaint, skillful questioning in her deposition may lead her (and her lawyer) to the realization that a custody contest will not be the effortless rout she had been anticipating. If a father who fears that a mother is planning to banish him from his children's lives hears the mother testify under oath that she believes him to be an excellent parent (albeit a terrible husband), the father may decide that some sort of shared-parenting arrangement could indeed work.

In many custody cases settled during discovery, neither parent experiences a change of heart. It is the litigation process itself that imposes a degree of sanity. The fierce inner fire needed to withstand the pressures of legal confrontation cools quickly as fees mount and emotional trauma deepens.

Other Evidence-Gathering Options

Many domestic relations lawyers focus so intently on the specific charges and countercharges in a custody case that they overlook obvious, readily accessible sources of potentially valuable information. Your attorney may want to consider sending the office paralegal out on some general discovery missions.

Obtaining and examining the mother's medical records may reveal that her mental or physical health should be an issue in your contest. While these records are normally considered to be privileged and, as such, beyond discovery, by seeking sole custody, the mother has likely made questions about her health fair game for investigation. Consulting the *Physician's Desk Reference* or a knowledgeable pharmacist may yield a wealth of useful data about the prescription drugs the mother uses.

The mother's personnel file, obtained by subpoena from her employer, may indicate personality or character traits that reflect negatively on her parental fitness. The personnel file is also a good source for evidence of unreliability or a substance-abuse problem.

The children's complete school records (which usually include material not in the mother's possession) can be obtained directly from the school under the Family Educational Rights and Privacy Act.

Telephone records are kept not only for long-distance calls but for local calls (minute-unit details) as well. A careful review of these records may suggest a pattern of social, business, or criminal activity helpful to your case. Phone company records may also indicate if the mother is using "caller ID" or "call blocking" to interfere with your right to speak to your children. The existence of call blocking is strong support for a denial-of-access claim. A user of call blocking (the mother, for instance) provides a particular phone number (the father's number, for instance) to the telephone company. Whenever a call from the designated phone is received, a recorded message advises the caller that the line is "not in service."

The driving record of the mother (and of any boyfriends) is available from your state's Department of Motor Vehicles. Drunk or reckless driving convictions are, obviously, an effective foundation for questioning the children's safety if the mother is awarded custody.

A check of local, state, and federal data banks may uncover evidence of criminal activity involving the mother or a close associate.

Bank records and credit-card receipts may show spending patterns inconsistent with a mother's claim that a father is neglecting his children's financial needs.

THE PRIVATE INVESTIGATOR

If you're a devoted Raymond Chandler buff or addicted to *Rockford Files* reruns, you may jokingly suggest to your attorney that a smart, savvy private eye could "crack this (custody) case wide open." You know what? You may be right. Sometimes, using the services of a private investigator is an excellent idea.

Specifically, your lawyer may recommend a private investigator if there is reasonable cause to suspect that your children's mother is engaging in behavior damaging to her parental image. If your spouse frequently leaves the children alone while she parties the night away; or if she relies on corporal punishment to discipline the children; or if she abuses drugs or alcohol; or if she exposes the children to sexual activities; or if she fails to maintain a safe, clean, and healthy home, an investigator's services may provide the best means of collecting usable proof of the mother's dangerous or inappropriate conduct.

A diligent search of the mother's garbage may uncover evidence that decides a close custody case. Photos, video- and audiotapes, and a respected investigator's testimony are often used to decimate the sworn statements of the mother and her corroborating witnesses.

While you will of course participate in the decision to hire an investigator, choosing *which* investigator to retain is a responsibility that's best left to your attorney. Most fictional PIs are brilliant, streetwise, and cool. In the real world, honest, effective, and reliable investigators share their profession with a legion of incompetent, unscrupulous slugs. You must rely on your lawyer's experience and contacts to distinguish between the helpful and the useless.

Although you'll be paying all the fees (naturally), your attorney should hire the investigator and closely supervise all aspects of the investigation. This policy takes advantage of "work product" privileges that do not exist if you retain an investigator yourself.

If your lawyer engages an investigator and then simply turns him or her loose to find "whatever's out there to find," consider changing lawyers. Specific instructions, including the nature of the investigation (what to look for, and where and when to look), how much time the investigator is allowed to spend, and preset limits on compensation must restrict the scope and budget of the investigative effort.

Competent investigators are expensive, but an experienced professional will usually be able to determine rather quickly if any meaningful results can be obtained within the time and money constraints you and your attorney have established.

If the private investigator will be testifying at trial, an untarnished reputation, a presentable image, and experience on the witness stand will be essential to his or her credibility. You don't want the judge to discount crucial evidence because your investigator is perceived to be shifty or disreputable.

PIX AND FLIX

Photos and videotapes are excellent supplementary vehicles for documenting the tone and quality of the father-child relationship. The judge who will hear your custody case doesn't know you or your children. Pictures and videos of your day-to-day interactions with the kids allows the judge to "meet" the children and "see" the bond you share with them.

A custody trial (or any trial, for that matter) is basically a high-level "show-and-tell" exercise. Most family court judges are just like the classmates you enthralled with your pet frog back in third grade—they'd much rather be shown than told.

Beginning in the earliest stages of the dissolution process and continuing through all the various stages of litigation, take pictures—a roll of film a week, if you can. Make them candid shots, not posed, artificial setups. Whenever possible, have friends, relatives, or accommodating passersby behind the camera so that you and the children can be shown together. Photos of you and the kids making a pizza, or washing the car, or sledding, or flying a kite—and obviously having a fine time in each other's company—are invaluable visual aids for trial. Pictures of you and the children at outings with the children's friends and the friends' parents are also effective.

If you have a friend or family member who is adept with a video camera, or if you can afford a professional, compiling a videotape chronicling the activities you and the children typically share may also be a good idea. This "Days in Our Life" presentation should be no more than thirty minutes long and graphically depict a wide range of interactions involving you and the kids. To capture the variety you'll need, arrange for selective taping on several separate occasions.

Limit footage from special events; concentrate on scenes of everyday life. A judge can relate to a video showing you and the children shopping, playing Monopoly, or toasting marshmallows at Uncle Billy's backyard barbecue. Tapes of a Caribbean cruise or a hot air balloon ride are inappropriate. Focus on activities that judges and their children are likely to have shared.

Witnesses

Two types of witness are used to present evidence in a custody trial: experts and witnesses of fact. Experts are permitted to offer opinions about the issues under dispute; witnesses of fact can generally testify only to what they've seen or heard.

THE EXPERTS

In a child custody case, the influence exerted by expert custody evaluators can be formidable. Often, the opinions of these professionals are a crucial centerpiece in the court's decision-making process. In more than a few jurisdictions, there are family court judges who simply rubber-stamp the expert's conclusion and give little or no consideration to any other evidence.

Who are these people with so much power over so many lives? The custody evaluation expert is a mental-health professional, ideally a pediatric psychiatrist or a child psychologist. In some jurisdictions, general psychiatrists perform assessments. In other regions, psychiatric social workers are recognized as custody experts.

A pediatric psychiatrist is a medical doctor who has completed three or four years of postgraduate training in psychiatry and an additional two years of child psychiatry. This curriculum may have included formal training in custody evaluation, but only a few of our medical schools currently offer custody assessment classes.

Child psychologists who serve as custody experts usually have a doctorate in clinical psychology. Most also have experience in treating developmental disorders in children and general mental-health problems in adults.

Social workers called upon to perform custody evaluations typically have a master's degree in social work. Unless they have completed additional classes on their own, these evaluators usually have received only minimal education in child psychology. Social workers with comprehensive, concentrated training in custody evaluation are rare.

Unfortunately, the law has established no firm criteria for certifying custody evaluation experts. In practice, some experts are far more qualified than others. Some family court judges recognize a valid expert opinion when they hear one; some do not.

In the early stages of custody litigation, the judge will often ask the lawyers to agree to the court's appointment of a custody evaluation expert. The decision to accept or reject this request rests squarely on the shoulders of your attorney. If your lawyer is an experienced and active domestic relations practitioner, he or she will be familiar with the qualifications and tendencies of most of your jurisdiction's custody experts.

Because the expert's recommendations can carry such substantial weight in family court decisions, the appointment of a competent, ethical, gender-neutral evaluator is essential to your case. If your attorney knows that an expert that the court has suggested is notoriously pro-female or otherwise troublesome, your lawyer will likely withhold agreement to the appointment and ask the court to provide the names of three or four other evaluators. Working with your spouse's attorney, your advocate can usually settle on a qualified expert acceptable to both sides.

In large, densely populated jurisdictions, a custody expert proposed by the court may be someone your lawyer doesn't know well enough to accept or reject. When this uncertainty arises, the court will usually permit your attorney (and your spouse's lawyer) to briefly investigate the expert's credentials and experience.

Assuming that your advocate is appropriately vigilant, this screening will be thorough. Your lawyer will obtain the potential expert's resume and inquire about the evaluator's general practice. If the expert is a "professional witness"—someone who makes a living serving the judiciary—your attorney might not be pleased. Too many of these "experts" are incompetent drones. A divorcing father's custody claim will generally be reviewed much more fairly by a practitioner who works in the real world, with all sorts of families.

Your lawyer will also be interested in the expert's training and experience, especially in the administration of custody assessment protocols. The best available custody experts (based purely on skill levels) are generally board certified in pediatric psychiatry. (A board-certified psychiatrist has completed extensive postgraduate work at an accredited institution and has passed a series of examinations conducted by a national board of review. Only about half the psychiatric professionals in the United States are board certified.)

While it's always dangerous to rely on generalizations, there seems to be some validity to the theory that the more qualified the expert, the better a father is likely to fare in the expert's evaluation. Apparently, education dissolves, or at least dilutes, bias. Additionally (and an important consideration for dads who care about their kids), children are usually treated more sensitively and respectfully by highly qualified evaluators than they are by civil service hacks.

Inquiries concerning the proposed expert's experience and his or her custody "philosophies" will be geared to help your attorney detect both harmful prejudices and useful idiosyncrasies. A review of the expert's custody evaluation history should show no predictable trends. His or her record should include recommendations of sole custody for mothers in some cases, for fathers in others, and some evidence that the expert has advised joint custody when appropriate.

If your lawyer is reluctant to accept any court-appointed custody evaluator and suggests that you hire your own expert witness, you should probably resist for a couple of good reasons. First, any expert in your employ will almost never have the degree of credibility a court-appointed evaluator commands. Despite his or her qualifications and presentation skills, most judges will drastically discount the value of testimony offered by your "hired gun." Second, if you hire an expert, your spouse will likely do the same. You and your kids will be subjected to two rounds of tests, interviews, and role-playing exercises instead of only one. The additional evaluations inevitably result in higher costs and more trauma than the dueling experts' tainted conclusions are worth.

This is not to say that you won't need the assistance of your own expert consultant at some point in the litigation process. As we'll discuss shortly, an expert's services may be useful in preparing you for your sessions with the court's expert and possibly in mounting a challenge to a court-appointed evaluator's unfavorable conclusions.

If your mental health, or your spouse's, is an issue in your custody dispute, the court may expand the scope of the custody evaluation to include a psychiatric examination of the parent whose emotional stability has been questioned.

The psychiatrist who is assigned this task must first determine if the alleged disorder really exists. If it does, the evaluator's next objective is to estimate the illness's effects (if any) on the children and the parent-child relationship. If a mental illness creates a present or potential danger to the children, the impact on a custody decision is obvious. If a parent's emotional disorder is being treated successfully with medication and/or psychotherapy, the evaluating professional will regard the illness simply as another factor to be considered in assessing parental capabilities.

It's important to emphasize that seeing a therapist is not regarded as evidence of mental illness. The million and one varieties of stress engulfing and defining modern life have made visits to psychotherapists and counselors as commonplace as visits to the dentist. Generally, only allegations that a parent is suffering from severe disorders such as schizophrenia, chronic paranoia, severe depression, or an overpowering addiction require a professional's validation or refutation.

Incidentally, if you have been seeing a therapist, you may be tempted to ask him or her to testify in support of your parental competence claims. This is usually not a good idea. Because it will rarely be viewed as objective, your therapist's testimony has limited value. And, by involving the therapist in your custody case, you are waiving the normal rules of doctor-patient confidentiality. Your spouse's attorney will be able to ask all sorts of questions you may not want to hear the answers to in open court. You also risk screwing up a professional relationship it may have taken you months, or years, to build.

Similarly, if your children are receiving counseling, try to keep their therapists out of the case also. Respect your children's privacy. Especially if the divorce is the reason they are seeing a therapist, do not disturb their treatment unless it is absolutely necessary.

The court's custody evaluator will consult with your children's therapist (and yours). Since the court's expert is the expert the court will rely on, generally so should you. If your children's therapist knows that they would prefer to live with you, and your therapist believes that you are a loving, caring parent, let the court's evaluator discover and present that information.

THE CUSTODY EXPERT'S EVALUATION

A competent, thorough custody evaluation will usually include at least the following:

- Clinical interviews with each parent and child.
- An in-depth observation of parent-child interaction.
- IQ, personality, and academic achievement tests for the children.
- Psychological and personality tests for the parents.
- Interviews with pediatricians, teachers, day-care providers, therapists, and anyone else likely to have information useful in resolving custody issues.

Most divorcing fathers become apprehensive as their scheduled interview with the custody evaluator approaches. This concern is well placed. The fate of the dad's case and his relationship with his children may hinge on the evaluator's opinion.

You and your attorney may find it helpful to engage a custody expert of your own at this stage of the proceedings. Hire the best professional you can afford. Well in advance of the court-ordered evaluation, your expert can explain the standards custody evaluators rely on in your region, discuss any idiosyncrasies of the expert you will see, administer tests similar to those used by the court's expert, and conduct a realistic preview of your upcoming interview.

Afterward, your consultant will critique your attitudes and presentation skills. While what you learn in these meetings may or may not significantly impact the image you'll convey to the court's evaluator, you will at least become comfortable with the evaluation process, and you'll certainly know how to avoid antagonizing the evaluator.

As I've preached often in these pages, a divorcing father seeking custody cannot succeed unless he learns to detach himself from the emotional upheaval of divorce and to focus intently on the needs and interests of his children. Self-control and maturity are especially critical qualities in the custody evaluation interview.

A custody expert wants to see a wise, concerned, even-tempered parent—a man capable of dealing constructively with his own feelings and the broken relationship with his former mate.

Answer all the evaluator's questions truthfully and completely. If you don't know the answer to a particular question, say so. Express your regrets that your kids are entangled in your marital conflict and your hope that you can shield them from further trauma. Show a sincere concern for your children's welfare. Keep your complaints about your spouse's attitudes and behavior to yourself. Be ready to discuss your active involvement in all phases of your children's lives.

If asked, describe your custody plans in detail: child-care arrangements, how you will adjust work and leisure routines to accommodate the kids' needs, your participation in the children's education, religious training, and social activities. Make it clear that, if you are awarded custody, you will be cooperative and flexible in arranging liberal visitation for the children's mother.

You will not like some of the evaluator's questions, and you may find the evaluation process degrading and intrusive. Recognize these as natural reactions, and do not display your outrage at what is happening to you and to your children. Present yourself as a concerned, compassionate father, not as a wild-eyed zealot. Don't lecture or whine or castigate your spouse. Save your righteous indignation for another day, another place. Be what the custody evaluator would find if he or she were to look up "a good father" in the dictionary.

Resist the impulse to "rehearse" the children for their sessions with the custody evaluator, but prepare and comfort them to the extent that their interviews will not frighten or upset them. Most custody experts are adept at recognizing parental manipulation and hold the tactic against a parent who uses it. So don't coach the kids. Tell them that you'll be happy and proud of them if they simply tell the truth. Assure the children that they are free to speak frankly about you and their mom. Promise them that they will never have to tell you or their mother what they've told the evaluator.

An important element in the custody evaluation process is the expert's observation of the children's interaction with each parent. Typically in this exercise, the parent and the child are invited to play together while the evaluator watches. Despite the artificial setting and the fact that the parent will be aiming to please, an experienced custody evaluator can learn quite a bit from these sessions. Often, a startling contrast in the parent-child relationship is noted. For example . . .

A mother spends an hour idly watching her daughter play with dolls and tiny plastic critters. There is little conversation and the mother never really *plays* with the child. The mother seems stiff, uncomfortable, bored.

The father of the same child spends most of his session with his daughter down on the floor with her. Together, they rearrange doll-house furniture and design a variety of faces for Mr. Potato Head. The dad seems to be having a pleasant afternoon, and so is the child. They tease each other and chuckle together when one or the other says something silly.

Identifying the parent likely to prevail in this phase of the evaluation doesn't present much of a challenge, does it?

To make the most of the observation exercises, a father should be as much like himself as he can be under the circumstances. Behave as you usually do when you're playing with the kids at home. The evaluator isn't looking for the perfect dad. He or she just wants to see how you and your children relate to each other. A competent clinician can usually tell when "parental behavior" is being staged, so gratuitous hugs, kisses, and baby talk are unnecessary and possibly harmful to the case.

After testing and interviewing both parents and the children, and observing all the various relationships within the family dynamic, the court's custody evaluator may also speak with the children's teachers, pediatrician, and day-care providers. When the expert feels that sufficient information has been accumulated, he or she will analyze the data and prepare a written custody opinion.

A concerned, committed professional will not take the custody evaluation responsibility lightly, so don't expect a quick end to the process. If prepared conscientiously, the expert's report will generally include a review of who was interviewed and for how long; a summary of any additional sources the expert has consulted; descriptions of the clinical sessions the expert has conducted; a general assessment of each parent's child-rearing skills; analyses of the parent-child relationships observed; and, finally, the expert's conclusions and custody recommendations. The report will be delivered to the judge, and, depending on the court's policies, a copy may be sent to the parents' lawyers.

In some family courts, the custody battle is for all practical purposes over. Litigation may continue, but unless some amazing evidence turns up at trial, the judge's custody decree will closely mimic the evaluator's recommendations.

Often, at the court's insistence, or with its encouragement, the custody expert will offer to discuss the evaluation's conclusions in a joint conference attended by both parents and their attorneys. If a meeting of this kind is offered to you, by all means go. Unless you have participated in mediation, this will be the first time that your custody dispute has been exposed to the scrutiny of an objective (and knowledgeable) third party.

If the expert has concluded that both you *and* your spouse are competent, caring parents, he or she may recommend some form of joint custody. Don't view this suggestion as a cop-out. The evaluator is usually not trying to dodge a difficult, troublesome responsibility. The joint custody suggestion almost surely evolved through careful analysis.

Parental capability and commitment can't be measured empirically on any numerical scale. But pretend for a moment that such a scale does exist. Imagine also that the world's worst parents would score "1" on this scale, while the world's best moms and dads would earn a "10." Let's further agree that in the eyes of the law and society a parent who receives a score of "5" is an "adequate" parent. Can you think of any defensible reason why the law should be allowed to govern the relationship between an adequate (or better) parent and that parent's children? Neither can the professional expert who suggests joint custody.

A shared-parenting recommendation means, in effect, that the evaluator has found little or no difference in the parental abilities of the parents "tested." It doesn't matter if you are a 7.0 and your spouse a 6.5, the expert is saying. You are both excellent parents. Your children will benefit from the positive qualities you share and from valuable talents and perspectives unique to each of you.

The evaluator's report is often the first time that it becomes clear to contentious parents that their animosity for each other has absolutely no relevance in assessing what is best for their children. Hearing a respected authority present their children's needs and fears often inspires warring parents to suspend hostilities and take a fresh look at what their custody fight is doing to their children.

Sometimes, a newfound willingness to settle has a less noble genesis. The expert's opinions cause a litigant who believes that he or she is clearly the superior parent to experience a humbling shock. The parent realizes that the resounding victory that once seemed certain has now been reduced to a huge, frightening "maybe."

When a move toward settlement is the end result of an expert's suggestion, the evaluator will frequently volunteer to assist the parents in working out equitable custody arrangements.

If the cooperation necessary to implement joint custody is an impossible dream, the court's expert will probably make a sole custody recommendation. If one of the parents seems to be unfit, the evaluator will say so. When one parent seems only slightly more preferable, the evaluator will likely recommend liberal visitation for the parent not given custody. There will usually be an undercurrent of reluctance evident when an evaluator believes that both parents are competent, as the following excerpt from a real expert's report demonstrates:

> Unfortunately, in this case, joint custody is out of the question. Mrs. Reed is adamantly against it, the parties disagree strenuously on many issues, and there is no evidence of the commitment necessary to make joint custody work. Therefore, sole custody of the children should be awarded to Mr. Reed. He has demonstrated superior parenting skills, and seems more aware of the children's needs than their mother. Mr. Reed relates to the children with warmth and humor, even in the midst of these stressful proceedings. Although Mrs. Reed clearly loves her children, her demonstrated level of concern for them is noticeably lower than Mr. Reed's. She is an important part of the children's lives, however, and should be granted liberal visitation.

Occasionally, a custody expert's report is so convincing that the judge, both lawyers, and both parents accept its recommendations without reservation. Litigation ceases and the parties address themselves to the technicalities involved in merging the expert's conclusions into the final divorce decree.

When the custody evaluator's appraisals are disputed, the trek toward trial resumes. If the court's custody expert believes that you should have custody of the children, you will, naturally, be pleased and relieved, and your lawyer will likely ask the expert to testify for you at trial. If the expert concludes that the children should live with their mother, you and your lawyer must decide how best to challenge the expert's opinion.

One technique you might use to cast doubt on an unfavorable evaluation is to employ a respected custody evaluator of your own to conduct a "peer review" of the court expert's appraisal. The potential value of this approach can be seen in the following case history.

A court-ordered custody evaluation in litigation involving Mr. and Mrs. Green was performed by Nathan Davis, a child psychologist. Davis, after interviewing the Greens and their children several times, issued an opinion recommending that sole custody be awarded to Mrs. Green.

Mr. Green's lawyer asserted that Davis's custody evaluation was deficient and prejudicial. He asked the judge if Davis's report could be reviewed by Dr. Stephen Smith, an eminent board-certified pediatric psychiatrist. The judge consented.

After examining the evaluation in question, Dr. Smith spelled out its inadequacies for the court as a rebuttal witness:

- Davis had provided almost no data comparing the parental capabilities of Mr. and Mrs. Green.

- A meaningful analysis of the quality of the relationship between each parent and the child was also missing.

- The report made numerous references to each parent's opinion of the other's parenting skills, but no description of parental behavior observed independently by Davis.

Apparently, Dr. Smith concluded in his critique of Davis's report, Trent had unconsciously taken sides in the Greens' conflict. Mrs. Green was telling the truth, Davis had obviously decided, while Mr. Green was a liar and a scoundrel. This subjective stance, Dr. Smith pointed out, prevented Davis from doing his job: evaluating each parent's competence in child rearing.

Although Mr. Green's lawyer attacked the custody evaluation in vigorous cross-examination of Davis at trial, the use of Dr. Smith to impeach the "expert's" report was a far more effective strategy. Smith, a respected professional with impeccable credentials, was not involved in the custody contest itself. Smith's status, logic, and his neutrality impressed the judge. He immediately declared that Davis's report would not be used by the court and ordered a new evaluation by another custody expert.

Because courts often consider the experts they appoint to be impartial allies, your lawyer will be especially careful in challenging the abilities or objectivity of these witnesses during trial.

Possible launching sites for effective and entirely appropriate probes include:

Qualifications. Is the expert licensed to practice in your state? Is he/she board certified? Is he/she a pediatric psychiatrist (or psychologist), or simply a general mental-health practitioner? How long has he/she been practicing? How many custody evaluations has he/she performed? Has he/she completed any training courses recommended by the American Academy of Psychiatry and the Law (or any other national forensics group)?

Bias. In all the cases in which this expert has been involved, how many decisions resulted in a custody award to the mother? Does he/she have any particular child-rearing philosophy (as indicated in speeches, articles, or previous testimony)? Is he/she a divorced parent? If so, who has custody of the children? Is he/she the child of divorced parents? If so, was his/her custodial parent the mother or the father?

Limited Knowledge. Does the expert have children? Is he/she aware of the stresses, leverages, and intrafamily dynamics of custody litigation? How many times did he/she see the children, and for how long? Did he/she observe the children in their home environment?

The Evaluation Process. Were the children sick, anxious, or fearful during tests, interviews, or observation periods? Did the expert follow standard (and accepted) evaluation protocols, or has he/she "invented" variations? Do the expert's notes, statements, analyses of test results, and so forth support his/her conclusions?

No attempt to discredit a court-appointed expert is likely to succeed unless it is supported by the results of an extensive investigation of the expert's background and methodology. Admittedly, this is expensive, burdensome homework. But to change a judge's opinion of information that could very well destroy your case, it's an assignment that must be completed.

THE SOCIAL SERVICES INVESTIGATION

In many jurisdictions, custody litigation prompts an investigation conducted by a court-ordered social services representative. This inquiry usually includes a series of interviews (with each parent, teachers, neighbors, pediatricians, and so forth) and an inspection of the parents' homes.

The overworked, undertrained social workers charged with completing these investigations are not likely to be custody experts.

Nevertheless, a divorcing father must treat them as such because their reports often exert substantial influence in the court's custody decisions. Theoretically, the social services investigation provides the judge with an objective view of the parents' practical parenting aptitudes and an appraisal of the home environments in which the children will be raised. Unlike the mental-health professionals appointed as custody evaluators by the courts, social services personnel are not generally qualified to assess the emotional nuances of the parent-child relationship. They can't tell a judge if the children they see have the love and guidance kids need, but they can report on an absence of cornflakes in a parent's pantry and the presence of a crack house next door.

Many domestic relations attorneys (including me) believe that the social services investigation is an overused and overrated procedure that gives poorly prepared civil service "lifers" far too much power over the fathers and mothers and children of divorce.

I am not aware of any scientific standards or uniform procedures that govern the social services investigation. Typically, the caseworker's conclusions favor the more congenial and articulate parent or the parent whose child-rearing philosophy most closely conforms with the investigator's own preconceptions and prejudices. Flagrant hearsay that would never be permitted in trial testimony is often presented as absolute fact in the social services report, and then used as evidence or even the basis for some custody recommendations.

Despite its generally obvious (and often outrageous) deficiencies, the social services report is difficult to impeach. Family court judges and court-employed social service personnel work together every day. Most judges treat the caseworkers assigned to their courts as colleagues and view their subjective appraisals as valuable evidence.

In deference to this special relationship, any attack on an unfavorable caseworker's report must target the report itself, not the competence or bias of the investigator. Inadequacies in the report, your attorney will emphasize, must be the result of time constraints imposed by a heavy caseload, because, as everyone in this jurisdiction knows, social worker Smith usually performs splendidly in a difficult, demanding job, etc., etc., etc. (Sometimes, ironically, this puffery is true.)

Flaws in the social services report likely to cast doubt on the investigator's conclusion may include one or more of the following:

- Too much time was spent with one parent, not enough with the other.

- The report contains statements not supported by facts.

- The report conflicts with the court-appointed evaluator's conclusions.

- Only a cursory inquiry occurred.

- Opinions and hearsay are treated as fact.

- One parent was interviewed at home (with the children present), the other at the office (without the kids).

- The investigator did not interview teachers, day-care providers, or others aware of the children's relationships with their parents.

You must prepare for the social services investigation in much the same manner as you readied yourself for all the other annoying and degrading examinations of your parental fitness.

Meet with your attorney for a review of the investigator's preferences, prejudices, and idiosyncrasies.

In many jurisdictions, a questionnaire is sent to parents in advance of the social services interview. If this "investigation in writing" technique is used in your area, consult with your attorney while formulating your replies.

(These inquiry forms are rarely revised. Your lawyer may have a "preview" copy for you.)

The court will allow your attorney to request a list of all witnesses the social worker plans to interview. Some judges permit parents' lawyers to lobby for their clients. Your advocate should know how much contact with social services personnel is customary in your region, and, within these parameters, he or she will attempt to emphasize your merits briefly and eloquently, I hope. Your attorney may also direct the investigator's inquiry toward issues in which you hold an advantage, propose interviews with witnesses who support your claims, and suggest specific questions for the investigator to pose to your spouse and other witnesses.

Neither you or your attorney should allow "nonparallel" appraisals. If the caseworker interviews your spouse at home with the children, your interview must also be conducted at home with the kids present. If you or one of the children is sick at the time scheduled for the investigator's visit, reschedule.

As soon as you learn that a social services inquiry has been ordered, be ready to welcome the investigator into your home at any time. Some social workers believe that an unannounced visit provides a more accurate picture of the child-rearing environment.

Your home should be clean and free of potential hazards to the children's safety (cleaning fluids and medications stored securely out of reach, no exposed wiring, and so on). Adequate locks and smoke detectors should be in place. Furnish the kids' rooms appropriately, and display their toys without seeming to do so. A well-kept yard with a sturdy fence is a plus.

Be able to tell the social worker the location of your children's school, the nearest parks, and the closest hospital emergency room. When asked for your custody plans, present a feasible child-care schedule, with no gaps in which your children are alone or inadequately supervised. If you've revamped your employment and leisure-time routines to implement your custody plan, say so. Show an interest in the children's education and social development, and be prepared to answer questions about the kids' schoolwork, friends, and activities.

Present yourself as a concerned, caring dad, doing the best he can under the circumstances. Exhibit a calm and charitable attitude toward your spouse. Don't criticize her in the investigator's presence.

If possible, schedule the home visit for a time when you and the children are preparing dinner or doing homework together. Allow the social worker to observe a warm, easy interaction between you and the kids. Avoid staged, overdone displays of affection.

GUARDIAN *AD LITEM*

A guardian *ad litem* ("guardian for the suit") is a person appointed by the court to serve as the children's advocate in a custody dispute. Usually a lawyer experienced in custody matters, the guardian acts as an objective fact-finder and a buffer between the litigants and their attorneys. In a handful of states, the appointment of a guardian *ad litem* is mandatory in all contested custody cases.

The guardian often conducts a separate investigation of unresolved custody issues and, when appropriate, makes an independent recommendation to the court. In some jurisdictions, the guardian is much more active, often serving as the children's lawyer.

In addition to reviewing the reports of expert witnesses and interviewing parents, teachers, and others having relevant information, the guardian may cross-examine witnesses at trial. Sometimes, the guardian acts as a mediator in an attempt to help litigating parents reach a settlement that (in the guardian's opinion) serves the children's best interests.

Proponents of the guardian *ad litem* approach believe that when custody litigation becomes a street fight between two angry adults too involved in their own personal agendas to recognize their parental responsibilities, appointment of an advocate free of emotional baggage and having no legal allegiance to either parent is a necessary safeguard for the rights of the children.

Critics of the concept argue that the guardian introduces another troublesome variable to an already complex and confusing equation. Like the other "experts" used by family courts, the guardian may or may not be qualified to address custody issues and may or may not possess the objectivity necessary for the effective advocacy of children's rights.

If a guardian *ad litem* is appointed in your custody litigation, rely heavily on your attorney's advice regarding communication with the guardian. It's usually a good idea to allow your lawyer to initiate contact with the guardian. Using brief and specific examples, your attorney should summarize your parenting attributes and explain why living with you will enrich your children's lives. Significant events involving the children should be discussed and facts detrimental to your case addressed openly. Your lawyer may arrange for you to meet with the guardian or ask the guardian to visit you and the kids in your home.

Presenting yourself and your custody goals to the guardian requires the same behaviors and attitudes you exhibited in your discussions with the court's custody evaluator and in the social services interview. Be polite; don't denigrate your spouse; underscore your concern for the children and your willingness to do whatever needs to be done to protect and serve their interests.

WITNESSES OF FACT

Your lawyer will point out that any number of people who know you, your spouse, or your children may be able to corroborate your custody claims. The testimony of your children's teachers, pediatrician, coaches, and child-care providers may be particularly useful in building your case. Clergymen, neighbors, friends, business associates, or law-enforcement officers may also have knowledge that reflects positively on your parental image or illuminates your spouse's shortcomings.

These individuals are considered to be "witnesses of fact"—persons able to offer specific firsthand accounts of events and behavior relevant to the resolution of your custody dispute.

Teachers, pediatricians, school guidance counselors, and some professional day-care providers are sometimes viewed as "quasi experts." Technically, these witnesses aren't legally qualified to comment on the overall parental competency of the litigating parents, but because of their vocational backgrounds, the information they bring to court is almost always seen as more valuable and more credible than the testimony of "lay" witnesses.

A teacher who testifies that you, and not your spouse, is the parent who consistently and actively participates in parent-teacher conferences is, in effect, offering a "quasi expert" opinion that you are more involved in your children's education than your spouse is. A pediatrician who tells the court that you, not your spouse, is the parent who customarily brings in the children for checkups and the only parent who has ever called with questions about medications or illnesses implies that you, not your spouse, is the concerned, caring parent. A day-care worker who describes the warm, playful interaction between you and your child that occurs *every day* when you pick the child up after work is providing valuable parental images for the trial record.

While anyone who has observed events and behavior that support your case's central themes are potential witnesses of fact, the testimony of your relatives and close friends has limited value. Witnesses with whom you share no family or financial bond are most credible to the court and, thus, most effective. When attempting to identify possible witnesses for your side, forget about cousin Ralphie and your lifelong buddy Bob. Concentrate on coaches, dance instructors, scoutmasters, your children's friends (if they're old enough), the parents of your children's friends, librarians, police officers, and similar people.

After screening your list of potential witnesses, your attorney will choose a manageable number to participate in your case. Remember that when it comes to presenting witnesses, less is more. Calling twenty people to testify about five events you feel are relevant to your custody claim is far less effective than being able to produce five witnesses able to corroborate twenty favorable occurrences. A judge is not amused when a dozen people show up in his courtroom to swear that they saw Dad walking his kids to school one Tuesday morning.

Your attorney, *not you,* should choose and prepare your witnesses. Your role in this effort should be limited to telling your lawyer who can testify about what and then notifying potential witnesses that your attorney will be contacting them.

When your advocate talks to your witnesses, he or she will assure them that what the court needs to make a responsible custody decision are facts. Witnesses should never be asked to testify "for" you or "against" your spouse. The fact that you are seeking custody should not be presented as a personal crusade that you must complete successfully at all costs, but as a necessary duty that you have reluctantly assumed for the children's sake. The attorney's most important objective in these witness interviews is to determine what the witness knows and how best to use that knowledge.

Your lawyer will contact your witnesses once or twice more before custody proceedings begin to prepare them to testify. What each witness has seen or heard will be reviewed in detail. Important courtroom basics concerning dress, demeanor, and what to expect in cross-examination may also be discussed.

THE TEMPORARY HEARING

Way back in chapter 3, I described a situation fairly typical of the early stages of the dissolution process: two divorcing parents living in the same home, each fervently wanting the other out, each refusing to leave.

Lawyers representing mothers in custody matters frequently believe that there is an easy way to break this stalemate. Often relying on ultraflimsy or nonexistent justification, these attorneys file petitions asking a family court to give their clients exclusive possession of the family home and temporary custody of the children. A motion requesting temporary custody may also be filed when one of the parents moves out of the family home without first obtaining an adequate separation agreement. The parent who remains in the home with the children claims abandonment or seeks court validation of the "status quo" (the way things are).

Under the law (and a competently drawn temporary joint custody order should always affirm this fact), both divorcing—but not yet divorced—parents share custody of their children jointly, *until a court decrees otherwise.*

A temporary custody petition is an attempt to force a family court to make an immediate custody decision without the careful consideration of the evidence and circumstances that a determination of this magnitude requires. As I warned in chapter 3, the "temporary" orders sometimes issued in response to these petitions are often permanent. If your spouse requests temporary custody of the children, you are facing a serious threat. You must respond swiftly and vigorously.

If you and your spouse are occupying the same residence, her petition for temporary custody is valid only if there is clear and convincing evidence that you are an unfit parent or a threat to the safety of your spouse and/or your children. Allegations that living with the tensions and hostilities associated with the dissolution of your marriage is harmful to the children (even if true) are not enough. If you and your spouse are living apart, the petition for temporary custody is probably an attempt to restrict your access to the children and thus strengthen your spouse's position as "the more involved" parent. If your spouse has left the family home and the children are living there with you, the request is obviously an attempt to reverse those circumstances.

Regardless of the situation, a motion for temporary custody should not be shrugged off. Don't allow an exchange of pleadings and affidavits or a judge's conference with the attorneys to decide the matter. Instruct your lawyer to insist on a hearing.

A temporary custody hearing is very similar to a custody trial, only shorter and more condensed. If the opposition is not prepared for a "mini trial" at this stage of the litigation process, their petition may be withdrawn or buried in a lengthy continuance.

Assuming that your lawyer has been down this road before, preparation for a temporary hearing will be just as thorough and just as intense as preparation for trial. Unless you live in a crowded urban jurisdiction (where nothing will happen for months), time may be a problem. You will have to compress your case, focusing on your strongest arguments and presenting only your most important witnesses and documentation.

If you win temporary custody of the children, let the remainder of the litigation process play itself out at its normal pace (a speed halfway between "unbelievably slow" and "no perceptible movement" in most regions of the United States). Until the case reaches trial, you are in control.

Don't be a sore winner. Give your spouse liberal access to the children. Cheerfully accommodate her visitations. Don't allow yourself to be drawn into verbal or physical confrontations. Don't denigrate her in the children's presence. Don't let your advantage dissipate. Stay involved in your children's lives. Help them with their schoolwork; be active in their extracurricular functions and social activities. Build an extensive, diversified parental portfolio.

Whenever an impulse to move your custody case to its conclusion strikes you, remind yourself that the longer the children live happily with you before trial, the more reluctant a judge will be to disturb their stable, familiar environment.

If the temporary custody question is decided in your spouse's favor, don't despair. The hearing provided your lawyer with an extremely useful preview of your spouse's case, and your custody claim has been officially filed. Unless your parental fitness has been completely discredited, you will have visitation rights. Use the months between the temporary hearing and trial to strengthen your parental image and to polish your parenting skills.

Help coach the soccer team; become a chauffeur for the Girl Scout troop. Volunteer as a teacher's aide on field trips, and offer your baby-sitting services whenever your spouse needs time away from the kids. Be fatherly.

Your attorney will work with you to supplement and reframe the evidence presented at the temporary hearing. Whether your case needs a tune-up or a major overhaul, there will be plenty of time to complete the work required. So don't give up.

Sexual Abuse Allegations

Every day, Sally Jesse Raphael, Jerry Springer, and a legion of lesser talk-show hosts appear to empty out our nation's trailer parks to unleash an endless parade of geeks, freaks, sleazoids, and sociopaths. The panoramic range and deep depravity of the demented behavior these "regular people" admit to startles and shocks some Americans (including a sizable number of legislators).

Not me. Since 1981, I've been a combatant on the front lines of matrimonial law—an arena in which many evil, rabid mothers routinely level false allegations of sexual abuse to destroy the lives of innocent men. The fact that deploying their children as weapons in these sick, twisted vendettas often risks the children's sanity does not deter these "ladies" for a moment.

The use of false sexual abuse allegations to win custody suits has become almost a standard tactic among disturbed mothers and unethical divorce lawyers. Its widespread usage has earned this despicable "strategy" its own special place in the lexicon of mental health professionals. Since the early 1990s, the identifier Sexual Abuse In Divorce Syndrome (SAID) has been used by psychologists to describe a series of interrelated conditions that competent investigators must consider when attempting to confirm the veracity of sexual abuse allegations that arise in the midst of custody disputes.

The fact is that without reliable witnesses or unambiguous physical evidence, a sexual abuse charge can never really be substantiated. If one or more of the following factors is found in the context of an accusation associated with a divorce action, however, an experienced investigator will realize that the SAID syndrome, and not inappropriate sexual behavior, may be the source of the abuse charge:

- There were no abuse allegations while the parents were married.

- Interrogatories, the mother's deposition, and other discovery completed earlier in litigation included no mention of sexual abuse.

- The mother (not the child) was the first to report the alleged abuse.

- Acrimonious divorce litigation has been under way for some time.

- There are unresolved custody and visitation issues, or recent changes in custody and visitation terms have given the father more access to the child.

- The father has recently become involved in a serious relationship with another woman.

- Money issues related to the divorce have not been resolved.

- The mother who reports the alleged abuse presents herself as a victim of manipulation, coercion (physical or social), or sexual abuse during her marriage.

- The mother who reports the alleged abuse is hostile, emotionally driven, vindictive, and dominant. She insists that punitive measures, including criminal prosecution, must be taken immediately, even before an investigation has been completed.

- The mother exhibits borderline psychotic tendencies, makes outrageous and implausible charges, and becomes irrational when attempts are made to obtain details of her claims.

- The child/victim's account of the alleged abuse closely matches the mother's report in phrasing and narrative structure.

- The child, when questioned about the alleged abuse, gives responses that appear to be rehearsed, coached, or conditioned.

- The child uses verbal descriptions of the alleged abuse not appropriate for his or her age, and demonstrates little or no comprehension of what he or she is saying.

- The child offers spontaneous and automatic reports of the alleged abuse without being asked questions soliciting this information.

- The child is not uncomfortable or nervous in the presence of the alleged abuser.

- The child demands punishment of the alleged abuser (usually banishment from the family) and criticizes the alleged abuser forcefully and publicly. (Actual sexual abuse victims tend to be embarrassed and traumatized by what has happened to them, not vindictive and outraged.)

It's important to emphasize that the presence of some—or even several—of these SAID syndrome characteristics does not mean that a sexual abuse accusation will be dismissed. Based on a well-meaning "better safe than sorry" policy, abuse investigators often accept an abuse charge as fact and consider the accused abuser guilty until proven otherwise. The SAID syndrome "red flags" noted above, however, should alert law-enforcement officials and the mental-health professionals who work as "abuse validators" that they may be dealing with a false allegation. The more SAID indicators found, the more likely that possibility becomes.

The first reaction of most divorcing fathers falsely accused of sexual abuse is shock, followed closely by outrage—an almost uncontrollable anger that, unless moderated quickly, will almost always be held against him.

If your spouse makes a false charge of sexual abuse against you, it is absolutely imperative that you control your emotions in your dealings with the psychiatrists, social workers, guardians *ad litem,* law-enforcement personnel, and family court judges who will soon be closing in from all sides. A man unable to hold his emotions in check is often perceived as being unable to control his actions as well and, thus, probably capable of deviant behavior. This is not a logical thesis, I know, but because it is a common presumption, you must conduct yourself accordingly.

Project an image of cooperative concern. Be courteous but firm in your interactions with court and law-enforcement officials. Flashes of bad temper, impatience, or anger may cause negative comparisons between you and your accuser.

In coping with the rage within you, remember that you are a father and that it *is* possible that your child has been sexually abused (by the mother's boyfriend, a relative, or a baby-sitter). It's also possible that the child mistakenly believes that he or she has been molested.

As soon as you learn of a false sexual abuse charge, respond quickly and aggressively. You'll have two objectives at this point: to protect your child from further trauma and to defend your innocence, emphatically and logically.

If your divorce attorney is not experienced in fighting false abuse charges, and, certainly, if criminal prosecution seems imminent, you will require additional representation. You'll need a professional with expertise and a proven track record in sexual abuse matters. An advocate with these credentials will be expensive, but incompetent or inexperienced counsel may cost you your children, your reputation, and your freedom.

Be active in your own defense and in defending your child. Consult your case journal. You may find entries that will lead to evidence and/or witnesses demonstrating your innocence. Learn as much as you can about the allegations, and advise your attorney of all inconsistencies (or impossibilities) you discover in the accounts of the alleged abuse.

For your child's sake, petition the court to restrict the number of interviews, interrogations, and evaluations that he or she is forced to endure. Lobby for a single, gender-neutral "validation" examination, the results of which can be shared by the family court, the prosecutor's office, and the litigants' attorneys. Insist upon the appointment of a respected, experienced mental-health professional with a record of objectivity, extensive training in sexual abuse evaluation, and *no* association with any law-enforcement agency. (Too many police department experts operate with a presumption of guilt.)

Agree to participate in the validator's investigation only if the inquiry will also include an evaluation of your spouse's mental state and behavioral history and a full exploration of the context in which the abuse allegation surfaced.

The competence and experience of the professional chosen to investigate the charges are a vital concern to you, your attorney, and, I hope, the courts. According to guidelines published by the American Professional Society on the Abuse of Children, credentials of a qualified abuse validator should include *at least:*

- An advanced degree (M.D., Ph.D., or master's) in a relevant field (psychiatry, psychology, family counseling or psychiatric social work).

- A minimum of two years' experience in working with children.

- A minimum of two years' experience treating sexually abused children.

Equally important to the investigation that the validator will undertake is the evaluation process used. There is no standard protocol, but there are a number of effective procedures that competent abuse validators usually incorporate into their appraisals.

Before the evaluation begins, the professional should acknowledge to all concerned that he or she is acting as an *investigator,* not a therapist. Therapy is (generally) only necessary when abuse has occurred. A desire to help the child must be put aside until that determination has been made.

A competent abuse investigation will typically include:

- Separate interviews with the mother and father to establish the interpersonal dynamics in operation at the time of the alleged abuse.

- Interviews with the couple's attorneys and family court personnel to understand the status of litigation at the time the abuse allegation was made.

- Interviews with relatives, doctors, teachers, and friends of the children—anyone who has had frequent contact with the child recently.

- "Free play" and "structured play" sessions with each parent and the child.

Usually, the validator will interview the child alone only after completing the steps outlined above. At least two interviews are required. The first session is designed to establish rapport, measure the child's developmental status, and test memory capabilities. The abuse allegation won't be mentioned.

In the child's second interview, the validator will ask about the charges. These questions should be as open-ended and nondirective as possible, and become point-blank requests for specific information only if all other forms of inquiry have failed.

At some time during this session the validator must attempt to determine if the child has been coached. (An experienced professional knows the verbal and nonverbal cues to watch for.)

Depending on the validator's technique, drawing materials, dollhouses, and other toys may be used in the abuse assessment. The use of anatomically correct dolls is a controversial issue. Some professionals believe that these dolls are useful if the child is older than five. Other experts feel that the dolls often stimulate sexual fantasies. Some states bar evidence obtained with the dolls because there is no reliable procedure for their use.

Obviously, the validation process will take time. And, until the evaluation is complete, most courts will be reluctant to uphold your custody or visitation rights. If the court denies you access to your child during the abuse investigation, volunteer to see the child under the supervision of a neutral adult third party. Without continuing contact with you, your spouse's opportunity for negative programming is completely unimpeded. Don't tolerate unnecessary delays in the validation process. Remind the court that any laxity in resolving the abuse issue will be extremely detrimental to the child.

The most damaging result of the validator's assessment, of course, is an opinion that the abuse charge seems to have merit. This finding is not judicially conclusive, however. It is simply a piece of evidence, subject to dissection, challenge, and refutation.

A more likely outcome is that the abuse allegation is unfounded. That conclusion can be based on several factors. The evaluator may discover that the child, prompted by a hysterical mother, misinterpreted a normal display of parental affection. Or the child was indeed abused, but not by the father. The mother might be attempting to avoid responsibility for molestation the child suffered while in her care. Or the child (typically an adolescent in this scenario) is attempting to punish the father for breaking up the family, or is using the abuse charge to escape the constraints of normal and proper parental control.

If the sexual abuse allegation is found to be false *and* the result of a mother's manipulation or devious legal "strategy," the slanderous charge will become a huge obstacle that a mother seeking custody may find impossible to overcome. Over the past decade, the indiscriminate use of false abuse allegations has created a judicial backlash in many jurisdictions. In addition to exposing herself to criminal charges, a mother who subjects her child to the short-term trauma and potential lifelong damage caused by the allegation proves, in the eyes of most courts, that she is an unfit parent.

Surviving the Litigation Process

Involvement in a custody case almost always means prolonged emotional distress. Family court congestion, the ponderous pace of discovery, the invasive stress of psychological evaluations and social service investigations, the 106 motions to admit this and exclude that, or to modify "A" so that it becomes "B," the loopy obstinacy of some litigants, the obsessive compulsions of your spouse's attorney (or yours), the huge stacks of paper filling your den and your basement, the laziness and incompetence of family court hacks—in short, every single aspect of the pretrial process seems to have been designed to drive you crazy.

Perhaps the worst aspect of litigation is that everything seems to take forever. You ask your lawyer how much more of your life your custody fight is going to devour, and the answer you get, more often than not, is a shrug. And that's an honest, realistic reply. There are too many variables at play to allow anyone to accurately predict how many months, or years, will fade into history between the beginning of custody litigation and its ultimate resolution.

To complete this legal marathon with most of your mind intact, you are going to have to adopt a holistic approach to the litigation process. Try to keep the custody fight in perspective. You cannot allow the case to absorb every moment of your time and every molecule of your being. Resist the need to become an expert on every custody decision handed down since the Eisenhower administration.

Take care of yourself. Eat wisely and sleep well. Exercise regularly. Avoid excessive drinking. Alcohol may anesthetize you for a few hours, but when you wake up the next morning you'll still be a guy entangled in a custody dispute—a guy with a fifty-pound head and a tongue that tastes like Styrofoam.

When you are at work, concentrate on the task at hand. Don't allow your mind to drift toward this strategy or that witness. Use the long empty stretches between legal events to broaden and refine your parenting skills. When you are with your children, be their father, not a litigant.

Help the kids understand what is happening. Avoid drawing them into your conflict with your spouse, but acknowledge that the ongoing litigation will affect them. Assure the children that both you and their mother still love them, but because you two can't agree on who will live where, you have asked a judge to decide. Make it clear that no matter what the outcome of the custody case, you and their mother will always take care of them.

Divorcing parents often turn to their children for support and strength during the litigation process. Don't give in to this natural urge for solace and understanding. Your children can't be your "best friends" without being damaged emotionally.

Answer the kids' questions about the custody contest honestly but carefully. Explain what judges and lawyers do, but don't delve into legal strategies or the charges and countercharges you and your spouse have been exchanging. It's a good idea to tell the children that the judge may want to talk to them at some point in the proceedings. Assure them that a talk with the judge is nothing to be worried about; it's just one of the things judges do to figure out what's fair.

You will probably feel a strong temptation to recruit your kids as allies in your custody dispute. You must resist that urge. Morally and ethically, neither you nor your spouse has the right to ask your kids to choose one parent over the other. As a father, your goal should be to reduce, not heighten, the anxiety your children are experiencing.

The Trial

The odds that your custody dispute will reach a courtroom are slim (nine to one against on most tote boards). You, your spouse, or both of you will run out of money or patience. The need to move on will overwhelm the desire for vindication and validation. Obsessions with a painful past will evolve into hope for a brighter future.

The dry, dull reality of the legal process eventually dissolves the fantasy that a swift, easy victory is only a motion away. If your lawyer and your spouse's are domestic relations veterans, subtle musings that settlement wouldn't be a bad idea might come up at least once a week. If you live in a densely populated area with a high divorce rate, you can also expect pressure to settle from a harried family court judge desperate to clear his or her crowded calendar.

If your custody dispute does reach trial, don't be surprised by the adrenaline rush and keen anxiety you will experience almost simultaneously as you enter the courtroom. The visceral "fight-or-flight" instinct that kicks in when a human senses danger or impending combat is especially strong at the beginning of a custody hearing.

Your accelerated heartbeat and that queasiness in the pit of your stomach are a normal reaction to the realization that the posturing and positioning and bluster are over. It's showtime.

Maybe.

The trial, you will be disappointed to learn, is subject to the same delays and disruptions as the rest of the legal process. There's no telling when the proceedings will actually get under way or how long they'll last. I can guarantee only that your custody hearing will be much longer than a Perry Mason episode and much shorter than the O. J. Simpson extravaganza. There will be pretrial conferences and motions and paperwork and discussions of ground rules. There will be continuances and recesses to accommodate the schedules of expert witnesses, other trials, or because the judge has other duties (or a vacation) to attend to. Your trial will take however long it takes.

Not long ago, Johnnie Cochran, Marcia Clark, F. Lee Bailey, and Christopher Darden spent several months in America's living rooms demonstrating the trial process. In the event you've forgotten, this is what happens. . . .

Proceedings begin with an opening statement by each attorney. These introductions provide the judge with a preview of the issues that each side will present and the contentions each will attempt to prove. Outrageous claims cannot be made in the opening argument. Everything said must be supported by evidence to be offered in the trial.

Don't expect the passion or eloquence of TV or movie law. Most custody cases are tried by a judge. Dramatic flourishes and emotional pleas that might impress or influence a jury have no effect on seasoned, weary family court judges.

The plaintiff's side presents its case first. (In some jurisdictions, the plaintiff is called "the petitioner.") The plaintiff's attorney questions his or her witnesses and presents documentary evidence to support the validity of the plaintiff's custody claims. This is *direct* testimony. The attorney representing the defendant (or "respondent") then *cross-examines* the plaintiff's witnesses in an attempt to negate or neutralize the witnesses' testimony. If cross-examination reveals new information or triggers the need to clarify statements made by the plaintiff's witness, the plaintiff's attorney may choose to reexamine the witness. This is called *redirect*. Its use allows *recross* by the defendant's lawyer. And so it goes, witness by witness, until the plaintiff's case has been presented in its entirety.

The defendant's side follows the same your-turn-my-turn format to present its case. Each lawyer then offers a closing statement highlighting the strengths of his or her case and pointing out the flaws in the opponent's presentation. You may be disappointed to learn that a reading of the verdict almost never occurs at the end of a custody trial. Typically, the judge won't get around to making a decision for weeks.

YOUR STAR WITNESS

Your testimony is vital, very likely to make or break your case. Prepare for trial carefully and thoroughly. With your attorney, review the facts you will present, your case's central themes, and areas vulnerable to cross-examination by your spouse's advocate.

Recognize that your appearance, on the stand and in open court, is a performance. You, starring as the capable, concerned dad, must present yourself and your case in a manner designed to provoke understanding and, perhaps, a grain or two of sympathy.

Appearance and demeanor are important communication accessories. Some judges will be more impressed by how you look and act than by what you say. Dress as you would for an important business appointment. Wear a dark suit and a quiet tie. Observe courtroom etiquette. Don't mutter, whisper, whistle, snicker, or sigh in disgust while other witnesses are testifying. Doing so will almost certainly annoy the judge. If you have a question or information for your lawyer, pass a note. Never speak directly to your spouse or her attorney while court is in session. Don't react to unfavorable or deceitful testimony by groaning, grimacing, or smacking yourself in the forehead or pounding the table. Never lose your temper in the courtroom. Expect to be insulted and lied about; don't respond to these attacks.

Assuming that you and your lawyer have done your homework, your direct testimony should flow smoothly. Speak clearly and confidently. Don't use slang or vulgarities. Your attorney's questions and your answers will emphasize your positive parenting skills and achievements and attempt to neutralize any negatives your spouse's attorney is likely to probe.

If you became extremely angry and verbally abusive when your eight-year-old used your ninety-dollar tennis racquets for snow-shoes, for example, you will be able to admit—and mitigate—your loss of control. Questioning about the incident will allow you to express how badly you felt when your outburst reduced your child to tears, and to explain the changes you've since made in your approach to discipline.

Remember that you, not your attorney, must tell your story. Your lawyer can't ask you leading questions. Instead of "On May fourth, did you see your wife slap your oldest child in the face and knock her to the floor?" expect this:

"What, if anything, occurred between your wife and your children on May fourth?"

Under the rules of evidence, you can generally only testify to events or actions that you personally saw or heard. Your opinions and interpretations are of no consequence. While you can state that on specific dates you arrived at the family home to find your children running around naked and dirty, you can't state that these circumstances prove neglect attributable to your spouse. It's the judge's job to reach that conclusion.

You also can't testify to information you learned secondhand. If, for instance, the cable guy told you in April that he saw your spouse hit your son with a lawn rake, you can't repeat those remarks in court. It is hearsay and, as such, probably inadmissible. To place his observations on record, the cable guy must testify himself.

After your direct testimony is concluded, your spouse's attorney is entitled to cross-examine. No matter how confident you are in your case, you will find cross-examination to be a stressful, disconcerting experience.

In your direct testimony, you had a security blanket—a carefully structured progression of questions and answers. If your spouse's lawyer is any good at all, he or she will not give you the opportunity to tell your story a second time. Instead, your spouse's attorney will zero in on areas of perceived weakness or inaccuracy. Questions will be fired at you, or slipped in unexpectedly, in no discernible sequence and in a variety of tones: from polite, to sarcastic, to openly hostile. The cross-examiner's goal is to confuse you, to trick you into stumbling, to force you to make damaging admissions, or to contradict yourself.

As I mentioned, you can't be asked leading questions during your direct testimony. During cross, however, your spouse's advocate *is* permitted to pose questions like, "Is it not a fact that you used money your spouse was saving for your daughter's oboe lessons to purchase malt liquor and pork rinds?" The law assumes that during cross you are a hostile witness, reluctant to admit to damaging facts. Leading questions are allowed in cross to help lawyers to present both sides of disputed issues.

There are cross-examination techniques that are not permissible under the law. You should not be required to answer a question if the inquiry is found to be:

A Compound Question. A query such as "Did you not force your children to watch six consecutive hours of *Green Acres* reruns and soon thereafter commence a romantic affair with Rosetta Delgado, a cashier at Arby's?" is unmanageable and likely to confuse a witness. An attorney is allowed to ask only one question at a time.

Argumentative. The question "Do you mean to sit there and tell this court that you do not spend eighty-seven hours a week bowling?" is intended to influence the judge, not elicit information. It is also inflammatory, almost forcing a belligerent response from the witness.

Repetitive. A witness cannot be asked the same question over and over again, no matter how cleverly that question is rephrased.

A Presumption of Facts Not in Evidence. "Loaded" questions are prohibited. The most famous example of this improper form of inquiry, "When did you stop beating your wife?" surely originated in some ancient divorce trial. Unless a history of regular beatings was undisputed by both parties, the question assumes a fact not in evidence.

Irrelevant. Questions not related to the issues of the trial are not permitted.

As you were advised in our discussion of the deposition process, always wait a moment before answering any question from opposing counsel. Give your attorney time to object. If the objection is sustained, you don't have to answer the question; if your lawyer's objection is overruled, you do.

A number of techniques that I suggested you might find helpful in your deposition are equally useful in testimony at trial. Be as concise as possible. "Yes," "No," "I don't know," and "I can't recall" are all fine answers. The briefer your responses, the less material the cross-examiner will have to build on and the harder you will be making him or her work. Always be truthful and you will avoid major inconsistencies that could damage your credibility.

Finally, don't let me leave you with the impression that your only function during cross-examination is to absorb abuse. Be alert for opportunities to slide in opinions and hearsay you could not bring up during your direct testimony. You can respond to a "Why?" question, for example, in almost any way you like. If you are asked why you didn't invite your spouse to your daughter's ballet recital, you can say, "Because it was a Thursday night and I know my wife drinks grain alcohol and shoots dice with sailors on Thursday nights." Your answer, a baseless assumption under the rules of evidence and, as such, never admissible in your direct testimony, becomes part of the record on cross because the examiner "opened the door."

YOUR SUPPORTING CAST

If a court-appointed custody evaluator has recommended that you be given custody of your children, your lawyer may wish to call the expert to testify in your behalf at trial. If you feel that the evaluator's report speaks for itself (and is already in evidence or will be) and you can see no reason to incur the considerable expense required to add the expert to your roster of witnesses, your concern may be valid, unless:

- The judge prefers live testimony to the written word.
- The expert can expand and amplify the evaluation report's conclusions.
- The judge will be impressed by the expert's credentials, experience, methods, and narrative style.
- Your attorney anticipates a challenge to the expert's report and wants to solidify the evaluator's stature with the court *before* that challenge is mounted.

In addition to offering credible testimony favoring you as the custodial parent, the expert's participation in your case may prove useful in the formulation of the questions that your lawyer will pose to your spouse at trial.

While an expert witness's opinions and impressions are acceptable at trial, the testimony of teachers, neighbors, and other witnesses of fact must be restricted to accounts of events and behaviors they saw or heard firsthand.

Even if your pediatrician believes that you are a much better parent than your spouse is, he probably won't be able to say so at trial, at least not directly. But he may be able to offer credible observations that could lead a judge to believe that perhaps you are a superior parent.

The pediatrician's testimony might unfold something like this. . . .

Q: How often have you seen Tommy Tuttle during the past two years?
A: Six times, for his regular checkups.
Q: Who, if anyone, accompanied Tommy on these visits?
A: His father, Timothy Tuttle.
Q: On all the office visits for the past two years?
A: Yes.
Q: Did you speak to Mr. Tuttle on any of these occasions?
A: Yes, on all of them.
Q: Can you tell us the nature of those discussions?
A: Yes. Our chats were about Tommy's health. The usual doctor-parent topics: nutrition, vitamins, growth spurts, and so forth.
Q: Aside from these office visits, was there any other contact between you and any member of the Tuttle family during the past few months?
A: Yes. Mr. Tuttle called me at my office on two occasions. In February, to ask me about a bad cough Tommy had, and in May, to ask my advice about a blister on Tommy's heel.
Q: Do you know Mrs. Tuttle?
A: Yes.
Q: When is the last time you spoke to Mrs. Tuttle regarding Tommy's medical care?
A: I haven't spoken to Mrs. Tuttle in more than four years.
Q: How old is Tommy Tuttle?
A: Six and a half.

An experienced attorney will mold meaningful facts into a powerful mosaic of images that strongly support the client's central
themes. The sample testimony that follows illustrates this technique. . . .

The foundation of Ben Barton's custody case is the assertion that
Ben, and not his soon-to-be ex-wife Sandra, has been their son
Scott's primary parent. For the past two years, Sandra has been obsessed with her career, although not so preoccupied that she hasn't
had time for a series of affairs with various men. Ben's attorney believes that he can show the court a marked contrast between Scott
Barton's parents using brief testimony from two witnesses.

Mr. Pasko is Scott's sixth-grade teacher and his basketball
coach. Pasko tells the court that Scott's father, Ben, has attended
several parent-teacher conferences and the school's academic
awards ceremony.

"Before these proceedings began, I had never met Mrs. Barton,"
Pasko reveals. Further questioning establishes that Ben has attended all twelve of Scott's basketball games, and Sandra, none. Important background firmly established, Ben's attorney soon arrives
at the heart of Mr. Pasko's testimony. . . .

Q: What occurred on February 24th at around 3:00 P.M.?
A: The Happy Valley Little Guys All-Star Game.
Q: Did Scott Barton play in that game?
A: Yes, he did.
Q: Was there anything unusual about his behavior?
A: Yes. I noticed that Scott seemed distracted. Whenever there
was a stoppage in play, I saw him scanning the bleachers.
Q: Did you speak to him about this?
A: Yes, at halftime I asked Scott who he was looking for.
Q: What did he say?
A: He said he was looking for his mom.
Q: Describe Scott's demeanor after the game.
A: He was a little down. Very quiet.
Q: Did you speak with him?
A: Yes. I told him to cheer up, and that he'd played great.
Q: And how did he respond?
A: He kind of sighed. And he said he'd thought his mom was
finally going to get to see him play, but she hadn't shown up.
Q: Was Mr. Barton at the game?
A: Yes.

Richard King, a private investigator, follows Mr. Pasko to the stand. Here is some of King's testimony. . . .

Q: Did you have Sandra Barton under surveillance at around 3:00 P.M. on February 24th?

A: Yes.

Q: What, if anything, did you observe on that occasion?

A: I saw Sandra Barton entering room 214 at the Polynesian Paradise Motor Lodge.

Q: Was she with anyone?

A: Yes. She was with a man. He had his hand on her buttocks.

Q: Have you since learned who that man is?

A: Yes. His name is Sonny McCracken. He operates the Tilt O' Whirl at Pokey's Playland on Route 6.

Q: How long were Mrs. Barton and Mr. McCracken in room 214?

A: Three hours and eighteen minutes.

Q: Did you see them leave?

A: Yes.

Q: Did you observe any physical contact between them?

A: Yes. As Mrs. Barton got into her car, Mr. McCracken kissed her and squeezed her right breast.

Q: Did you observe anything else?

A: I saw Mr. McCracken toss a paper bag into the dumpster behind the motel.

Q: What did you do then?

A: I retrieved the bag from the dumpster.

Q: What, if anything, was in it?

A: An empty tequila bottle and two used condoms.

By linking the testimony of Coach Pasko and investigator King, Ben Barton's attorney was able to make several salient points very efficiently:

1. Ben Barton demonstrated a consistent interest in, and support of, his son Scott's educational and extracurricular activities.

2. Sandra Barton was absent from several significant events in her son's life, including at least one special occasion Scott obviously wanted to share with her.

3. Sandra, on at least one afternoon, preferred the gratification of sleazy sex to participation in an activity her son perceived as important.

Additionally, if the judge in the Barton case happens to believe (consciously or unconsciously) that a woman who sleeps around can't possibly be a good mother, the paired testimony becomes even more damaging to Sandra's parental image.

THE CHILDREN

Whether or not your children will participate in your custody hearing depends on the interplay of several variables. In some courts, it's strictly a matter of age. Many judges don't want to involve children under eight in the trauma of legal proceedings. Some family court arbiters believe that they have a special affinity for kids and will ask to speak to any child able to communicate meaningfully, regardless of age. Generally, most courts will want to hear from children eight through twelve, if the children are articulate, if they have expressed an interest in testifying, or if issues are raised that only the children can resolve. Children older than twelve will almost always be required to appear.

While children occasionally testify in open court, an interview *in camera* (in the judge's chambers) is the approach most judges favor.

If your children are summoned for a meeting with the judge, don't coach them or attempt to use them as advocates. Judges will ask—and children will tell—every detail of either parent's pre-interview instructions.

Assure the kids that going to court doesn't mean that they're in any trouble. Tell them what a judge does and that the judge needs their help to solve a tough problem. Explain that it's against the law to lie to a judge, but as long as they tell the truth, they can say whatever they want. Promise the children that whatever they tell the judge will always be a secret that they'll never have to tell you. Indicate that you'll be proud of them if they answer all the judge's questions honestly and completely.

Most children of divorce are willing (or eager) to talk to anyone who might be able to end the stressful emotional crossfire that prolonged parental conflict inevitably creates. If your children feel differently—the prospect of going to court causes panic, for example—the judge will either find some other way to speak to them or not require their testimony.

Eleventh-Hour Settlements

Shortly before the official beginning of a custody hearing, and at any time during the trial, a family court judge may pressure the litigants into "voluntary" settlement of their dispute.

In high-caseload/low-efficiency jurisdictions, the reason for this pressure is obvious. Settling a case requires much less of a judge's time and effort than a custody trial. Even without a congested calendar prompting them, many experienced judges feel that they have a duty to try to mediate a custody contest rather than allow parents to rush helter-skelter into the severe trauma of trial. Other judges believe that custody litigation needlessly deepens and extends the anxieties of the couple's children. Some judges are just plain lazy. A settlement saves them a great deal of work.

If the judge in your case favors settlement of your custody issues, your first indication of this opinion is likely to come when your attorney emerges from a pretrial conference held in the judge's chambers.

In the pretrial conference, each lawyer presents the most compelling features of his or her case and cites perceived weaknesses in the opponent's position. Crucial documents and other strong evidence is discussed with the judge. If settlement of the dispute is his or her preference, the judge will manage to convince *both* attorneys that their cases are weak and their positions tenuous. This slap in the face often causes on-the-spot reevaluation of hard-line stances. Formerly confident, fully committed advocates suddenly become much more objective. Losing is a very real possibility, the attorneys realize. When the judge asks, "Can't you settle this?", it's not unusual for the lawyers to reply, "We can certainly try."

If both parties in the suit seem to be adequate parents, the judge often proposes some form of shared parenting. (This approach is common in states favoring joint custody.) Other settlement options are also likely to be discussed, with the judge using his objectivity (and his considerable power) to guide the lawyers toward a "package" that includes some benefits for both sides.

If your lawyer brings you a settlement offer fashioned under the judge's direction and with the judge's participation, listen carefully. Your attorney should be able to explain why acceptance of the proposal's terms are in your best interests. After you've analyzed that information, it will be up to you to decide how much more there is to gain (or lose) at trial.

After the trial is under way, and until the moment the judge reaches a decision, settlement remains an open option.

Why settle in the middle of a case? There are lots of reasons, some understandable, some silly. Expert testimony that your spouse's lawyer promised her would be valuable comes up valueless. Or a witness who your lawyer feels is crucial to your case can barely string two words together. Or during a two-week delay squarely in the middle of your lawyer's cross-examination of your spouse, she decides she'd rather settle than return to the witness stand. Or both of you decide it looks too close to call.

Regardless of the circumstances leading to a settlement offer, if a proposal that meets your custody goals becomes available, go for it.

If no acceptable offer materializes, present the case you have prepared. Cross your fingers, pray, hope for the best. There is nothing else you can do.

6
The
Aftermath

There will be no heart-stopping moment of suspense. No jury foreman will stand up in a hushed courtroom to announce your fate. Instead, your uncertainty and anxiety will continue for weeks after the end of your custody trial. Eventually, the judge's decision will arrive in the mail or by way of a phone call from your attorney.

If you win, expect a rush of conflicting emotions. Initially, you'll experience intense relief, then joy, pride, and satisfaction. (You aren't losing your children. A judge has declared you the superior parent. The terrible things said about you in court were lies and exaggerations.) Later, don't be surprised if negative emotions arise. You may feel resentment. (The judge didn't go far enough. For years the bitch made life miserable for your whole family. She should have been stripped of all parental rights, banished completely from the children's lives.) Surprisingly, guilt is also common. (Your children love their mother; why did you put them through this?)

If you lose the custody fight, a mourning process similar to the progression of emotions triggered by the death of a loved one begins. You may feel devastated, confused, angry, and profoundly sad. You may be enraged at your ex-spouse and convinced that you have been betrayed by the legal system. You may also experience various fears—the fear that you've lost your children, the fear that your life will become meaningless and empty, the fear that you'll never be happy again.

Win or lose, allow yourself a period of emotional adjustment. If you've prevailed in your custody dispute, don't plan a victory bonfire on your ex's front lawn. If you've lost, don't snatch the kids and take off for New Zealand. (And don't launch an appeal. Unless the judge in your case has erred frequently and flagrantly, appealing the decision will be a futile and extremely expensive exercise. Instead of buying your attorney a new Lexus, spend the appeal funds on your children.)

When your custody case ends, don't do much of anything until you have established the internal equilibrium and pragmatic perspective essential to the reconstruction and renewal phase of the dissolution process. Rash behavior of any kind can be detrimental to your children and may result in several more months or even years of burdensome litigation.

Moving On

Divorced parents who survive the rigors and horrors of custody litigation are usually surprised to discover that the end of courtroom hostilities brings little peace of mind and no real closure. No matter what a judge's decision asserts, parents and children remain linked by a natural bond as old as the earth. A court's attempt to redefine family relationships rarely brings about the changes in behavior and attitudes necessary for reconstruction of a viable family unit.

A new family structure can't be formed until parents and children accept the reality imposed by the court's custody orders and adapt to the changes in their lives that will inevitably occur.

Unless extreme circumstances have been proven, no family court is likely to completely exclude a parent from the lives of his or her children. An award of sole custody to one parent is almost always accompanied by a grant of visitation rights to the other. When a judge (or an expert custody evaluator) concludes that both parents are competent and caring, an order mandating liberal visitation for the noncustodial parent is becoming more and more common. Apparently, the valid concerns of family scientists, social scholars, legal professionals, and fathers' rights activists are finding an audience. In several jurisdictions, courts have acknowledged that the children of divorce want and need continuing access to both parents.

If you are awarded custody of your children, don't let the toxic emotional residue of litigation infect your parenting approach or your plans for the future. Recognize and accept the fact that your ex-spouse will continue to be your children's mother. Remember that children's ability to heal the wounds inflicted by their parents' divorce is directly dependent on the frequency and quality of their unimpeded access to both parents. If you treat your children's mother as an outsider or behave as if she doesn't exist, you may inflict serious harm on your children and provide your ex with grounds for a custody modification action.

While it may be difficult to do, offer your former adversary some form of conciliation. Be generous with visitation arrangements and don't interfere with her visits. Try to reach an agreement on child-rearing issues such as discipline, education, and social development. As the custodial parent, you will, of course, usually have the final word in most of these matters. But unless you and your ex agree not to undermine each other's parenting efforts, the children will quickly learn how to manipulate both of you.

As you plan for your ex's visitations, an effort to accept the fact that visitations will occur is not enough. Remind yourself that your children *need* to see their mother regularly.

When discussing your ex's visitation with your kids, be upbeat, natural, and relaxed. Let them know that you know how important their mom's visits are to them. Tell the children that you'll think about them when they're gone but that you want them to enjoy themselves. Indicate that you'll be fine and that you'll be there when they get back.

Never speak disparagingly about your ex or display any anger or displeasure with an upcoming visit. Don't require the children to phone you during brief visits, and don't try to sabotage visits with remarks like, "If you want to come home early, just call me." If they ask, admit to the children that you'll miss them, but don't imply that you'll be sad or miserable or lonely while they're gone. During visitation, don't make unnecessary phone calls to your ex or disrupt visits in any way.

After visitation, welcome the children home casually and comfortably. Don't ignore your ex or treat her rudely in your children's presence. While you don't have to invite her in for dinner, a moment or two of civil conversation is appropriate. Never interrogate your children about visits or about details of their mother's life. If something that happens during visitation disturbs or puzzles the kids, they'll usually let you know. Ignore complaints like, "Mom made us eat brussels sprouts." Truly troublesome information ("Why does Mommy drink so much Jack Daniel's?") should be discussed with your ex, not the children.

To the extent that you can, blend your ex's visitations into your family's routine. As difficult as it may be, share your children with their mother. With the passage of time, you may discover that your selflessness will end (or significantly reduce) hostilities that might have otherwise lingered for years. More important, by adopting a sensible attitude about visitation, you are taking a vital first step in rebuilding your children's lives.

The Visiting Father

If you lose your custody dispute, visitation will be your only access to your children. I won't lie to you. Forging and maintaining a viable, meaningful parent-child relationship through visitation is often a lot like building a functional beach house using Popsicle sticks, wet sand, and duct tape. It can be done, but it ain't easy.

While remaining involved in your children's lives is at least possible with a reasonable visitation schedule, the limited time, artificial setting, and erratic frequency that characterize some visitation arrangements are a prescription for disaster.

Keep in mind that a court order awarding sole custody of the children to their mother does *not* terminate your parental rights. In conjunction with its custody decree, the family court that decides your custody case will almost always issue a visitation order.

Lazy or naive judges may attempt to dodge the visitation issue completely by awarding "reasonable visitation" (no specific schedule is set) to the noncustodial parent. This cavalier dismissal of a parent's right to maintain specific and regular access to his children often places a noncustodial father at his ex-spouse's mercy. He may see his kids if and when she feels like allowing him to do so. "Reasonable visitation," the definition of which depends on whom you ask, almost always results in conflict, confusion, and a renewal of litigation.

Your attorney should ask the court to set specific visitation provisions before the custody judgment is finalized. If the schedule you request places no undue hardship on the custodial parent, it will likely be granted. Very few judges will allow an adequate parent who loses a custody dispute to leave court empty-handed.

In the order that ends a custody contest between two competent parents, a responsible, compassionate judge (and they do exist) will affirm the noncustodial parent's access rights and instruct the parties to formulate a visitation schedule that respects those rights. If the parents can't agree on visitation, or if the court finds visitation terms proposed by the custodial parent unacceptable, a specific visitation schedule will likely be imposed.

Generally, a father with a typical court-ordered visitation schedule can expect to see his children:

Weekends. Every other weekend is the traditional award, with the weekend defined as the period beginning Friday afternoon and ending Sunday evening.

Midweek. If the parents live close to one another, visitation on one day during the week (from after school to bedtime) is now a common order.

Holidays. The noncustodial parent will usually have the children on alternating holidays. Holidays are defined either as federally recognized holidays or as days treated as holidays by the children's school. Birthdays (the children's and the parents'), Mother's Day, and Father's Day are usually dealt with separately.

Vacations During the School Year. Shorter vacations and extended holidays typically are split evenly. Spring break is spent with one parent one year, the other the next. Whichever parent has the children for spring break usually receives a smaller slice of Christmas vacation for that year.

Thanksgiving and Christmas. Sometimes Thanksgiving and the day after are alternated between parents; sometimes the children spend part of turkey day with one parent and the evening with the other. Most judges split Christmas into Christmas Eve and Christmas Day, and, travel conditions permitting, require the parents to arrange Christmas festivities accordingly.

Summer Vacation. The noncustodial parent can usually expect to have the children for four to eight weeks each summer.

In addition to visitation specifics, standard access provisions of a typical custody decree permit frequent mail and telephone communication between the noncustodial parent and the children. More often than not, the court will also require the custodial parent to immediately notify the noncustodial parent of all medical emergencies involving the children. Guaranteed access to the children's grades and other educational information is another common access order.

If you are the noncustodial parent, you will have to make a concentrated, consistent effort to keep your rightful place in the lives of your children. To the extent possible, restructure your work, vacation, and social schedules to accommodate your children's visits with you.

As you begin to piece together a new relationship with your children, you will probably find the role of visitor/dad awkward and artificial. Believe it or not, if you focus on being a father, these feelings will eventually fade (as will the hostility and other negative emotions spawned by your divorce).

Until time and the practical pressures of single fatherhood restore your predivorce poise and common sense, force yourself to be civil and low-key when you pick up your children for visitation. The children's transition from their mother's home to yours should be as free of tension as possible. You want your kids to smile when you arrive, not cringe.

At the beginning of each visit, give the children time to adjust to being with you. As the visitation routine becomes more familiar (to the kids, and to you) this adjustment period will become progressively shorter.

Set aside a room or a distinct area in your home specifically for the children. You want them to become accustomed to having their own space and their own personal part of your life.

Young children (especially during their first few visits) often need to reassure themselves that their mother won't disappear while they are spending time with you. To ease those fears, remind the kids that they can call Mom whenever they want to.

Make your children's time with you easy and natural, as much like the family life you shared before the divorce as possible. Hang out with your kids. Plan activities at home as well as outside. Cook for them. Teach them how to ride a bike or fly a kite or play checkers. Show an interest in the children's schoolwork, friends, sports, and hobbies. Help them make and keep friends in their "visitation" neighborhood. Include chores and homework in your lists of things to do.

Frequently, your children's activities (sports, Sunday school, hanging out with friends, and the like) will conflict with your access time. While the law dictates that none of these competing activities should ever replace visitation, be as understanding as possible. Balance your right (and need) to be with the kids with their need for a normal childhood. Structure your visits to accommodate their interests whenever it's practical to do so.

Don't interrogate the children about their mother's life. Your kids aren't spies. Nor are they messengers. If you have something to say to your ex, tell her yourself. And never criticize or complain about your ex to the children.

Be a parent to your children, not their best pal or their recreation director. Don't spend your visits dragging the kids around to every amusement park, video arcade, wave pool, and cineplex in the tricounty area. And don't overload the children with expensive toys and gifts. You don't have to buy their love; they're your kids. Don't launch a concentrated effort to "win" your children away from their mother. Remember that children want and need both their parents.

Normal and reasonable discipline should be in effect during all visits. Work with your children's mother to formulate consistent standards of behavior for the children, and predictable, appropriate parental responses if these standards aren't met. Regardless of how you and your ex feel about each other, you must present a united front on authority issues. If you don't, one or both of you will spend most of your parenting time dealing with conflict and rebellion. Worse, your kids may grow up confused, out of control, and resentful of all legitimate authority.

As each visit ends, let the children know how much you have enjoyed being with them and tell them when you'll see them again. When you return them to their mother, be polite and pleasant. Don't trouble the children with whatever friction still exists between you and your ex.

Be prompt and reliable in picking up the children for visitation and in returning them. In exchange for your ex's flexibility in finetuning the logistics and details of your visitations, be equally accommodating in accepting minor alterations to your parenting time schedule.

Part-time parenting is a difficult, frustrating role, and many fathers simply cannot bear its heavy burdens. If your first stumbling attempts at the pseudo-fatherhood the court has forced upon you end badly, you may be tempted to give up.

Don't.

Your children need as much of you as they can get. Appreciate them when they're with you. Love them openly and abundantly.

Teach them solid moral values by example. Listen to them. Offer help and guidance. Encourage them in all their interests. Stimulate their intellect and natural curiosity. Show them what you know about basic life skills.

In other words, be your children's father. Overcome the obstacles of time and distance and the loss of a parenting partner. Maybe it's true that the odds are stacked against you, but you can beat the odds—because you must. Your children need to know that you'll be close by whenever they need you.

As hard to believe as it may seem during your first few weeks as a divorced dad, it's unlikely that your existence will feel like 3:00 A.M. in a suburb of hell forever. Over a period of time (and it may take years), natural healing or positive changes in your life (success at work, a new love, a rebirth of character and self-confidence) may improve the relationship between you and your former spouse.

A strict by-the-numbers visitation schedule may evolve into a less formal, more cooperative arrangement. As your children grow up, they may feel comfortable moving freely between two caring, supportive home environments. The animosity of your divorce may dissolve to respect, or at least tolerance.

No, it's not fantasy. Reconstruction and reinvention of a broken family can happen, and it does.

On the other hand . . .

Post-decree Litigation

A significant number of custody disputes never really end. These case files remain active for years, growing thicker and denser and meaner as each new charge and countercharge is filed. Even after a judge has judged and court orders have been issued, some angry mothers will not, or cannot, give up their dark dreams of revenge and vindication.

The legal proceedings that formalize the dissolution of a family often trigger volatile, unpredictable chain reactions. Desperate losers and vengeful winners create their own definitions of justice. Again and again, for months, or years, a weary court system is called upon to revisit disputes that refuse to remain resolved. For more than a few divorced couples, litigation lasts longer than marriage.

A widely publicized custody skirmish involving O. J. Simpson prosecutor Marcia Clark provides an all-too-common example of the petty bickering that often disrupts—and sometimes destroys—the postdivorce phase of the dissolution process.

Marcia and Gordon Clark were married in 1980 and divorced in 1994. A joint custody agreement was fashioned to provide for the couple's two children, ages three and five. The children lived with Marcia, but Gordon saw them often, and Marcia assured Gordon that the divorce would not damage his relationship with his children. "She said I could see the kids as much as I wanted," Gordon told *Newsweek* magazine.

In the fall of 1994, when Gordon moved into a home of his own, he noticed a change in Marcia's attitude. "The kids were at my house often, and now they could spend the night," Gordon said. "I think she had a problem with it. She started to lessen my time with the boys."

Three months later, Marcia filed a request for primary custody and an increase in child support (from $650 a month to $1,100). Exhibiting a startling lack of judgment, Marcia argued that she needed the additional funds for hair styling and clothing expenses associated with her lead role in the Simpson trial and to cover increased child-care costs incurred while spending "16 hours a day and weekends" on the case.

Gordon's reaction to Marcia's petition was predictable. "I was devastated," he said. "I just wanted to be with my kids and she's saying, 'Not only can you not be with them, I'm going to hire baby-sitters and you have to pay them.' And she needed more money to improve her Hollywood glitzy image. She wanted me to be a bank, not a father."

Despite his anger, Gordon countered Marcia's demands with what seemed to be a reasonable proposal: He would assume primary custody of the children until the Simpson trial ended. "If she can't be there, that's okay. I can be," said Gordon. "My priority is the kids."

Marcia rejected Gordon's offer.

Why?

"It's my feeling that Marcia refuses to give an inch," Gordon said. "It's like she's still in court and I'm being prosecuted."

The Clarks' inability to resolve an apparently simple parenting problem should serve as a clear warning for divorced fathers who believe that a custody decree will bring an end to conflict and confrontation. The Clarks are well-educated, middle-class professionals earning $150,000 a year between them, not semipsycho lowlifes. Post-divorce dementia spans all the rungs of the socioeconomic ladder.

"There shouldn't be a new court battle every time there's a shift in the wind," David L. Levy, president of the Children's Rights Council reminds us. "Court battles are not good for kids."

Levy is correct, of course, but in many situations, postdecree filings *are* justified, driven by the need to rescue children endangered, threatened, or disadvantaged by unfit custodians or negligent, myopic courts.

CUSTODY MODIFICATION

Generally, a family court's custody orders can be modified only if it can be proven that there has been a change in circumstances that *substantially* affects the children's best interests. The modification process has two distinct phases. First, a change in parental behavior or environmental factors that have created a serious impact on the children's lives must be demonstrated. Second, the court must decide which parent can best serve the children's interests based on the changed circumstances.

In some states, no modification of a custody decree will be considered until the original court orders have been in effect for a reasonable length of time, unless, of course, the children are facing imminent danger. This "settling in" period is specified by statute in some jurisdictions and in others is a matter of common law or well-established local custom.

Changes in behaviors, attitudes, or environment likely to be viewed as serious enough to warrant a court's consideration of a custody modification based on the "best interest" standard include:

- A de facto change in custody has already occurred and has been in effect for some time. For whatever reason, the children are now living with the "visitation" parent most (or all) of the time, and the custodial parent has not challenged the change in residence.

- A de facto joint custody agreement has been established by the actions of the parents and the children, who now spend about half their time living with each parent.

- The child wants to live with the noncustodial parent. This preference alone rarely results in custody modification, especially if the child is under fourteen years of age.

- Serious stepparent problems have arisen. Many children perceive (sometimes accurately, sometimes not) that a stepparent is treating them like second-class citizens (the "Cinderella Syndrome"). Evidence of a damaging conflict with a stepparent is best presented by a qualified mental-health professional.

- The custodial parent has been convicted of a crime.

- The custodial parent, members of the custodial parent's household, or the children themselves are using illegal drugs.

- The children are frequently exposed to adult nudity and/or flagrant sexual behavior.

- The custodial parent is negligent or provides inadequate child care. Frequent periods of time during which young children are left alone are significant, as may be "latchkey" arrangements in which no adult is present to supervise children after school. Leaving children too often and for too long with baby-sitters is also a practice some courts find to be unacceptable.

- Health care provided by the custodial parent is inadequate, harmful, or potentially harmful.

- The custodial parent is mentally ill or emotionally unstable. (The testimony of qualified psychiatric experts will be necessary to prove this.)

- The custodial parent or someone in the custodial parent's household is abusing the child physically, psychologically, or sexually. Credible evidence of abuse is generally much more persuasive when presented by physicians, mental-health professionals, or abuse "validators." False or unconvincing abuse allegations usually turn the court against the complaining parent and can cause that parent to lose custody.

- The children's school performance is abysmal, as shown by academic failures, truancy, or severe behavioral problems.

- The custodial parent frequently and flagrantly denies the children access to the noncustodial parent, or engages in a campaign calculated to alienate the children from the noncustodial parent.

- The custodial parent has moved to an unsafe or otherwise inappropriate area. A high crime rate, the close proximity of toxic waste or other dangerous pollutants, and the inferior quality of schools in the new neighborhood are among the environmental factors courts have deemed to be significant.

- When a custodial parent moves and takes the children far enough from a noncustodial parent to affect that parent's access to the children, relocation *generally* provides a change of circumstances sufficient to reopen the question of custody.

If a parent can show that circumstances have substantially changed, custody modification proceedings generally focus on the same standard that governed the original custody litigation: the best interests of the children. As they did in the initial custody contest, each parent again attempts to prove that he or she is the better custodian. The same evidence used to demonstrate the gravity of changed circumstances can be offered for the court's consideration in identifying the children's best interests.

Inertia is among the most powerful forces in family law. Most judges strongly believe that children should not be taken from a familiar environment unless there are compelling reasons for a custodial change. Stability is valued so highly that a noncustodial parent seeking modification of a court's original custody decree must prove that the proposed change is *necessary* to ensure the children's health, safety, well-being, or development.

Divorced fathers who have been awarded primary custody of their children can best protect their custodial status by recalling the simple advice of the ancient sage Henny Youngman:

> PATIENT: Doc, it hurts when I do this.
> DOCTOR: So, don't do that.

The Youngman Principle, adapted, extrapolated, and distilled for use by divorced dads with custody, goes like this:

1. Go back and review the behavioral and environmental conditions likely to justify a custody modification action.
2. Don't allow these conditions to exist.

A noncustodial father contemplating custody modification litigation must analyze the interplay of several factors before filing suit. Accurate and objective answers must be formulated for questions like these:

- If a child's preference is the basis for the custody transfer request, are the child's motives valid or manipulative? Is the child truly upset or endangered by the custodial mother's behavior, or is the child playing one parent against the other for personal reasons? Is the child's need to escape the current environment real or an attempt to blackmail Mom?

- Can dangerous, negligent, or otherwise unacceptable behavior attributed to the mother be corroborated by independent witnesses or documentation?

- Can social workers, psychiatrists, law-enforcement personnel, physicians, or abuse "validators" substantiate suspicions of physical, emotional, or sexual abuse?

- Does the father's definition of unacceptable or inappropriate parental behavior correspond with the values and standards accepted by the court and the community?

- If sufficient cause to consider a custody modification is demonstrated, what evidence can the father present to support his contention that he can provide the children a healthier, safer, richer, or more stable life?

- Will reopening custody litigation expedite or hinder the post-divorce reconstruction process?

When the claim that a custodial mother is unfit is the basis for a father's modification petition, a consistent pattern of abuse or negligence must be proven. Photos, detailed entries from the father's journal, and the child's own testimony may all prove useful in meeting this requirement. If his child is in immediate danger from a custodial mother, the father need not (and should not) wait for the court to schedule a custody modification hearing. After filing a "child in need of care" action with the appropriate state agency, the father should immediately seek the court's intervention on behalf of the child.

If long-distance relocation of the mother and children is the issue, extensive analysis usually is unnecessary. The father must seek modification of custody and visitation orders to maintain contact with his children. The stability factor that typically favors the custodial parent changes shape in relocation cases. The lives of the children will be disrupted whether they move with the custodial parent or change residences to live with the parent who is not going anywhere.

A review of recent decisions in relocation cases reveals no definite trends. It seems to be a "jump ball" situation. Some courts seem to have adopted a "pro-mobility" stance, declaring that a custodial parent has the right to move wherever he or she wishes, regardless of the hardships imposed upon the visitation parent. Other judges respect noncustodial parental access rights and recognize that children need two parents. These courts require a hearing to determine how (or if) the noncustodial parent can maintain contact with the children after their relocation. A change in visitation schedules may be ordered (with the noncustodial father receiving fewer but lengthier visits), or the relocating mother may be required to pay all transportation costs associated with the father's visitations.

In more than a few cases, long-distance relocation of a custodial mother has resulted in a transfer of custody to the father. These decisions were all based on the best-interests-of-the-children standard. If, by moving to the father's home (as opposed to leaving the area with their mother), the children remain in the same school and are able to maintain well-established social and extended family ties, there is an excellent chance that the father's custody modification request will be granted.

VISITATION MODIFICATION

Substantial changes in circumstances can also affect visitation provisions of the initial divorce decree. Visitation may be reduced, restricted, or eliminated entirely if the noncustodial parent is convicted of a crime, exposes the child to overt sexual conduct, neglects or abuses the child in any way, indulges in drug or alcohol abuse, or involves the child in hazardous or unacceptable activity.

The court, not the custodial parent, decides what constitutes harmful behavior. However, custodial parents frequently attempt to reduce or restrict visitation because they find the noncustodial parent's visits to be "disruptive" to the household routine, or because the children return from visitation "excited, emotional, and unable to settle down," or because the custodial parent disapproves of the children's activities during visits.

None of these complaints is likely to persuade an experienced family court judge to alter a visitation order. The noncustodial parent's access rights should supersede any minor inconveniences caused by visitation. And, while it's true that the transition from one home to another frequently stimulates children, the "excitement" they exhibit as they adapt to the change in routines is completely normal (and very similar to the behavior of any child who has recently returned from vacation, or computer camp, or an overnight stay at Grandma's). Finally, unless the visitation parent encourages or condones illegal or unsafe activities, what the kids do during visits is a matter left entirely to the noncustodial parent's discretion (unless there is a court order to the contrary).

Generally, courts will completely eliminate visitation only in extreme cases (the noncustodial parent is unfit, dangerously unstable, violent, and so forth). Reduction or restriction of visitation is more common.

A frequently cited justification for the reduction of parental access is the unavailability of the noncustodial parent. If children spend all (or most) of their visitation time with baby-sitters or if the noncustodial parent consistently fails to appear for scheduled visits, many courts impose a "use it or lose it" edict. Unless the visitation parent's level of commitment to the children immediately increases, his or her time with the children will be severely reduced or restricted.

When a noncustodial parent's residence is found to be an unsuitable environment for children (a plywood cubicle behind the furnace in the basement of an adult bookstore, for instance), visitation may be restricted to more appropriate venues (Grandma's house, acceptable public areas, and the like). Limiting visitation to the custodial parent's home usually is impractical and uncomfortable for both parents and the children.

Supervised visitation is generally ordered when a noncustodial parent's conduct or lack of stability causes a clear and present endangerment to the children. A suitable "supervisor" is an adult third party acceptable to both parents or the court.

Several conditions may prompt a request to expand a noncustodial parent's visitation, including:

- A visitation parent has eliminated the objectionable behaviors, unacceptable associations, or unsuitable environmental factors that caused access restrictions in a previous visitation order.

- Rehabilitation of a visitation parent once afflicted with mental illness, drug or alcohol dependency, and so forth has been verified by a court-approved expert.

- Young children mature and become less dependent on the custodial parent.

- The visitation parent is available to assume child-care duties currently performed by baby-sitters.

- The children profess the desire to spend more time with the noncustodial parent.

A custodial father who finds it necessary to demand reduction, restriction, or elimination of his ex's visitation rights must demonstrate the damage (or potential damage) to the children likely to occur if the visitation schedule currently in effect isn't altered. As is the case in most domestic relations proceedings, independent validation of the father's contentions will be necessary.

Noncustodial fathers seeking expansion of visitation should first attempt to negotiate the changes they desire. If an agreement with the custodial mother can't be reached, the father's petition for modification should include a comprehensive recitation of all factors being relied on to justify the request. The benefits that expanded visitation offer to the children (*not* the father) must be stressed.

As an illustration of this principle, let's examine the postdivorce circumstances encountered by a guy we'll call Al.

Six months after custody and visitation issues had been resolved by a family court, Al's ex-wife, Betty, takes a job that keeps her away from home from 9:00 A.M. until almost 7:00 P.M., Monday through Friday. Bobby, the divorced couple's seven-year-old son, stays with a neighborhood baby-sitter each schoolday from 3:00 P.M. until Betty returns from work.

Al, a bus driver, arranges to work "the dawn patrol," from 5:00 A.M. until 1:30 P.M. He then asks the court to modify its original visitation order. Al's petition points out that he is now available to be with Bobby each day after school. Al also asserts that he can provide more competent and more attentive child care than the teenage girl Betty has hired. Bobby's best interests (specifically, his safety and his educational development) form the foundation of Al's request—not just Al's desire to spend as much time as possible with his son.

VISITATION ABUSE

When Kevin and Alice were divorced two years ago, a family court imposed a traditional custody/visitation arrangement. The couple's two young children would live with Alice and spend Wednesday evenings and every other weekend with their father.

Alice has consistently failed to comply with the court-ordered visitation schedule. Several times, she has called Kevin to cancel his visits, offering reasons ranging from ballet lessons to too much homework to a stubbed toe. On numerous other occasions, Kevin has arrived for visitation to find Alice's home dark and empty. His attempts to reach his children by telephone are usually thwarted by an ever-vigilant answering machine.

Kevin, like thousands of other disenfranchised fathers, is a victim of visitation abuse. Theoretically, at least, a divorced father's access to his children is a right protected by law. And in some jurisdictions, judges will indeed punish frequent and blatant visitation denials with fines, contempt-of-court citations, and custody modification orders. Much more often, unfortunately, a custodial mother who obstructs visitation will face minimal legal sanctions, if any. Family courts are dead serious about enforcing child support orders, but sometimes alarmingly casual in punishing visitation violations.

A divorced dad who finds himself being excluded from his children's lives by visitation abuse must take immediate action to assert his access rights.

Begin by trying to reason with her. This approach is often difficult, because a mother who interferes with her children's relationship with their father is frequently driven by irrational forces (jealousy, the neurotic need to punish past sins, the compulsion to control, and so forth). Nevertheless, you must be conciliatory. Remind her that although your marital relationship is over, your parental partnership is not. Ask her not to involve the children in whatever emotional issues she hasn't yet resolved, and suggest (carefully) that no responsible, caring mother would push her children's father out of their lives. State dispassionately that a court has upheld your parental access rights, and confirm that, if necessary, you will reopen litigation to enforce those rights. Help your ex recall how expensive and emotionally taxing the initial round of legal action proved to be.

If your attempts at rational dialogue fall on deaf ears, *do not* resort to the withholding of child support. Although support and access issues are not supposed to be linked, they most certainly are in the minds of some family court judges. If you do not fulfill your support obligations, attempts you make to redress your visitation grievances might not receive serious consideration.

Initiate your campaign to document your ex's denial of visitation with a simple certified letter—something like this:

> My attorney suggested that I send you this letter so that there will be no misunderstandings about my parental time (visitation) schedule with Tommy.

As you know, our divorce decree indicates that I am to have Tommy on Thursday evening between 6:00 P.M. and 9:00 P.M., and on alternating weekends. I feel that it is very important to maintain my parenting time with Tommy, so I am writing to confirm my intention to exercise all parental rights awarded to me in our divorce decree.

The decree states that I will have Tommy on the following dates:

(Fill in court-ordered visitation dates for the next six months.)

I will pick up Tommy at 5:00 P.M. on the Fridays listed above, and return him at 6:00 P.M. on the Sundays listed above. Please have Tommy ready for his time with me.

I am anxious to cooperate with you in the raising of our son, so please let me know, in writing, if you disagree with the visitation dates I have listed. Also, please inform me in writing of any reasons why my time with Tommy may not occur as scheduled.

Thank you for your attention.

If your letter elicits no positive response, and visitation obstruction continues, you or your attorney may file a Notice of Exercise of Parental Rights with the court. This uncomplicated document is an official notification to your ex that you will be expecting her to comply with the court's visitation orders. The notice recounts (verbatim) all relevant aspects of the visitation award, including the times and dates when you will be picking up the children, an inventory of the clothing, medicine, homework, toys, and so forth you will require to be sent with them, and the address and telephone number of the visitation location. The notification (delivered by certified mail or a process server) concludes with a request for your ex's cooperation "in permitting [you] to exercise [your] lawful parental rights."

Unless your access to your children immediately improves, bring a witness to your next several visitation attempts. Hire an off-duty policeman, deputy sheriff, or some other neutral and credible third party. The witness should remain at a distance throughout the attempted exercise of your rights, but close enough to see what occurs.

Arrive for visitation *on time*. Bring a copy of your divorce decree and a tape recorder. Turn on the recorder as you approach your ex's residence, and don't turn it off until you leave (if allowable in your jurisdiction). As you approach the residence, record the following facts:

- Your name.

- The address you are approaching.

- The visitation provision you are attempting to exercise (as found in the court order).

- The name of your witness and why he/she is with you.
- The date and time.

If your ex and/or the children are not in or they refuse to come to the door, record that fact. If your ex is in, tell her, "I'm here to exercise my court-ordered visitation." Recount the time and date specified in the visitation award.

If you are told that you cannot see the children, reply, "I have a copy of our divorce decree, which clearly states that this is my (weekend/evening) with the children. I miss them very much and I want them with me."

If illness is claimed, ask the nature of the illness, and then say, "I'll bring their medicine with us and make sure that it's taken as prescribed." If that suggestion is rejected, tell your ex that you'd like to see the children for a moment, and ask for the name of the doctor who is treating them. If a doctor's name is offered, verify the children's health status as soon as possible. If they haven't been to the doctor, ask your ex why not. If you are not allowed to see the kids, leave—with the recorder still running in plain view. Summarize what has occurred on tape.

If told that the children "have other plans," offer to take them wherever they're going and to restructure your time with them to accommodate their activities.

No matter what your ex says or does, remain calm. Use a dispassionate and persistent reiteration of your access rights to induce her to admit that she opposes your visitations. Don't argue with her, and refuse to exchange insults or obscenities.

As you leave after an unsuccessful visitation attempt, describe briefly any significant behavior or observations that may not be apparent from a review of the tape. (Your ex threw a beer bottle at you, your son waved to you from a window, and the like.)

Keep a calendar of each denied visitation and a record associating a tape and a witness's name with each denial. Use a new tape for each attempted visit. Keep in mind that submission of a tape as evidence may place the entire tape (and everything on it) in the court record.

When you and your attorney feel that you have enough documentation to establish a clear pattern of visitation interference, determine if your state has a criminal law for visitation abuse, and seriously consider calling the authorities. Otherwise, a civil notice of access violation and a motion for enforcement of parental rights can be filed. Your petition should include a request for the recovery of all your documentation expenses and attorney's fees, and also a demand for the court's assurance that these financial penalties will be automatically assessed if future visitation violations occur.

If the court agrees that your visitations have been unlawfully obstructed, what happens next depends on the judge and the severity of the access violation. Civil penalties range from a mild slap on the wrist to contempt-of-court convictions punishable by fines, expanded visitation, or, if visitation abuse also includes evidence of parental alienation attempts, custody modification.

While relying on the courts for the preservation of parental access rights is often expensive and always burdensome, the litigation process has been, until recently, a divorced father's only legal remedy for visitation abuse. As I've pointed out frequently, failure to pay child support can be a criminal offense. A custodial mother who is owed support has a free, far-flung enforcement apparatus at her disposal. However, in January 1994, the state of Illinois enacted a pioneering law to criminalize visitation abuse. Under the terms of the Unlawful Visitation Interference statute, a custodial parent's first two visitation violations are classified as petty offenses, subject to fines. The third obstruction is a misdemeanor, carrying a heavier financial penalty and the possibility of incarceration for up to one year.

The law's cosponsor, State Representative Cal Skinner, Jr., characterized the interference statute as an "educational" vehicle. "It's not about putting people in jail or fining people," Skinner said. "It's telling people that society thinks it's important that children have access to both parents, even if the parents hate each other."

In the first three months following passage of the visitation obstruction law, 411 complaints were logged. Of these, 365 were found to be valid. As the experience of Ed Reedy suggests, involvement of law-enforcement personnel tends to solve visitation problems much more quickly (and certainly much more cheaply) than domestic relations litigation.

For six years after Ed and Gretchen Reedy divorced, Ed was barred from his children's lives for months at a time. A school district janitor, Ed could not afford to take legal action to assert his parental access rights. "There was nothing I could do," Ed said. "But then I heard about the visitation law."

When Ed's next visitation attempt was thwarted by Gretchen, he returned an hour later with a police officer and eventually Gretchen was charged with unlawful visitation interference. "Ever since, I've had no trouble with her whatsoever," Ed said.

Until all states pass tough criminal laws recognizing the value of the father-child relationship—and effectively punishing custodial mothers who attempt to destroy this vital bond—a divorced dad must rely on his own financial resources and the civil courts to protect his access to his children. Although more family courts than ever before are acknowledging that the best interests of children include stable and consistent involvement with both parents, the ingrained impact of a century of pro-mother bias still exists throughout our legal system.

PARENTAL KIDNAPPING

Although specific technicalities vary from state to state, parental kidnapping (sometimes called child abduction, child stealing, or custodial interference) generally is defined as "the taking, keeping and concealment of a child by a parent (or someone acting in the parent's behalf) in violation of the custody rights (*including visitation rights*) of another parent."

In the United States, more than 350,000 children a year are abducted by parents or other family members. Some form of parental kidnapping occurs in approximately one of twenty-two divorce cases. Children between the ages of three and nine are the most frequent targets of parental abduction. Typically, these abductions are motivated by revenge, outrage, or a pathological attachment to the child.

Careful examination of thousands of parental kidnapping cases suggests that most of these abductions could probably have been prevented. More than 60 percent of these kidnappings were preceded by threats or an unsuccessful abduction attempt. Fathers who attempt to kidnap their own children tend to do so in the early stages of the dissolution process. Mothers are more likely to attempt abduction after a court's custody orders have been issued. An FBI profile of the typical child abductor describes an individual with dual citizenship, who lacks close ties with family and community, and who is either financially independent or able to find work easily regardless of location. Many child abductors have criminal records.

Divorced fathers can (and should) take precautions to reduce exposure to parental kidnapping.

1: As we discussed earlier, a custodial father should not impede or interfere with the access rights of a noncustodial mother. In fact, the father should actively promote a healthy mother-child relationship. Most child abductions attempted by noncustodial mothers are prompted by the mother's belief that she has been excluded from her children's lives (by an unacceptable court decision or a spiteful father). The best defense against parental kidnapping is a flexible, cooperative shared-parenting environment.

2: If an abduction is threatened, immediately report the threat to the appropriate law-enforcement officials. The police or a local prosecutor will probably advise the would-be abductor that child snatching is a crime punishable by fines, imprisonment, or both. Additionally, your attorney should seek court-ordered injunctive relief prohibiting removal of the child from the state you live in and forward a certified copy of the court's order to the U.S. Department of State (Office of Citizens Consular Services) in Washington, D.C. Your lawyer should also seek a court order directing that the mother's and children's passports be turned over by their lawyer to the court immediately, with a prohibition against duplicates being issued. Never ignore abduction threats, and treat them even more seriously if your ex has recently quit her job, sold her house, or divulged plans to move out of state or out of the country.

3: Certified copies of your divorce decree should be placed in your children's school files and given to teachers, day-care providers, and baby-sitters. Make everyone who supervises your child in any way aware of your custody and access rights. Immediately relay any abduction threats you receive to these individuals. Ask to be alerted if your ex (or anyone purporting to be a family member, a baby-sitter, a friend, and so forth) makes an unscheduled visit to the school or day-care facility. Instruct school and day-care personnel that the children are never to be released to anyone without your permission. If your children normally walk or ride a bus or van to school or day care, be sure that school officials and day-care providers know in advance which days the children will not be present. Request immediate notification whenever your children do not arrive where they are supposed to be on schedule.

4: Teach the children to use the telephone. Make certain that your kids know their full names, your telephone number, and area code. Show them how to make a collect call and have them practice doing so. Teach the children to call home immediately if someone (including Mom) tells them that you are dead, in the hospital, on your way to Hawaii, or the like. Assure the kids that you will always love them and want to be with them, and that anyone who tells them that you don't is lying. Be sure that they know not to talk to strangers, even if the stranger claims to be "Daddy's friend."

5: Keep a current record of the addresses, telephone numbers, and birthdays of your ex's relatives and friends. Make note of your ex's Social Security number, license plate number, employer's address and phone number, and credit-card issuers. Know your children's Social Security numbers, height and weight, and any distinguishing physical characteristics (such as moles and scars). Keep current photos and videotapes of the kids. Have several copies of your custody or visitation orders close at hand.

In most states, parental kidnapping is a criminal offense—a felony in some jurisdictions, a misdemeanor in others. You may be able to press charges against the abductor and anyone who aids in the abduction. Prison terms and financial penalties vary by locale. Some states require a convicted child abductor to make restitution for the costs of locating and recovering the children. In felony cases, the Federal Bureau of Investigation can assist in apprehending abductors.

If criminal prosecution is unsuccessful or ends in an unsatisfactory verdict, a victim of parental kidnapping may file a damage suit. The abductor and anyone helping her in the kidnapping or concealment of the child can be sued for damages to compensate the victims for expenses incurred and suffering caused by the act.

Several resources are available to help a parent search for his children and their abductor. The computerized Federal Parent Locator Service (originally established to find child support delinquents) can trace child snatchers through their Social Security numbers. The FBI will enter descriptions of missing children into its National Crime Information Center (NCIC) system even if the abductor has not yet been charged with a crime. Most states have clearinghouses to help parents find kidnapped children, and in some areas, special school registries have been initiated to identify missing kids.

The National Center for Missing and Exploited Children (NCMEC), a federally funded resource center, operates a toll-free hot line and maintains a staff of attorneys with expertise in child abduction cases. The NCMEC, in association with the American Bar Association, has prepared a comprehensive handbook for parents whose children have been abducted.

Here, adapted and condensed from those recommendations, is what to do if your children are kidnapped by their mother:

- File a missing persons report with your local police department.

- Ask local authorities to have the FBI enter your children's description in their National Crime Information Center (NCIC) computer system.

- Call the National Center for Missing and Exploited Children (NCMEC) toll-free hot line (1-800-843-5678) to report the children missing.

- Actively participate in the search for your children. The NCMEC will furnish you with a list of agencies and individuals to contact for help.

- Meet with your local prosecutor and decide whether or not to press criminal charges. If the abductor will be charged with a felony, the warrant will be entered into the FBI's NCIC system, and if the abductor has fled the state, obtaining a federal warrant will enable the FBI to assist in the search.

- If you don't already have primary custody, obtain a temporary custody order immediately. If you are the custodial parent, get extra certified copies of the custody decree from the clerk of the court. When your children are located, promptly send a copy of your custody order to the family court in the jurisdiction where they are found.

- Ask the police to help you retrieve your children when the abductor is apprehended. In most states, police are not required to return your children to you. You may need to petition the family court where your children are located to enforce your custody rights. To prevent the abductor from fleeing when notified of the impending enforcement action against her, you can request a "pickup" order, which directs police to place the children in the court's care.

If your children have been taken out of the United States, you will probably need the services of a private investigator to locate them. Once the children are found, you may face an uphill battle in a foreign court to force their return. If the country where they are living abides by the Hague Convention on the Civil Aspects of Child Abduction, a thick jumble of red tape is eliminated. Under the Hague

Convention treaty, abducted children taken to a signatory nation must generally be returned home for a custody determination. In the United States, the Office of Citizens Consular Services of the State Department is responsible for administration of the Hague Convention agreement. If you believe that your children have been abducted to a foreign country, contact this office to learn how to proceed.

SUPPORT ISSUES

Fathers who fall behind in their child support obligations will quickly discover how the enforcement process works. Adjusting support levels to offset changes in economic circumstances not present when the original support order was issued, however, is pretty much a catch-as-catch-can proposition. Generally, a divorced father may be able to petition a family court for a review of his support obligations if:

- He shares (on an equal or nearly equal basis) most day-to-day child-rearing duties and expenses.

- He encounters unusual transportation expenses in exercising his visitation rights (assuming these expenses are the result of a custodial mother's relocation).

- His ex's income has grown significantly.

- He pays certain expenses directly (such as the mortgage on the mother's home, extraordinary health-care costs, private school tuition, summer camp fees, violin lessons).

- His income and/or child-care expenses have changed significantly since the original support decree was issued.

A father whose only complaint about his child support obligation is that not enough of his money actually reaches the children will be hard-pressed to prove or remedy the misdirection of funds that he suspects is occurring. It is unlikely that a family court adjunct or state agency would bother to verify that support payments are in fact used to meet children's needs. Support enforcement tools are sadly lacking. Unless a custodial mother recklessly flaunts her inappropriate spending habits, there is nothing a father can do. Until a practical system of audits and accountability can be established, a custodial mother can generally use support funds in any way she pleases.

While statutes strengthening a father's position in many custody and access issues are at least under consideration in many states, I see no strong support reforms on the horizon.

SUMMARY

For couples with children, the final phase of the dissolution process cannot end until both fathers and mothers accept the new family framework imposed by divorce. Even after a court ends their marital relationship, a parenting partnership of some sort must endure. The sooner that both parties recognize and adapt to their new roles, the sooner the healing process can begin. A father determined to build a new life for himself and his children must be prepared to overcome the emotional damage typically inflicted by divorce and concentrate on his children's needs. While he must be willing to compromise frequently for the children's sake, he must also be vigilant in protecting his place in his children's lives.

7
Paternity
Issues

As we've demonstrated, a divorced or divorcing father determined to play a meaningful role in his children's lives must traverse a virtual minefield of bias, insensitivity, apathy, and incompetence. Fathers of children born out of wedlock face even more daunting obstacles when they attempt to assert their rights.

The paternal rights of single fathers are routinely violated by legislatures, social agencies, and judiciaries all over America. In most states, an unwed mother intent on keeping her child and the child's father apart will find few impediments to doing so. In fact, a mother who wants her child's father out of her life can usually find help to achieve that aim, and sometimes incentives as well. Public-aid entitlements are often higher when a child's household includes no father. And arranging for the adoption of a child is certainly more convenient when a father is unaware that he has a child and the mother has no obligation to tell him.

In recent years, thousands of middle-class couples desperate for children have made private adoptions a flourishing industry. As we might expect in a business that often treats children like commodities, success in the private adoption marketplace is not always measured by moral, legal, or ethical standards.

The law defines adoption as a statutory procedure that establishes a legal parent-child relationship between a child and (one or two) adults who are not the child's biological parents. To create parental rights for the adopting parties, the parental rights of the child's biological parents are terminated. If the adoption is not contested, the termination procedure involves little more than completing some forms and obtaining the approval of a circuit court. In some jurisdictions, adoption of a child born out of wedlock does not always require a father's consent. In fact, the natural mother is usually under no obligation to furnish the court, the adoptive parents, or anyone else with the father's name. Possibly because he might object to the adoption, a serious effort to notify an unwed father that his child is about to be adopted is rarely undertaken.

The widely publicized (and widely misinterpreted) Baby Richard case powerfully illustrates the torment and heartache that can result from the possible callous disregard of a father's rights.

BABY RICHARD

In 1989, Otakar and Daniella began living together in Chicago. Daniella became pregnant in June 1990. For the first eight months of the pregnancy, Otakar supported Daniella and their unborn child. In January 1991, Otakar went to Czechoslovakia for two weeks to care for his seriously ill grandmother. At some time during Otakar's visit, Daniella received a phone call from a relative advising her (erroneously, it turned out) that Otakar had rekindled a past romance with another woman.

Upset by this false report, Daniella left the couple's apartment. When Otakar returned to Chicago, Daniella refused to see him or speak to him. At about this time, in the words of the Illinois Supreme Court, "A conspiracy was undertaken to deny the natural father any knowledge of his son's existence."

A social worker encouraged Daniella to give up her unborn baby for adoption. The social worker called her personal attorney for help in "placing" the infant. The attorney was a friend and the employer of Jane Doe, the woman who soon became the adoptive mother in the case.

At the suggestion of Jane Doe, her husband John, and their attorney, Daniella gave birth to the child who became known as "Baby Richard" at a different hospital than the facility Daniella and Otakar had originally chosen. The mother surrendered Baby Richard to the Does four days after the child's birth. In consenting to the adoption, Daniella acknowledged that she knew the identity of the baby's father but refused to divulge that information.

In the days and weeks after Baby Richard's birth, Daniella and her relatives tried to ward off Otakar's persistent inquiries about the child by telling the father that his son had died shortly after being born. Otakar didn't believe these stories. He launched an intensive search for the truth. On the fifty-seventh day after Baby Richard's birth, Otakar learned that his son was alive and in the process of being adopted. The father hired an attorney and contested the adoption.

The trial court ruled that Otakar was an unfit parent, and as such, had no standing to contest the adoption. Otakar was declared unfit because "he had not shown a reasonable degree of interest in the child within the first 30 days of [the child's] life." By finding Otakar unfit, the court was able to terminate his parental rights. By terminating these rights, the court was able to permit the Does to adopt Baby Richard without Otakar's consent. In the eyes of the court and the state of Illinois, the Does became the child's parents.

The disenfranchised father appealed the circuit court's decision and a legal battle that would last three years began. Eventually, the Baby Richard case made its way to an Illinois appellate court. Otakar lost again. Agreeing with the trial judge, the appeals court concluded that Otakar's parental rights were "properly terminated" because he had "failed to demonstrate a reasonable degree of interest, concern or responsibility as to the welfare of a newborn child during the first 30 days after its birth."

By this time, Baby Richard had been living with his adoptive parents for more than two years. This circumstance prompted the appeals court to claim additional justification for its decision. Keeping the child with the only family he'd ever known was in the child's best interests, the court declared. Because the interests of the child were "paramount," the question of whether or not Otakar's parental rights were properly terminated was now merely a nagging technicality.

According to the appellate court decision, "[Baby Richard] has not touched or seen [his birth mother] since four days after his birth, and he has never spoken a word to her. Nor has he touched, seen, or communicated with [his biological father]. In fact, he is totally unaware of the existence of [his biological parents]." Comparing the parental status of Otakar and Daniella to that of Baby Richard's adoptive parents, the court noted that since the child "was a newborn, John and Jane Doe have done everything with [Baby Richard] that is the essence of being parents."

Despite the setback, Otakar pressed on. Finally, in June 1994, more than three years after Baby Richard's birth, the Illinois Supreme Court demonstrated to Otakar—and to disenfranchised single fathers all over the United States—that the law, although often imperfect, and almost never swift, sometimes fulfills its promise. The lower courts' decisions were reversed; Otakar's parental rights were restored, and Baby Richard was returned to his natural parents (since reunited).

Declaring Otakar unfit at the original adoption hearing had been a grave error, the state supreme court asserted. "The finding that the father had not shown a reasonable degree of interest in the child is not supported by the evidence," the court said. "In fact, [Otakar] made various attempts to locate the child, all of which were either frustrated or blocked by the actions of the mother. Further, the mother was aided by the attorney for [the Does] who failed to make any effort to ascertain the name or address of the father. . . . Under the circumstances, the father had no opportunity to discharge any familial duty. . . . On the 57th day following the child's birth, the father learned of his son's existence and of the pending adoption. On that day he hired a lawyer and contested the adoption of his son by strangers. One may reasonably ask, what more could he have done? What more should he have done? The answer is he did all he could do and should do."

Noting that the lower courts had "patently distorted and slanted the facts" and "grossly misstated the law," the Illinois Supreme Court also disposed of the argument that remaining with the Does was in Baby Richard's best interests. "If the best interests of the child are to be the determining factor," the court pointed out, "persons seeking babies to adopt might profitably frequent grocery stores and snatch babies when the parent is looking the other way. Then, if custody proceedings can be delayed long enough, they can assert that they have a nicer home, a superior education, a better job, or whatever, and the best interests of the child are with the baby snatchers. . . . The law, thankfully, is otherwise."

The Illinois Supreme Court's decision in the Baby Richard case sparked widespread outrage. The governor of Illinois and his wife condemned the court, as did hundreds of newspaper columnists and editorial writers. NO JUSTICE FOR A CHILD! lamented one headline. DAMN THEM ALL, cried another. Talk radio was aflame with anti-Otakar, anticourt hostility. "How can those idiot judges take a three-year-old from the only home he's ever had?" Annette from Peoria wanted to know. "How could that father inflict such pain and suffering on the Does and that baby?" Rita from Rockford asked. "What the hell is this country coming to?" Tony from Waukegan wailed.

The Does' petition for a rehearing on the Baby Richard matter presented the court with an opportunity to respond to the inflammatory and misleading rhetoric. The court refusal to reopen the case, Justice James D. Heiple wrote:

[T]he adoption laws of Illinois are neither complex nor difficult [to apply]. These laws intentionally place the burden of proof on the adoptive parents . . . Illinois law requires a good faith effort to notify the natural father of the adoption proceedings. We call this due process of law. . . .

The best interest of the child standard is not to be denigrated. It is real. However, it is not triggered until it has been validly determined that the child is *available* for adoption. And, a child is not available for adoption until the rights of his natural parents have been properly terminated. Any judge, lawyer, or guardian *ad litem* knows [that]. . . .

[T]his case cannot be decided by public clamor . . . Neither can it be decided by its popularity or lack thereof. . . . That is a judicial function pure and simple. For the Supreme Court to surrender to this assault would be to surrender its independence, its integrity and its reason for being. . . .

As for the child . . . It will not be an insurmountable trauma for a three-year-old child to be returned, at last, to his natural parents . . . It will work itself out in the fullness of time. As for the adoptive parents, they will have to live with their pain and the knowledge that they wrongfully deprived a father of his child . . . They and their lawyer brought it on themselves. . . . When the father, . . . 57 days after the baby's birth, . . . demanded his rights as a father, the [adoptive parents] should have relinquished the baby. . . . It was their decision to prolong this litigation. . . .

If there [has been] a tragedy in this case, as has been suggested, then that tragedy is the wrongful breakup of a natural family and the keeping of a child by strangers without right. We must remember that the purpose of an adoption is to provide a home for a child, not a child for a home.

The Baby Richard case offers fathers valuable (if ominous) insights. While we applaud the courage and wisdom of the judges who finally did the right thing, we realize that few fathers have the resources and resolve Otakar exhibited in enforcing his rights as a father. Too often, we know, expedience triumphs over justice. We see that the legal and family service professionals who operate within, and preside over, the adoption process often exclude fathers from adoption and child-rearing decisions. Terminating a natural father's parental rights, we find, requires only minimal effort and, even when accomplished illegally, rarely brings disapproval or reprisal.

A broader, more distressing perspective emerges when we examine the overwhelmingly negative public reaction spurred by the decision to return Baby Richard to his natural father. Rather than being hailed as a heroic figure for his arduous, determined pursuit of his parental rights, Otakar was cast as some kind of demon, publicly vilified and privately detested. Instead of being commended for bringing an end to what some have called "a state-assisted kidnapping," the justices of the Illinois Supreme Court were scorned and abused by much of the media and the populace.

It seems obvious that many of our social agencies, a wide cross section of our judiciaries, and most of our fellow citizens have little respect for fathers or fatherhood. "Until you can conceive them, carry them for nine months, and give birth to them, you have no rights," a single mother once told her children's father. Apparently, she was speaking for a sizable segment of society.

When a marriage is dissolved, there usually is no question of a father's parental status. A divorcing father may have to go to extraordinary lengths to preserve his legal link to his children, but at least no one denies that the link exists. Much like his legally married brethren, an unmarried father who sees his relationship with his children's mother coming to an end must be prepared to battle feverishly and tenaciously for his natural rights. Before he can do so, however, he often will be forced to fight his way onto the battlefield.

Establishing Paternity

Bob and Bonnie decide to live together. Bonnie becomes pregnant. Four months before their child is born, Bob and Bonnie break up. Bonnie banishes Bob from her life and declares that the baby she is carrying is hers and hers alone. Maybe she'll give the child up for adoption, maybe she'll keep it. Either way, she tells Bob, it's none of his business.

Ray and Regina have lived together for almost five years. They have a two-year-old son. Regina dumps Ray to marry Vince. She wants Vince to adopt her child, and she wants Ray to hit the road.

Larry and Lois have a brief affair. Soon after the affair ends, Larry learns that Lois is pregnant. He contacts her to ask if the baby is his. Lois claims it's not, but Larry doesn't believe her. A few weeks later, Lois disappears.

These troubling vignettes are not soap-opera plot summaries. They are accurate abstracts of everyday life in America. Almost two-thirds of the babies born in many major U.S. cities are born out of wedlock. More than 80 percent of these children will grow up without meaningful contact with their natural fathers.

A father who is not married to his child's mother must act swiftly and decisively to assert and protect his parental rights. As soon as it becomes apparent that his relationship with his children's mother is ending, an unwed father should seek the advise of counsel to establish legal paternity.

In 1983, the United States Supreme Court warned that the parental rights of unmarried fathers are perishable. For single dads, the court ruled, fatherhood is an "opportunity" that a father who wishes to participate in his child's life must "grasp in a timely manner."

In most states, an unmarried father whose children are more than six months old can likely establish parental status if:

- He was married to the child's mother on or within three hundred days prior to the child's birth;

- He has maintained contact with the child throughout the child's life and contributes to the child's financial support; or,

- He openly lives with the child and publicly acknowledges that the child is his.

For single fathers of children less than six months old, the prenatal period and the first thirty days of the child's life are critical. A father who openly lives with and supports a child's mother during pregnancy and makes a good-faith effort to pay birth expenses and child support during the first month of a child's life meets the legal parentage standards of most jurisdictions.

As a supplement to—but not in place of—parental behavior, an unwed father can establish paternity through a court order. In most jurisdictions, obtaining an order of paternity is a simple process requiring only the completion of a short "boilerplate" affidavit, the child's birth certificate, and the parents' signatures. In some states, a request for a paternity order can be signed in the presence of a notary public. Other states require the parents' signatures to be witnessed by the clerk of the court or a judge.

Primarily to provide for the support of children born out of wedlock (so that these children don't become public charges), most states have streamlined the process of establishing paternity. In many communities, all the paperwork required to identify unmarried parents can be completed before the newborn leaves the hospital. Paternity forms are presented to the parents shortly after the child's birth. If the parents sign the straightforward declarations, then the forms, along with a copy of the baby's birth certificate, are sent to the appropriate circuit court. A judge reviews the documentation and enters a paternity order.

Remember that a child from a nonmarital relationship generally has the same rights as a child born to married parents. Although the purpose of a paternity order usually is to provide children born out of wedlock with legal access to a father's financial support and his estate (including insurance, pension, and Social Security benefits), the order also affirms the father's parental standing in the eyes of the court. An order of paternity is generally a necessary precursor to settlement (or litigation) of child support and custody issues.

If his children's mother abandons the family, takes the children and leaves, or refuses to participate in obtaining a paternity order, an unmarried father can establish paternity by initiating a parentage action, which is a simple, relatively inexpensive lawsuit.

During the course of a parentage suit, it may be necessary for a father to establish paternity through blood or DNA analysis. In most jurisdictions, submission to testing is mandatory in any case where parentage is disputed. Refusal to comply with test procedures usually will result in a default judgment against the party who refuses.

No blood or tissue test is 100-percent accurate in determining paternity. If properly collected and processed, however, scientific evidence can show with biological certainty when a man is *not* a child's natural father. In attempting to demonstrate that a man is a child's father, test results are used to formulate a "paternity index."

Blood samples taken from the man and the child are subjected to a human leukocyte antigen test (HLA). Approximately eighty markers within the blood's white cells are studied and then compared with an index that weighs "plausibility of paternity" factors against a "cumulative chance of exclusion" indicator. If the index resulting from this procedure is 99.9 or higher, the man is presumed to be the child's father.

A similar mathematical quotient is used in DNA testing. Because DNA tests can isolate a biological father's "genetic fingerprint," DNA results are considered to be much more accurate than blood analyses, and in many jurisdictions, DNA evidence has replaced blood-test results as the primary indicator of paternity.

DNA is taken from the white cells present in a specimen of whole blood. Every person, except identical twins, has a unique genetic code, including a maternal allele and a paternal allele. If a child doesn't possess the allele found in an alleged father's genetic makeup, that man cannot be the child's father. If the genetic codes match, a paternity index much more precise than the indicator used in blood tests is calculated to determine the likelihood of paternity. Unless blood and tissue samples have been collected and processed incompetently, DNA evidence is extremely difficult to refute.

Contesting Adoption

Once an unmarried father's parental status is legally affirmed, custody questions usually can be addressed in much the same manner as they are in a traditional divorce case. An unmarried father who fears that his recently born (or unborn) child may be placed for adoption, however, must contend with an additional set of legal chutes and ladders.

The steps that must be taken to protect the rights of a father who finds himself in this situation vary from state to state. Only an attorney experienced in adoption litigation can explain the specific actions necessary to contest adoption in any given jurisdiction. (At the very least, a certified letter advising the mother that the father will not consent to adoption must be sent.)

While most states require potential adoptive parents to conduct a "good-faith" effort to locate the child's biological father, enforcement of this mandate is casual at best. It is up to the father to make his existence (and his interest) known. Several states, including Illinois and New York, have created "father registries" to aid fathers in discharging this responsibility.

In New York, a father needs only to mail a postcard to register. In Illinois, completion of a simple two-page form is necessary. The New York approach makes it easier for fathers to register; the Illinois process provides more identification details.

These registries allow an unmarried father to notify the state of his parental claim either before the child's birth or within thirty days afterward. Anyone attempting to adopt an infant must present evidence that the registry has been searched, and, if appropriate, that the biological father has been notified of an impending adoption. Upon receipt of such notification, the father has a limited time (rarely more than thirty days) to file a parentage action and contest the adoption. Failure to file promptly can be valid grounds for terminating a father's parental rights.

A "thwarted father," in the jargon of adoption law, is a father who has not been informed of a mother's pregnancy, or a father from whom a mother conceals her pregnancy and/or her whereabouts. A "thwarted father" may be able to assert his parental rights, but only if he can prove that he made a prompt and concentrated effort to locate his child, and only if he is willing and able to assume full custody of the child immediately. In most cases in which a biological father has proven that a child's mother has intentionally excluded him from an adoption decision, the courts have awarded custody to the father.

Adoption law attempts to balance the rights of biological parents, adoptive parents, and, most important, children. Unless a natural father's rights are identified and asserted early in his child's life, his parental status may be superseded by the child's right to a stable environment.

It is important to stress that adoptive parents have rights, too. In 1983, the United States Supreme Court decided that a biological father who waited over a year to assert his parentage had waited too long. "The mere existence of a biological link does not merit constitutional protection," the court declared. An adoptive parent's "developed relationship and full commitment" to a child are also deserving of consideration and preservation.

8
Recommendations
for Reform

Several federal commissions and hundreds of studies undertaken by state and local governments have collected compelling evidence that the source of America's most urgent social crises is the erosion of the two-parent family structure and the resulting exclusion of millions of fathers from the lives of their children. Crime, educational deficiencies, declining mental health, increases in teen pregnancies, and a host of other serious problems have been linked strongly to father absence.

Countless recommendations have been offered to reconnect fathers and children. Hesitantly and sporadically, some excellent proposals have been put into practice by our legislators, courts, and social service agencies. Some progress is better than none, of course, but in view of the severity of the devastation caused by fatherlessness, too little is being done too slowly.

During the past three decades, discrimination against women, older Americans, and racial and religious minorities has generated intense media scrutiny, widespread public awareness, and relentless government intervention. It is time that disenfranchised fathers were extended a comparable level of advocacy and protection.

Objective and clear-headed application of existing laws would be a meaningful first step in bringing estranged fathers the equality they deserve. Additionally, our legislative and judicial bodies would be well served if they listened carefully to the serious warnings that fathers' rights activists and family scientists have been issuing for years: Keep fathers and children together or the foundation of our society will continue to disintegrate.

From my perspective, down here in the domestic relations trenches, I can guarantee that conscientious, consistent, and committed implementation of the following public policy recommendations (adapted from the findings of two recent federal studies of the American family) would greatly alleviate several severe problems currently confronting disenfranchised fathers:

Premarital Counseling. As a prerequisite for a marriage license, require premarital counseling. Offer a state and federal tax deduction to all couples who pay for and complete this program.

Divorce Counseling. In divorce cases involving children, require a meaningful waiting period coupled with mandatory participation in divorce counseling. This program should include parenting classes in which a divorcing couple learns the impact of divorce on children and how to minimize divorce's negative consequences for the family.

Paternity. Ensure that every child's birth certificate includes the name and Social Security number of both parents. Presume that the birth certificate establishes parenthood and conveys full parental rights. Reduce (or terminate) public-aid benefits to mothers who refuse to identify a child's father.

Custody. Require joint legal custody and a shared-parenting plan in all divorces involving children unless one or both parents is found to be abusive or negligent by clear and convincing evidence. Launch court-supervised educational programs to teach divorcing couples how to share their children and to emphasize the need for a two-parent family structure after divorce. Defer settlement of all financial and property issues until child custody questions have been resolved.

Visitation. Banish this degrading and inaccurate term from all family court orders. If one parent has primary physical custody of the children, award the other "parenting time" or "family time."

Support. Make both parents responsible for the financial support of their children. Base support obligations only on each parent's earning ability and the children's needs, and no other factors. Mandate accountability of child support payments. Recognize the well-documented reality that financial support and parental involvement are interrelated and equally important to the welfare of children. Enforce these rights evenhandedly.

Access and Interference. Impose serious sanctions, including jail time, on any parent who interferes with a former spouse's access to the children. Assess similar penalties when a parent alienates children from a former mate.

False Abuse Allegations. Establish laws that treat the filing of a false sexual abuse or domestic violence charge as a criminal offense, and enforce them. Declare any parent who uses this tactic in custody disputes unfit.

Although fathers' issues are beginning to command national attention—and I've never felt so encouraged about fathers' rights as I do now—I honestly don't know when our legislatures, our courts, and the American public will finally realize that fathers are vital elements in this nation's social infrastructure. Considering the experiences of other disadvantaged groups victimized by bias and apathy, I suspect that a lengthy, difficult struggle lies ahead.

Despite the efforts of fathers' rights advocates, legal-system reformers, and social scientists, we remain a society in which a nationally syndicated "family" columnist can write this:

"In custody decisions, a mother should have priority. . . . Women have closer biological ties to their children than do men and are far less likely to walk out or shirk responsibility for them."

Fortunately, we are also a nation in which the same newspaper that publishes this outrageous drivel will report a story like this:

Kenneth Hester didn't know he had fathered a baby girl until several days after the infant was found in a garbage bin. But on April 29, he stepped forward in court to claim her as his own.

The baby's mother, Germaine Hovland, awaits trial on charges of attempted murder filed after her baby was found in a garbage container at the Hoffman Estates Medical Center.

"I'm impressed with you, dad. You stepped up and fought for the custody of this child," said Cook County [Illinois] Juvenile Court Judge Michael Zissman.

Hester refused to think of his actions as anything special. "There's something wrong with you if you don't want your own child," he said.

The Cook County public guardian's office recommended Hester be awarded custody of the child after blood tests confirmed that he is the baby's father. Hester, who is divorced, successfully completed parenting classes, as did a baby-sitter he has hired to help care for the child.

Until truth, justice, compassion, and common sense prevail more broadly and more consistently, a father facing exclusion from his children's lives must plan carefully, negotiate skillfully, and fight fiercely to assert and preserve natural rights and constitutionally guaranteed freedoms that most Americans take for granted.

Often, the obstacles of gender bias, judicial inconsistency, and public apathy separating a father and his children may seem insurmountable. Believe me when I tell you that they are not. Ten years ago, fathers routinely walked away from custody disputes. They felt they had no chance of winning. Since then thousands of men have stayed the course and built new lives for themselves and their children. And every time a disenfranchised father is able to reconnect with his children, it quickly becomes evident—to the father, to the children, and to our society—that the ultimate rewards of the father's quest far outweigh the heartaches and hardships endured along the way.

Appendix

Men's / Fathers' Rights Organizations

ACFC (American Coalition for Father's and Children), 2000 Pennsylvania Avenue, NW, #148, Washington, DC 20008; (202) 835–1000; Fax (202) 835–1001

Alberta Men's Resource Centre, 53321, 10405 Jasper Avenue, Edmonton, AB T5J 3S2; Chris Cavanaugh (403) 988–3280

American Institute for Men, 21986 Cayuga Lane, Lake Forest, CA 92630

American Men's Studies Association, 222 East Street, Northampton, MA 01060

Battered Men's Shelter, George Gilliland, 1039 E. Bush Street, St. Paul, MN 55106; (612) 774–9577

Bethany Christian Services (Birth fathers' rights), National Office, 901 Eastern Avenue, NE, Grand Rapids, MI 49503; (616) 459–6273

Center on Fathering, 325 North El Paso Street, Colorado Springs, CO 80903; (800) MY DAD 34; (719) 634–7797; Fax: (719) 634–7852

The Children, Youth & Family Consortium, Dr. Martha Farrell Erickson, Director, 12 McNeal Hall, 1985 Buford Avenue, St. Paul, MN 55108; (612) 626–1212; Fax: (612) 626–1210

Children's Rights Council, 20 Eye Street, NE, Rm. 200, Washington, DC 20002–4307; (202) 547 6227; 1 (800) 787–KIDS

Coalition of Concerned Citizens, 5312 9th Avenue, NE, Seattle, WA 98105

Coalition of Free Men, P.O. Box 129, Manhasset, NY 11030; (516) 482–6378

Coalition for the Preservation of Fatherhood, P.O. Box 8051, Boston, MA 02113; (617) 649–1906

Concerned Women For America, P.O. Box 21130, El Cajon, CA; (619) 443–8371

Dad the Family Shepherd, Administrator: Norman Hoggard, P.O. Box 21445, Little Rock, AR 72221; (501) 221–1102

Dads Against Discrimination, P.O. Box 1275, Albuquerque, NM 87103

Dads Against Discrimination, P.O. Box 8525, Portland, OR 97207–8525; (503) 222–1111

Dads Against Discrimination, Smith Tower, Suite 1518, 506 Second Ave-nue, Seattle, WA 98104–2311; (206) 623–3761

Dads Against Discrimination, Pat Chandler, 12301 Manitoba, NE, Al-buquerque, NM 87111; (505) 299–2673

Dads Assisting Dads, P.O. Box 59063, North Redington Beach, FL 33708; (813) 393–9647

Dads Make a Difference, Minnesota Extension Service, Gary Greenfield, Ramsey County, 2020 White Bear Avenue, St. Paul, MN 55109; (612) 777–2869

Divorced Men's Club of Oregon, P.O. Box 171, Turner, OR 97392

Domestic Rights Coalition, 1849 Iowa Avenue E., St. Paul, MN 55119–4234; (612) 659–0640

False Memory Syndrome Foundation, 3401 Market Street – Suite 130, Philadelphia, PA 19104; (215) 387–1865; Fax: (215) 387–1917; (800) 568–8882 (Executive Director: Pamela Freyd, Ph.D.)

Families and Work Institute, James Levine, Ed.D., Director; Ed Pitt, M.S.W., Associate Director, 330 Seventh Avenue, New York, NY 10001; (212) 465-2044

Family Action Association, Rich Lustakow, 953 Woodside Avenue, Apt. 106, Rippon, WI 54971; (414) 745–2538

Family of Men Support Society, 363 Falshire Drive, NE, Calgary, Al-berta, Canada, T3J 1T8; (403) 242–4077

Family Preservation Alliance, P.O. Box 285, Mercer Island, WA 98040

Family Resource Coalition, 200 South Michigan Avenue, 16th Floor, Chicago, IL 60603; (312) 341–0900

Father and Son Survival Kit, c/o Journey's Together, P.O. Box 2615, Se-dona, AZ 86336

Father Policy Institute, Kirk E. Harris, J.D., Ph.D., Institute Director; David Pate, A.M., Lead Consultant, The Fatherhood Project, Bank Street College, 610 West 112 Street, New York, NY 10025

The Fatherhood Project National Practitioners, Network for Fathers and Families, 330 Seventh Avenue, New York, NY 10001; (212) 268–4846

FatherNet, part of Children, Youth and Family Consortium, 12 McNeal Hall, 1985 Buford Avenue, University of Minnesota, St. Paul, MN 55108. They run the Fathernet BBS (718) 494–1719

Fathers' Advocate, Suite 2001, Smith Tower, 506 2nd Avenue, Seattle, WA 98104; (206) 624–0883

Fathers Are Capable Too, 1995 Weston Road, Box 79513, Weston, Ontario, Canada M9N3W9 (W Metro Toronto); (905) 459 7970

Fathers Are Parents Too!, P.O. Box 704, Winterville, GA 30683; (404) 880–KIDS; aburke@athens.net

Fathers Behind Bars Inc., 525 Superior Street, Niles, MI, 49120

The Fathers' Center, 120 West Lancaster Avenue, Ardmore, PA 10993; (215) 644–6400

Fathers' Education Network (313) 831–5838; Fax: (313) 831–6353

Fathers for Equal Rights, Adolph Riebenack, 2517 Birchfield Drive, NW, Huntsville, AL 35810

Fathers for Equal Rights, Ed Wilson, P.O. Box 750, Montrose, AL 36559

Fathers for Equal Rights, 3623 Douglas Avenue, Des Moines, IA 50310-5345; (515) 277–8789

Fathers for Equal Rights, David Shelton, P.O. Box 50052, Dallas, TX 75250-0052; (214) 741–4800

Fathers for Equal Rights, Box 5114 Avenue NE, Bellingham, WA 98227

Fathers at Home Support Group, P.O. Box 27161, Seattle, WA 98125

Fathers' PAC, 10810 NE 67th Street, Vancouver, WA 98662–5404

Fathers' Resource Center, 430 Oak Grove Street, Suite B3, Minneapolis, MN 55403; (612) 874–1509; frc@winternet.com

Fathers' Rights, P.O. Box 5345, Tacoma, WA 98415

Fathers' Rights Association of New York: 1–800-YES-DADS (1–800–937–3237)

Fathers' Rights & Equality Exchange, 701 Welch Road, #323, Palo Alto, CA 94304; (415) 853–6877

Fathers' Rights Metro, P.O. Box 313143, Jamaica, NY 11431

Fathers United for Equal Justice, P.O. Box 1308, Nashua, NH 03061; (603) 808–9389

Fathers United for Equal Rights and Women's Coalition, P.O. Box 1032, Brick, NJ 08723; (800) 537–7697; jrinscheid@attmail.com (Jeffrey L. Rinscheid)

Fight Against Sexist Tyranny (FAST), 29637 S. Dixie Highway, Suite 325, Miami, FL 33033–3320; (305) 592–3064

First Class Male, P.O. Box 199055, Indianapolis, IN 46219–9055

FOCUS: Children and the Other Parent, Mike Zufelt, 71355 Angelsea Drive, West Jordon, UT 84084; (801) 566–2954

Fully Informed Jury Amendment (FIJA), P.O. Box 59, Helmville, MT 58843

Future Dead White Males, 3 Golf Center, #353, Hoffman Estates, IL 60195; (708) 924–0376

Gay Fathers Coalition, P.O. Box 50360, Washington, DC 20009–0360

Gay Fathers Unlimited, 625 Post Street, Box 283, San Francisco, CA 94109

Grassroots Washington, P.O. Box 7704, Olympia, WA 98507

Inside Men's Lives, c/o MAS Medium, P.O. Box 882, San Anselmo, CA 94960–0882

The Institute for Responsible Fatherhood and Family Revitalization, Contact: Stacie Banks Hall (202) 789–6376 or (800) 601–4609 (pager)

The Institute for Responsible Fatherhood and Family Revitalization, Charles Ballard, President, Institute for Responsible Fatherhood, 1090 Vermont Avenue, NW, Suite 1100, Washington, DC 20005–4961; (202) 789–6376

International Men's AntiDefamation Network (IMAN), 9 Front Street, Emo, Ontario, P0W 1E0, Canada; (807) 482–2838; Fax: (807) 482–3026

Island Men's Network, 35 Cambridge Street, Victoria, BC, V8V 4A7; (604) 383–MALE

Joint Custody Association, 10606 Wilkins Avenue, Los Angeles, CA 90024; James A. Cook, President: (213) 475–5352

Justice in Child Custody Inc., P.O. Box 790, Crowell, TX 79227–0790

Legislation for Kids and Dads, 1 Hiawatha Circle, Madison, WI 53711; (608) 274–1638

Madison Men's Organization, 2001 E. Dayton Street, Madison, WI 53704; (608) 249–5576

Male Liberation Foundation, 701 NE 67 Street, Miami, FL 33138; (305) 756–6249

Manitoba Men's Network, P.O. Box 26022, Winnipeg, MB R3C 1K9

MELD for Young Dads, Dwaine R. Simms, Program Replication Manager, 123 North Third Street, Suite 507, Minneapolis, MN 55401; (612) 332–7563

Men Against Domestic Violence, 32 West Anapamu Street, #348, Santa Barbara, CA 93101; Voicemail: (805) 563–2651

Men Assisting, Leading, and Educating, P.O. Box 460171, Aurora, CO 8004–01716; (303) 693–9930; 1 (800) 949-MALE (6253); Fax: (303) 693–6059

Men International, Ken Pangborn, 3980 Orchard Hill Circle, Palm Harbor, FL 34684; PangK@aol.com

Men's Action Network, Anthony Nazzaro, Executive Director, P.O. Box 645, Dobbs Ferry, NY 10522; (914) 693–7826

Men's Center Foundation, 102 2931 Shattuck Avenue, Berkeley, CA 94707

The Men's Center of Raleigh and Wake County, 723 West Johnson Street, P.O. Box 6155, Raleigh, NC 27628; (919) 832–0509

Men's Centre North Shore, P.O. Box 34–215, Birkenhead, Auckland, New Zealand

Men's Council Newsletter, Box 4795, Boulder, CO 80306

Men's Defense Association, 17854 Lyons Street, Forest Lake, MN 55025-8854 (*The Liberator*); MensDefens@aol.com

Men's Education Network, Box 10033, Kansas City, MO 64111; (816) 753–4725

Men's Health Network, P.O. Box 770, Washington, DC 20044–0770; (202) 543–MHN–1 (6461); Fax: (202) 543–2727; mensnet@cap.gwu.edu

Men's Information Network, Service of the NW Center for Men's Studies; (206) 328–0356

The Men's Network, 120 Santa Margarita Avenue, Menlo Park, CA 94025; (415) 323–3445; 1 (800) 479–2636 (local to SF Bay Area only)

Men's Network for Change, 17 Marley Place, London, Ontario, N6C 3S9; (519) 432–1286

Men's Network for Change, 456 Bagot Street, Kingston, Ontario, K7K 3C3

Men's Network News, 17 Marley Place, London, Ontario, N6C 3S9

M.E.N.S. Network Society, P.O. Box 280, Station G, Calgary, Alberta, T3A 2G2; (403) 251–1531

Men's Project, 440 Grand Avenue, Suite 320, Oakland, CA 94610

Men's Resource Center of Wayne, PA, 987 Old Eagle School Road, Suite 719, Wayne, PA 19087

Men's Rights, Inc., P.O. Box 163180, Sacramento, CA 95816; (916) 484–7333

Men's Rights, Inc., Equal Rights Amendment Project, David Ault, Co-Director, P.O. Box 31864, Seattle, WA 98103–1864

Men's Rights, Inc., P.O. Box 163180, Sacramento, CA 95816; (916) 484–7333

Men's Studies Press, P.O. Box 32, Harriman, TN 37748–0032; Fax (in USA); (615) 882–4562

Mentor, P.O. Box 10863, Portland, OR 97210; cmoberg@ultranet.com (Craig Moberg)

Mentors Action Network, David Lindgren, founder, 1735 North Ashland Avenue, Chicago IL 60622; (773) 252–7538; Fax: (773) 252–7694

MERGE (Movement for the Establishment of Real Gender Equality), 19502 61st Avenue, NE, Seattle, WA 98155; (206) 938–8385

Ministry to Men, Administrator: Keith Boyd, 860 Ridgelake Blvd., Suite 384, Memphis, TN 38120; (901) 761–7865

Missouri Center for Men's Studies, P.O. Box 1033, Kansas City, MO 64111; (816) 561–4066

Mothers Without Custody, Jennifer Isham, President, P.O. Box 27417, Houston, TX 77227–7418; (800) 457–MWOC

MOVE (Men Opposed to Violence and Exploitation), 21 Newton Street, Ottawa, Ont K1S 2S6; (613) 231–5138

Movement for the Establishment of Real Gender Equality (M.E.R.G.E.), Publication: *Balance* (Quarterly, $12.50 CDN, $10 US), 9768-170 Street, #366, Edmonton, Alberta T5T 5L4 Canada

National Association for Fathers (NAF), Bob Hassler, SYSOP, 1075-D N. Railroad Avenue #111, Richmond, NY 10306; (718) 494–1719; BBS: 1 (800) HELP–DAD; voicemail (718) 983–5575

National Center for Fathering, Ken Canfield, Ph.D., President, 10200 West 75th Street, Suite 267, Shawnee Mission, KS 66204; (913) 384–4661; 1 (800) 593–DADS; Fax: (913) 384–4665

National Center on Fathers and Families, Vivian Gadsden, Ph.D., Director, University of Pennsylvania Graduate School of Education, Philadelphia, PA 19104; (215) 686–3910

NCM (National Center for Men) (Men's) Reproductive Rights Project, Kingsley Morse, Jr., Chair, P.O. Box 555, Old Bethpage, NY 11804; (516) 942-2020

NCM Portland Oregon Chapter, James Pierce Whinston, Deputy Director, P.O. Box 6481, Portland, OR 97228–6481; JPWHINSTON@aol.com

National Child Abuse Defense and Resource Center, Kim Hart: (419) 865–0526; Fax: (419) 865–0526

National Coalition of Free Men, Tom Williamson, President, P.O Box 129, Manhasset, NY 11030; Phone: (516) 482–6378, Hotline: (516) 794–5151; ncfm@liii.com

National Congress for Fathers and Children, 851 Minnesota Avenue, P.O. Box 1675, Kansas City, KS 66117; (800) SEE–DADS; ncfc@primenet.com

National Fatherhood Initiative (NFI), Wade Horn, Ph.D., Director, 600 Eden Road, Building E, Lancaster, PA 17601; (717) 581–8860

National Institute for Divorce Research, P.O. Box 35741, Panama City, FL 32412

National Institute for Fathers and Families, Inc., Chicago, Il (312) 595–0077

The National Men's Resource Center, P.O. Box 800, San Anselmo, CA 94979–0800; (415) 453–2839

National Organization for Birthfathers and Adoption Reform (NOBAR), P.O. Box 50, Punta Gorda, FL 33951; (813) 637–7477

National Organization of Dads & Kid, Inc.s, 50 Janis Way, Scotts Valley, CA 95066

National Organization for Men, Inc., 11 Park Place, New York, NY 10007; (212) 766–4030

National Training, Consulting, and Service Organizations, Center for Health Services Vanderbilt Medical Center, Barbara Clinton, Director, Vanderbilt University, Nashville, TN 37232; (615) 322–4773

Northwest Center for Men's Studies, 927 15th Avenue, Seattle, WA 98122–4719; (206) 323–5375; Fax: (206) 323–5375, BBS: (206) 328–0356

Olympic M.E.N. (Men's Evolvement Network), 167 West Silverton Road, Sequim, WA 98382

The Orlando Men's Council, Contact: Jim Bracewell, P.O. Box 462, Winter Park, FL 32790; (407) 629–5868

The Panfaea Institute for Gender Studies, Box 862, Sebastopol, CA 95473

Parental Responsibility Project, 2326 Mystic Drive, Sarasota, FL 34232

Parents Without Partners (PWP), 401 N. Michigan Avenue, Chicago, IL 60611; (312) 644–6610

Promise Keepers, P.O. Box 18376, Boulder, CO 80308; (303) 421–2800 Fax: (303) 421–2918

Redwood Men's Center, 705 College Avenue, Santa Rosa, CA 95404

SAFAR (Society Against False Accusations of Rape), James Donald Anderson, #6952487, 3405 Deer Park Drive, SE, Salem, OR 97301–9385

SAFE (Single And Fathering Effectively), Glenn Cheriton or Robert Gagnon, c/o Eccles Street, Ottawa, Canada K1R 6S5; Fax: (613) 789–3491; or Allen Roth, Box 938, Unit 120, St. Catharines, Ontario L2R 6Z4

Seattle Men's Evolvement Network (M.E.N.), 4649 Sunnyside Avenue, N., Suite 209, Seattle, WA 98103; (206) 545–3736

Shared Parenting Association of Alberta, 315 10 Avenue, SE, Suite 202, Calgary, AB, T2G 0W2; (403) 262–4662

The Single Fathers Research Project, 2901 Jefferson Drive, Greenville, NC 27834

Society for the Preservation of Family Relationships, c/o 172 Berlin Drive Knoxville, TN; (423) 694–8834

Southwest Key Program, Juan Sanchez, Ph.D., Director, Southwest Key Program, 3000 South IH–35, Suite 410, Austin, TX 78704; (512) 462–2181

Stepfamily Association of America, (SAA), Kevin Ricker, President, Suite 212, 215, Centennial Mall, South Lincoln, NE 68505l; (402) 477–7837

Texas Fathers Alliance, 807 Brazos, Suite 315, Austin, TX 78701; (512) 472–3237

Texas Men's Institute, Director: Marvin Allen, P.O. Box 311384, New Braunfels, TX 78131–1384; (210) 608–9201

Toronto Fathers' Resources, Contact: Danny Guspie: (416) 861–0626, ext. 1

Toronto Men's Clearinghouse, c/o Greg Barsoski, 104 Spencer Avenue, Toronto, ON Canada M6K 2J6

United Fathers of America, 12304 Santa Monica Boulevard, Suite 300, West Los Angeles, CA 90025; 1 (800) 540–1273; (310) 442–8575; (213) 482–0804 (Divorce Lawyer Referrals)

United Fathers of Washington State, Smith Tower, Suite 1521, Seattle, WA 98104; (800) 689–7949 (ask for Gary Flanzer); (206) 623–5050; GFlanzer@medio.net

United Men's Coalition, 169–47 25 Avenue, Whitestone, NY 11357; (718) 352–2981

Vancouver M.E.N. (Men's Evolvement Network), 3392 West 34 Avenue, Vancouver, BC, V6N 2K6; (604) 290–9988

Victoria Men's Centre, Victoria, 1967 Oak Bay Avenue, Victoria, BC V8R 1E3, Canada

VOCAL (Victims of Child Abuse Laws), 16541 Redmond Way, Redmond, WA 98052; (206) 878–5135

VOCAL (Victims of Child Abuse Legislation): (800) 745–8778 or (303) 233–5321; Public Relations: Graham Jeambey (303) 770–5096

Washington Coalition for Family Rights, 415 E. Hamlet Street, Othello, WA 99334

Washington Coalition for Family Rights in King County, P.O. Box 12003, Seattle, WA 98102; (206) 328–7000

Washington Coalition for Family Rights in Spokane, P.O. Box 3331, Spokane, WA 99220; (509) 535–0002

Washington Coalition for Family Rights in the Tri-Cities, 2010 Tinkle, Richland, WA 99352; (509) 946–0589

Washington State Coalition Against Censorship, 6201 15th Street, NW, #640, Seattle, WA 98107; (206) 784–6418

West Palm Beach Men's Council, 443 Wilder Street, West Palm Beach, FL 33405

Wingspan, Journal of the Male Spirit, 846 Prospect Street, La Jolla, CA 92037; (619) 282–3521, Fax: (619) 454–4851

Wisconsin Fathers for Equal Justice, P.O. Box 1742, Madison, WI 53701; (608) ALL–DADS

Dick Woods, 3623 Douglas Avenue, Des Moines, IA 50310–5345; (515) 277–8789

Worldwide Christian Divorced Fathers, 1429 Columbia Drive, NE, Albuquerque, NM 87106–2632; 1 (800) MY–DADDY

Periodicals

Aladdin's Window, 28936 Shingle Creek Lane, Shingletown, CA 96088–9658

At-Home Dad, Peter Baylies, 61 Brightwood Avenue, North Andover, MD 01845–1702

The Backlash!, P.O. Box 70524, Bellevue, WA 98007; (206) 649–0892; Contact: Rod Van Mechelen; rodvan@nwlink.com

Everyman, Box 4617, Station E, Ottawa, ON K1S 5H8

Family Law Reform, 2547 Noriega Street, #333, San Francisco, CA 94122

Father Times, published by Father's Resource Center, 430 Oak Grove Street, Suite 105, Minneapolis, MN 55403; (612) 874–1509

Fathers' Rights Newsline, P.O. Box 713, Havertown, PA 19083

Full-Time Dads: The Journal for Caregiving Fathers, P.O. Box 577, Cumberland Center, ME 04021

The Gauntlet, 2129 General Booth Boulevard, Suite 103208, Virginia Beach, VA 23454

Heterodoxy, 12400 Ventura Boulevard, #304, Studio City, CA 91604

Ho!, A Men's Journal, P.O. Box 1029477, Van Nuys, CA 91408

Inside Edge, 33 Richdale Avenue, #122, Cambridge, MA 02238

Journeyman, 513 Chester Turnpike, Candia, NH 03034; (603) 883–8029

The Liberator, 17854 Lyons Street, Forest Lake, MN 55025–8854; Mens-Defens@aol.com

Male Call, Newsletter of the Unitarian Universalist Men's Network, Editor: Neil Chethik, 1240 Washington Road, Mt. Lebanon, PA 15228; (412) 561–6277; nchet@aol.com

MALE VIEW magazine (the magazine of the U.K. Men's Movement), The Pickwick Press, 9a St. Woolos Place, Newport, Gwent NP9 4GQ, United Kingdom.

M.E.N. Magazine, 7552 31st Avenue, NE, Seattle WA 98115

MEN's Advocate, a MENSA Special Interest Group, Publication: MEN's Advocate, 12819 SE 38th Street, #237, Bellevue, WA 98006

Menstuff: National Men's Resource Calendar, P.O. Box 800, San Anselmo, CA 94979–0800

Mentalk: Men's Center News, 3255 Hennepin Avenue, Minneapolis, MN 55408

Mentor Magazine, P.O. Box 11381, Portland, OR 97211

Modern Dad, 1525 Forest Avenue, Highland Park, IL 60035; elisak@aol.com

The New Edition Magazine, 2300 Yonge Street, P.O. Box 67058, Toronto, ON M4P 1E0 Canada

Nurturing Today, c/o The Fathers' Exchange, 187 Caselli Avenue, San Francisco, CA 94114

Oasis Center, 7463 N. Sheridan Road, Chicago, IL 60626; (312) 274–6777; (cataloge of cources)

Phyllis Schlafly Report, P.O. Box 618, Alton, IL 62002

QUEST, Men's Resource Magazine, 1592 Union Street, Suite 370, San Francisco, CA 94123; (415) 931–5332

Rogue Male Majority, P.O. Box 304, Red Hook, NY 12571

Single Parent Family Magazine, Published by Focus on the Family, James Dobson, President, Colorado Springs, CO 80995; (719) 531–5181

Transitions, P.O. Box 12930, Manhasset, NY 11030

Wingspan: Journal of the Male Spirit, 846 Prospect Street, La Jolla, CA 92037; wingspan@Znet.com

Various Individual Contacts

Theadora Ooms: (Author of *Young Unwed Fathers*), the Family Impact Seminar: (202) 467–5136.

David Pate, Director, Paternal Involvement Project: (312) 427–4830.

Tom Henry, Philadelphia Children's Network: (215) 686–7810

Index

Index